The

CONFIDENT
PARENT

The
CONFIDENT
PARENT

A Pediatrician's Guide
to Caring for Your Little One—Without
Losing Your Joy, Your Mind,
or Yourself

JANE SCOTT, MD

with Stephanie Land

A TarcherPerigee Book

tarcherperigee

An imprint of Penguin Random House LLC
375 Hudson Street
New York, New York 10014

Most TarcherPerigee books are available at special quantity discounts for
bulk purchase for sales promotions, premiums, fund-raising, and educational
needs. Special books or book excerpts also can be created to fit specific needs.
For details, write: SpecialMarkets@penguinrandomhouse.com.

Library of Congress Cataloging-in-Publication Data
Names: Scott, Jane, author. | Land, Stephanie, author.
Title: The confident parent : a pediatrician's guide to caring for your
little one—without losing your joy, your mind, or yourself / Jane
Scott, Stephanie Land.
Description: New York : TarcherPerigee, 2016. |
Includes bibliographical references and index.
Identifiers: LCCN 2016025802 (print) | LCCN 2016034130 (ebook) |
ISBN 9780399175879 (paperback) | ISBN 9780698405950 (ebook)
Subjects: LCSH: Parenting. | Child rearing. | Child development. |
BISAC: FAMILY & RELATIONSHIPS / Life Stages / Infants & Toddlers. |
FAMILY & RELATIONSHIPS / Parenting / General.
Classification: LCC HQ755.8.S365 2016 (print) |
LCC HQ755.8 (ebook) | DDC 649/.1—dc23

Printed in the United States of America
1   3   5   7   9   10   8   6   4   2

To all the parents and children

whom I have had the privilege to serve.

And to my endlessly patient husband,

who has always supported me in

my career and at home.

Contents

Introduction   ix

1: A Fresh Perspective   1

2: Caring for Your Newborn —and Yourself   23

3: Simple Ways to Boost Baby's Brain   55

4: Gather Your Village   86

5: Sleep Through the Night—Really!   109

6: Breastfeed (or Don't) the
   Worry-Free Way   139

7: Make Mealtimes Fun   162

8: Slow Down to Discipline   190

9: Play!   214

   Final Thoughts   237

   Acknowledgments   241

   Notes   243

   Index   256

Introduction

Not long ago I had to buy a new mattress. While getting ready to pay for my purchase, I noticed a young mother wandering up and down one of the aisles studying the price tags, carrying a small baby while her tiny son followed a few steps behind her. The toddler stopped and quickly scrambled up the side of one of the model beds. He bounced gently up and down for a few seconds, and then started to wriggle toward the edge. It was clear he wasn't sure the best way to get down. As he sat with his bottom on the edge of the bed and looked warily down at what to him must have seemed a long distance to the floor, the mother surprised me. Instead of rushing over to help her child, she casually called over from the other side of the room, "You might do better turning around and dropping off the side." And he did. He proceeded to quietly wander up and down the rest of the floor, climbing on and off mattresses, exploring his environment, while his mother spoke with a salesman. It might sound crazy, but I left the store thrilled by what I had just witnessed. This mother didn't try to intervene. She didn't hover. She didn't warn her little boy that he was going to fall or to stay close to her. She just offered a suggestion, then let him play while she got on with her life.

If I hadn't known better, I'd have thought this mom was an Aussie. She had a "she'll be right" attitude if I'd ever seen one. *She'll be right* is the Australian way of saying "don't worry," an attitude that implies that whatever isn't okay now will certainly be fine soon. It connotes a relaxed, optimistic, confident approach to life, one that, in the decade I spent living there, I found often translated to a relaxed, optimistic, confident approach to parenting as well. We don't see this kind of parenting very often here in the States, but I wish we did. As a pediatrician, I often wished I could prescribe a hefty dose of "she'll be right" to the parents in my clinic. They would have been happier for it, and their children probably would have been safer, too.

Why? Because in the twenty-five years since I started my pediatric practice before retiring from my clinic at the end of 2015, I encountered many well-meaning parents so determined to protect their children they wound up putting them in real danger. I met many babies whose heads were flattened and deformed because they spent too much time on their backs or strapped into strollers, carriers, and infant seats by parents too busy or too worried about their safety to give them unfettered time on the floor. I treated toddlers for vitamin D deficiency because their parents were so concerned about sun exposure the children didn't spend a minute outdoors unless covered head to toe in clothes and sunscreen. And I met an awful lot of kids with behavioral issues that I have reason to believe were triggered by the stress of living in schedule-driven, hypervigilant homes.

I saw parents put themselves at risk, too. The mother who

called me at three in the morning frantic with worry that the pimple on her baby's backside was the first sign of staph infection, the father who confessed to staying up all night watching his infant sleep, the parents tearfully expressing fear that their child may have attention deficit hyperactivity disorder (ADHD) because he wouldn't sit still in preschool—at a time when these parents should be enjoying their new roles as caretakers and protectors, they were instead being crushed by it.

New parenthood is not supposed to be this way. And in other countries that haven't allowed their cultural traditions and common sense to be hijacked by personalities and media outlets that profit off our fear, it isn't. I wrote this book because I want parents to see there are many more ways to raise a happy, successful child than our culture would have us believe. If we could break down our assumptions about what entails good parenting, we could benefit from a world of best practice that will release parents from the culturally imposed pressure and stress that has become a de facto parenting badge of honor, still turning out equally successful children, while inspiring far more family joy.

Some people say we should parent more like the French; others say Asians do it best. But after living in and raising my kids on four continents, I know that every country has its own tried-and-true traditions and methods that work, and work beautifully. By exploring all the ways in which children succeed and thrive around the world, I hope to give parents some new back-to-basic tools that will allow them to follow their instincts and parent with confidence and calm. It's an approach I taught families for twenty-five years, gleaned from my own experience living and raising children abroad. In fact, you could say I've been preparing for this book my whole life.

BEFORE I WAS a doctor, I was a mother. And before I was a mother, I was a child growing up in my grandmother Ann's house in Mombasa, Kenya. I loved Grandmother Ann's house. It was a large thatched cottage, open and airy, with no glass in the windows, as was typical for the warm, tropical region. Ann was an animal lover, so I grew up among a virtual menagerie of birds, monkeys, giant tortoises, goats, cats, dogs, bush babies, and parakeets. Though she employed a keeper to care for them all, Ann was skilled in veterinary care and would frequently tend to them as well as her friends' and neighbors' sick animals. She often let me accompany her, and even help. I learned early that compassion was useless to a suffering creature unless bolstered by clear, cool thinking. I also noticed that as Grandmother Ann cared for the animals, she cared for their owners, too. Her heart was big, kind, and generous. Her ability to heal made a huge impression on me, and she remains one of the greatest influences on my life.

My upbringing was decidedly British and formal. Yet I lived side by side with the African families that worked in our home, and while I played with their children I also observed their methods and traditions. The men would work in the house while the women spent the day outside washing or mending clothes or preparing food while their young children who were not yet attending school milled about and played.

There was not a great deal of structure, and few rules. I rarely heard the mothers raise their voices to reprimand their children and no one cared if the kids got dirty. I played freely with my African friends, but whereas they could come and go as they pleased, I was under constant supervision. In 1950, a nationalist branch of the Kikuyu tribe, resentful of British colonial rule, mounted an uprising. I was never allowed to go anywhere by myself for fear that I would be kidnapped and sold on the market. My nanny accompanied me everywhere, even to visit my girl-friend next door. The threat was real; entire families had been massacred in their homes. I woke up one night to find someone "pole-fishing"—slipping a wooden pole spiked with razor blades through the bars of my bedroom window so he could steal things from my room. The razor blades were there to slash your hands if you grabbed the pole to stop the thief from taking the goods.

Then, when I was ten, my father's work as a civil engineer brought us to England. After the heat of Kenya, with its blazing sun and intense blue skies, the cold, cloudy climate was quite a shock. I had never slept under multiple blankets, nor was I used to layering myself to stay warm, dressing in shoes, socks, coat, hat, gloves, and scarf every time I went outside. And there was another huge surprise. Not long after we arrived, I asked my British grandmother if she would take me to the corner shop so I could get a chocolate bar. Grandma told me to put on my out-door clothes, handed me a small purse with a few coins in it, and said I could walk to the shop by myself. After all my years of being carefully guarded, I could hardly believe what I was hear-ing. I'm sure my eyes were as big as saucers as I tiptoed cautiously out the front door and onto the pavement. Being on my own felt very strange. But after a few moments, I started to run, waving my arms up and down like I was flying. So this was freedom! No chocolate bar ever tasted as good as the one I bought that day.

My family then moved to Ireland, where children were tolerated but expected to stay in the background. I was older by the time we moved to Tasmania and didn't spend much time with small children there, but I was surprised by how early school staff started guiding their pupils into academic, technical, or trade tracks. It was a model that sought to identify teenagers' strengths early and prevent them from wasting time doing substandard work in areas that were clearly not their best fit or that they didn't enjoy. I did notice, however, that my classmates seemed more confident and satisfied than those I went to school with in the English and Irish systems, which funneled everyone down the same path, regardless of his or her gifts and strengths.

As much as I appreciated what each of these cultures had to offer, I continued to hold a huge respect and affection for the quiet, easygoing rhythms of the African family life I had witnessed as a young girl. And at a young age, I promised that I would make sure that my future children would experience the freedom and independence that had once been denied me.

At the age of seventeen, I left Tasmania to attend a medical school in Perth. As was typical in the British system, I pursued a six-year degree that combined a bachelor's and a medical degree in one. Four years in, I got married. When I showed up to finish my fifth and sixth year, the dean took me aside and informed me that I could no longer attend medical school. "You are married, you have obligations now," he said. "Your responsibility is to go home, support your husband, and bear him children." I told him I was going to get this medical degree; I'd simply apply to another school in one of the other states. He shook his head. "What you want to do is so against my belief I will make sure that if your application shows up anywhere else you will not get in." With no other options,

I left school and accompanied my husband, a geologist, into the Australian outback, where the nearest town had a total of thirty-five inhabitants and survival was an everyday challenge.

I gave birth to my first child, Cameron, in Australia, and my second and third children—Brendan and Julianne—in apartheid South Africa, where we lived in the desert. My children often ran around naked in these rural areas. When they got muddy, I used the hose to spray them off. We made music with sticks and buckets, and sang at the top of our lungs. A stay-at-home mother and often left alone for long stretches of time, I became close to the native women who worked for us. From them I learned to adapt to the challenges of raising children in a harsh landscape and political climate, confronting snakes, poor medical facilities, contaminated drinking water, and Rhodesian terrorists. But it was in America where my adventures truly began.

I got divorced, remarried, and had a fourth child, David. I spent the first month of that baby's life at his side in the neonatal intensive care unit (NICU). I decided to resume my medical studies and got my degree at last. Finally, inspired by my experience of bringing four babies into the world, all of whom experienced some medical complications at birth, I decided to specialize in neonatology, eventually founding the first Level 3 NICU serving Twin Falls, Idaho, while also practicing pediatrics in the hospital's outpatient clinic. Then, after fourteen years, my husband and I relocated back to Colorado, where my four adult children had settled, and where I continued my career working as an urgent care pediatrician and then creating a small business developing medical devices for infants, which would enable me to continue to pursue my passion to help babies for the rest of my working life.

In the end I'm glad I became a parent before I became a doctor because my experiences raising children around the world helped shape my medical practice. I watch carefully and I listen closely, not just to my little patients, but also to their parents. They're often surprised at just how much and for how long. But there is much to learn from parent–child interactions, and I know how frustrating it can be when your pediatrician is dismissive or won't listen. Parents are also sometimes surprised at how much I understand the issues faced by stay-at-home mothers, single mothers, and working mothers. I sympathize because I've been all three. I know how it feels to care for a severely sick child and still have to find the energy to tend to and comfort his siblings. I know what it's like to be torn between one's obligations at work and one's commitment to being an involved parent. The one thing I do not know is what it's like to feel stressed out, anxious, frazzled, or overwhelmed by the pressures of parenting—the feelings most commonly expressed by the parents I have met, as a mother and as a doctor, since moving to this country. When I started practicing pediatric medicine, I thought I would spend the majority of my time soothing children and making them feel better when they were ill. However, I found myself spending an almost equal amount of time soothing parents, even when their children were perfectly healthy.

Mom, Dad, you've been given the role of a lifetime, but your years with your children under the same roof are short, and they will go fast. Do you really want to spend them feeling anxious, cranky, and tired? Of course not! But that's what's happening because too many people believe that if they're not worrying, if they're not putting their children's needs above their own, if it's not hard, they're not really parenting. Much of the rest of the world knows this just isn't the truth. It's time we learned it, too.

IN EACH CHAPTER I break down what parents need to know about childcare—from the easiest breastfeeding techniques to the most effective way to get a preschooler out the door in the morning—however, *The Confident Parent* is not your typical childcare book. It will not encourage you to subsume yourself to the needs of your children; it will not make recommendations that require a complete upheaval of adult life; it will not encourage you to invest in a single toy, program, or piece of gear. Kids don't need any of that, not even the ones destined for the Ivies. What they need is a happy, stress-free home led by relaxed, confident, and consistent, caring parents. That's what will give them the greatest odds of becoming successful adults. You can create that kind of environment. You can be that kind of parent. And you can have fun doing it.

In the chapters that follow, I lay out the hard facts about what you need to worry about and what you don't; what you can control as your children grow and what you can't. Grounded in the pediatric research, I share all the advice and knowledge I've learned through my personal observations as a mother and now a grandmother and through my professional experience as a pediatrician and neonatologist. In addition, we'll explore fresh perspectives and alternative solutions to age-old problems, many inspired by my research into how families raise their children in other parts of the world, addressing the common problems that challenge parents, such as:

- Figuring out how to reconcile the ideal and the idyll of breastfeeding with the reality that for some women it's extraordinarily difficult and impractical
- Treating colic
- Establishing healthy sleep habits
- Understanding and managing a temper tantrum
- Creating a harmonious morning routine that has everyone looking forward to the day
- Coping with or better yet avoiding a picky eater
- Easing separation anxiety
- Understanding excessive whining
- Preventing aggression
- Encouraging and supporting children in making their own decisions
- Recognizing when to hold on, and when to let go

It takes optimism and confidence to parent this way, but we can get there by finding ways to take the stress out of modern-day parenting. It will make a world of difference.

My intent is neither to romanticize the traditions of other countries and civilizations nor demonize the American way. I am well aware that there are parts of the globe in which children are not thriving, where families are underserved and plagued by disease. I have seen it firsthand. Furthermore, my experience and research does not extend into countries in full-scale war. Our current discussion is relevant only in lands of relative safety and plenty, not in places where happiness is defined as a day when everyone has made it home safely and has something to eat. There are certainly too many families living in neighborhoods that fit that description right here in the United States, but this book is not meant to address the systemic problems that threaten their survival. Rather, it is for those parents I meet every day who have the things they need and yet still behave as though their children were in danger, and feel they are on the front lines against an enemy they can't quite name.

Addressing families with children ranging from newborn to the early grade-school years, *The Confident Parent* will offer practical, easy-to-follow advice to help parents raise happy, healthy, successful kids without the daily struggles, screaming matches, and stress that too many of us have accepted as a natural part of family life. Each chapter reveals how it is possible to prevent or reverse almost every typical early-childhood challenge, from colic to sleep resistance, from tantrums to separation anxiety, once we address and eliminate the source of our own fear and anxiety and learn to look at the root cause of the problem.

When you can finally recognize that the world is far more rich with opportunity than danger, you'll parent with more confidence, which will lead to a calmer home, a more joyful experience, and a happier you. Whether you're already a parent or about to become one, there is a place on the scale where you can find a perfect balance between your needs and those of your child's. This book will help you find it. My hope is that the lessons I impart will give parents permission to let go and have fun so that they can enjoy parenting more and, in turn, avoid many of the mistakes that can make raising children harder than it needs to be. Ultimately, *The Confident Parent* will teach you how to introduce small changes that will help you start parenting with less anxiety and guilt and more instinct and joy.

1

A Fresh Perspective

I'M GOING TO start by telling you something you probably don't hear enough: You are doing a great job. Whether this is the first parenting book you've ever picked up or the most recent of many, the fact that you care enough to read a book on parenting and think deeply about the subject means that you are most likely already, in fact, a good parent. Probably better than good.

I want you to let that sink in. I meet so many parents who beat themselves up because they believe they are letting their children down with their failures. The baby cried all night and they couldn't figure out why. One day they were too demanding, another day they were too lax. They have been known to heat a box of frozen fish sticks for supper. They have yet to chaperone a single field trip. So many are carrying around an image of the perfect parent and are painfully aware that they're not one. My hope is that by the time you're done with this book, you'll be okay with that.

The goal of this book isn't to make you a perfect parent. It's to make you a more optimistic, confident, lighthearted, and fearless one. It's for anyone who has ever felt stressed out, strung out, anxious, exhausted, frustrated, or flummoxed by the challenges and pressures of parenting young children and who believes this is the normal, unavoidable face of parenting today. I assure you it is not. Many of the parents I have spoken with around the world are just as busy and just as invested in their children as we are, yet I have rarely heard them express the complete exhaustion and frustration that is such a regular complaint for the parents I have met in my pediatric clinics in Colorado, Idaho, and other parts of the United States. And it isn't just because their governments provide social services like ample paid parental leave, free childcare, and universal preschool, although those benefits help tremendously. As I see it, the big differences between these populations and the average American parent seems to be simply that those parents aren't judged for putting their own needs on par with their children's, and they don't spend time worrying about what everyone else thinks or what they could be doing more or better. Free of that mental anguish and second-guessing, they seem better able to project a calm, positive, relaxed attitude. While some families and cultures are stricter than others, in general I have found that parents living in or hailing from many other parts of the world seem to have a more optimistic outlook, firmly believing that with a stable environment and a nurturing family, the kids really will be all right. The end result of this approach is not only happy, healthy kids, but also happy, healthy parents.

Why is this confident, laissez-faire parenting philosophy in such short supply in our country? It has been squelched by a culture of fear, one that gleefully finds new ways to scare parents every day and lays the responsibility for their child's every triumph and failure right at their feet. There are of course those who try to buck the trend by instilling independence in their children at an early age, letting them make mistakes, or simply refusing to be afraid, but they are increasingly taking a risk. Many find themselves judged harshly by their peers or, worse, confronted by Child Protective Services, such as the Austin woman whose neighbor had her investigated for child abuse after she allowed her six-year-old son to play outdoors unsupervised within view of his own front porch, and the Maryland couple charged with "unsubstantiated child endangerment" for allowing their six- and ten-year-olds to walk home alone from a neighborhood park.

You would be hard-pressed to find any American who would disagree that it is the parents' job to protect their children from any risk or danger, that children's outdoor activities must be monitored to keep them safe, that parents must assess and encourage their children's gifts and talents early or risk squandering their child's potential, or that parents must be actively engaged with their children's schools and academic life. To buck these "rules" is to be irresponsible, even negligent. And they sound reasonable. Yet upholding these high standards requires a level of time, commitment, and effort that was never expected of generations past. For many parents, especially mothers, the demands—and the guilt and anxiety that arise when they can't meet those demands—can be overwhelming, leading to stress, exhaustion, and depression. Now, if extreme caution and vigilance resulted in the healthiest, most well-adjusted kids on the planet, maybe one could make the argument that parental happiness really should be secondary to the success of the child. But the facts don't support that theory at all.

Much has been written about how our American form of fear-based parenting is leading to epidemic levels of stress and anxiety, making mothers (and many fathers) feel crazy and miserable, but so far, knowing that anxiety is deleterious to our health hasn't been enough to force us to change our parenting approach. But maybe this will: There is ample evidence that the way we parent today isn't just hurting us—it's hurting our growing children, physically and cognitively. In the United States, we have seen

- a 600 percent increase since 1992 in the rates of full-term babies suffering from flat head syndrome, many by their two-month well-child visit, which over time can result in cognitive delays and visual impairment as well as other medical problems.
- 1 in 68 children diagnosed with autism spectrum disorder
- 1 in 8 children diagnosed with an anxiety disorder
- increased rates of asthma
- a 50 percent increase in ADHD diagnoses for school-aged children since 2003
- increased levels of juvenile depression, even in children with good self-control and emotional awareness
- a 35 percent increase of type 2 diabetes and hypertension in youth aged ten to nineteen between 2001–2009, diagnoses almost never seen in pediatric age groups until recently

Curiously, "all-in" parenting and making safety our number one priority isn't making our kids emotionally or physically healthier. And similar consequences are being felt in other countries, like England and Canada, that are adopting our parenting standards and habits. In this book we'll explore how the stress and fear we invite on ourselves can exacerbate or even set the stage for these conditions in our kids.

We don't even have to look for extreme symptoms to see the damage our over-involvement and heightened state of anxiety can cause. I saw it in my office every day. So do parents, they just don't realize it. It often manifests itself in the form of babies who won't sleep through the night, toddlers who won't eat balanced meals, young children prone to temper tantrums and separation anxiety, and older children who resist discipline. Parents are assured that children are biologically wired to behave this way; that daily struggles, screaming matches, and stress are natural parts of family life. But if that were the case, parents around the world would be wrestling with these issues as frequently as we do. Yet you rarely see Asian or Scandinavian toddlers having temper tantrums. Few Indian children turn their nose up at their vegetables. It's unusual for parents in Holland or France to spend months in a row tending to their wailing infants or restless toddlers. Are American babies and children somehow physiologically different from others? Of course not. The truth is that much of the time, these "inevitable" issues are in fact quite preventable and more likely caused by environmental and cultural factors than by biological ones.

Through my travels and conversations, I have found that parents hailing from or living in countries that report high levels of parental satisfaction and family harmony embrace a number of principles that may seem counterintuitive and even shocking to many American parents:

1. It is not natural for mothers to be with their young children all day and night.
2. Nurturing a marriage or partnership is as important to child-rearing as nurturing the child.

3. Children are strong and resilient—unless parents teach them not to be.
4. Sometimes a parent's needs must come first.
5. Picky eating is learned, not innate.
6. There is such a thing as being too careful.
7. Raising successful children is about providing interaction, not just opportunities.

These are the principles that underlie much of the advice I have offered the families in my practice over the years and the ones that have seemed to make the most positive difference in their lives by preventing or reversing almost every typical early-childhood challenge, from colic to sleep resistance, from tantrums to separation anxiety.

A PROBLEM THAT TRANSCENDS CLASS

The knee-jerk reaction to any critique of the perfectionist pressure put on American mothers in particular and parents in general is that it is a problem for only a certain upwardly mobile, affluent demographic that has the time to wring its hands over such things. But this phenomenon is no longer limited to upper-middle-class white families, if it ever really was. I have served a broad swath of American families, from the relatively homogenous families in northwest Colorado to the urban and ethnically diverse communities in North Carolina to isolated, rural Idaho where 40 percent of the population was on Medicaid. I have treated the children of well-off professionals, middle-class couples, teen moms, and recovering meth addicts. Most of the parents I meet adore parenthood and describe this time as one of unbelievable love and joy. But across the board, they often qualify that description by adding that it is also a time of unbelievable anxiety, stress, and even exhaustion. Many even wear their fatigue and stress as a badge of honor. After all, no one said parenting would be easy, and everyone knows it takes sacrifice and hard work to raise a well-adjusted, healthy child.

But should it? Is it a universal given that good parents should be willing to give up just about anything for the benefit of their children or that good parenting is inherently stressful? As this book will show, no. Parents in many other countries juggle work and children. They want what's best for their kids. And of course they sometimes worry. But they are not consumed by it because unlike us, they are not bombarded with the message that parenthood is a trial, that childhood is a dangerous time for children, and that anything could happen at any time to destroy their happiness. It's often a subtle narrative, but we hear it all the time, and it is constantly reinforced by the multitude of rules we've developed to stave off our worst nightmares.

RULES MADE TO BE BROKEN

Nothing makes a risk-averse society feel better than a nice list of rules. Parents love them. Rules take all the guesswork out of decision making, offering parents a few moments of respite in a job that requires endless improvisation. They also give us an immediate way to categorize ourselves and other parents: Those who follow the rules are "good" parents; those who break them out of willfulness or ignorance are "bad," or at the very least, irresponsible.

I have a strong aversion to too many rules, especially when it comes to raising children. With the exception of the ones grounded in physiological facts, rules are generally culturally biased, and therefore completely subjective. For example, many Americans were appalled by the story of the Kaufmans, a young couple raising their one- and three-year-old daughters on a sailboat while embarking on a round-the-world trip, only to be rescued by the Coast Guard when they lost control of the boat and their younger daughter fell ill. In blogs and comments, people accused the Kaufmans of selfishness, negligence, and child endangerment. Because we live in a society that aspires to a certain level of material comfort and has established that children should be raised on terra firma, to many, the Kaufmans' actions seemed inexplicable and dangerous. They broke the rules, and many people thought they should pay.

And yet, families take their children on adventurous trips all the time—we just don't hear about them because the media aren't all that interested in family success stories. And really, their decision wasn't that wild, globally speaking. The Bajau-Laut and the Moken people of Southeast Asia raise their children in boats or in homes built over the water, and you won't find a life preserver anywhere. The Korowai tribe of New Guinea lives in tree houses, sometimes perched up to 150 feet off the ground. Does the fact that the Moken and the Korowai have different safety standards mean that families who sail should leave the lifejackets behind or that apartment dwellers with children should forgo window guards? Of course not. (The Korowai are said to still practice cannibalism, too, so they're not necessarily role models.) But clearly, with proper planning and preparation, humans can adapt to almost any living environment. The rules governing the "right" way to raise and care for children are far more flexible than people realize.

You might be surprised at how many rules invoked in the name of safety, and accepted by many American parents as dogma, are unheard of or taken with a grain of salt in other countries. For example, this one, emblazoned in big block letters on the label of every jar of honey sold in this country: Babies under a year old shouldn't eat honey. Everyone knows that, right? Yet around the world, in places like Greece, New Zealand, France, and the Middle East, parents feed it to their young children without a moment's thought, often mixed in dairy products or drizzled on toast or fruit. Is there something different about the honey they feed their children? Are our children particularly vulnerable to illness in ways that children in other countries are not? Not at all. The reason we see this stringent warning repeated over and over again is because at one point back in the 1970s, California saw a few cases of infant botulism, which is extremely rare. Later, researchers found traces of botulism spores in some samples of honey. Thus the Centers for Disease Control and Prevention (CDC) set the recommendation that parents avoid feeding honey to infants, whose gastrointestinal tracts are incapable of handling any botulism spores that might be present. Botulism, especially in a small infant, can be deadly. It's not a trivial matter. But let's put things in perspective:

- On average, there are only 80 to 100 cases of infant botulism reported in the United States per year out of approximately 4 million births per year. Of those cases, only about 20 percent are related to honey.

- Botulism spores can be found in dirt, water, and dust, including the dust from your vacuum cleaner.
- By the age of six months, children's intestinal tracts have matured enough to pass any botulism spores that could be present in contaminated honey, so they can't linger, germinate, and release toxins into the child's system. Pediatricians don't generally recommend that babies start to eat solid foods until six months anyway. This also explains why you'll see so many honey-flavored foods geared for babies in the supermarkets in other countries—by the time children are ready to enjoy these foods, their bodies are fully capable of handling them.
- Even if a child does contract infant botulism, it is rarely fatal and, barring serious complications contracted in the case of hospitalization, there are no permanent consequences after recovery.

So the risk of an infant contracting botulism is exceedingly low, and the risk of an infant over the age of six months getting botulism is even lower, yet American parents are given a blanket warning: No Honey for Babies under One Year Old under Any Circumstances. Apparently the CDC decided that it was easier to effectively scare parents with a general, easy-to-remember rule than to bother explaining the real risks. More important, taking such a conservative position absolves everyone in charge of setting guidelines about what is and isn't safe for children's consumption, as well as the honey producers, from responsibility should a child get sick.

Now, it's really not a big deal if American children don't get to taste honey until they're a year old. But it's worth dissecting the logic behind such a blanket warning, as it's just one of hundreds of rules like it to which parents feel obligated to give credence. Every day, through parenting magazines, social media, and television, parents are exposed to a litany of ways in which their child could be hurt or even killed (*Parents Magazine* has even published a feature called "It Happened to Me" devoted to these horror stories). Almost every story is accompanied by general advice that parents should follow to avoid such a thing ever happening to their child. The stories spread—"Did you hear...?" "Can you imagine...?" After a while, they get repeated so much they become the rule, not the exception. And that's how so many people get spooked and wind up following fear-based dogma.

Here's a sample of some common parenting "rules." How many have you heard?

- Childhood sunburns increase the likelihood of cancer, so children should never go outdoors in the sun without a layer of protective sunscreen.
- Crying stresses babies out, so babies should always be allowed to feed on demand.
- High fever can damage the brain, so any fever must be brought down as soon as possible.
- Most children don't get enough calcium, so children should primarily drink milk even after they are weaned. Conversely, milk makes sick children even sicker and should be restricted until the child is well.
- Your child stands a higher risk of developing allergies if you introduce anything but rice cereal once it's time to start solid foods.

I could fill a whole book with a list of paranoia-inducing rules just like these that have seeped into our collective consciousness and affected parents' outlook on child-rearing. Each recommendation was originally grounded in fact, but along the way important details were lost. For example:

- *Excessive* sun exposure can increase one's risk of cancer later in life. So while it is good practice to ensure your child wears sunscreen on exposed skin and covers up in light cotton clothing, there's no need to feel guilty if your child occasionally gets a little sun or leaves the house without sunscreen.

- Crying for *excessive periods of time* is hard on a baby, but it won't hurt your child to cry for a few minutes while you finish what you're doing and then tend to his or her needs. And for reasons I explain in chapter 6, if you schedule a feed every two and a half to three hours, you may actually have a happy, rested baby who cries far less often than if you breastfeed on demand.

- Fevers can cause brain damage *if they get uncontrollably high*. Some fever is the body's way of fighting infection. A low-grade fever, even one lasting several days, is nothing to worry about if it is unaccompanied by other worrisome symptoms, like severe abdominal pain or earache. I counsel parents to treat children who have a fever of 102°F or are aged six months or more with acetaminophen or ibuprofen simply to help make their children more comfortable. Once a fever rises above that, even to 104°F, it still won't permanently damage your child, but at that time she should absolutely be evaluated.

- It's true that calcium is an important nutrient and that most children don't get enough, but after a baby's first year it's preferable that he *eats* his calcium, not drink it. There are so many fun ways to get it through dairy products, and there are plenty of other foods fortified with calcium as well. I also frequently see the reverse problem: Though there is nothing in the medical literature to support the idea that milk increases the body's production of mucus, I constantly meet parents who restrict milk and dairy products as soon as their child gets a head cold. This is absolutely unnecessary, and it's the wrong time to restrict calories or deny the simple comfort many little children get from a cup of milk.

- Rice is favored as a first solid food for its easy digestibility and hypoallergenic qualities, but it's not your only option. In fact, many physicians and nutritionists are recommending that babies' first foods should be pureed vegetables. In British-influenced countries parents often incorporate egg yolks into baby food, such as might be found in a homemade custard or pudding.

Being aware of important details like these could make a huge difference in the way we raise our children.

THE BIRTH OF FEAR-BASED PARENTING

It is not more dangerous to raise a child in this country today than it was before. So why are we constantly made to feel like it is? Who benefits?

The media get blamed for a lot these days, but in this case, it's not unfair to say that the media have had a tremendous influence on the paranoia that has infiltrated American parenting practices, starting in the 1970s with the coverage of the tragic disappearance of little Etan Patz in New York City, who vanished the first day he walked to the school bus alone and ramping up a decade later with the murder of six-year-old Adam Walsh, kidnapped from a Florida department store while shopping with his mother. Since then, we've been flooded with a constant stream of stories about child abductions, abuse, freak accidents, and fatal product malfunctions.

The media, including parenting blogs, have a strong incentive to highlight worst-case scenarios. Fear sells; reason and subtlety do not. Nothing gets people talking (and coming back for more) like the scary stuff—the heartbreaking stories about children fighting for their lives, about traumatized yet triumphant mothers, about fathers advocating for their children against a slow-moving medical bureaucracy. Parents who are suffering are naturally more motivated to share their stories and to make a lot of noise, demanding change. And since fear makes people pay attention, it's in the magazines' and the Internet's best interest to give these parents the platforms they need to disseminate their message and play an incessant drumbeat: *The world is a dangerous place. Terrible things can happen. Don't let them happen to you!*

It's a fear that runs so deep it's hard to relinquish even when you think you've freed yourself. Miriam, who grew up in the States but now lives in Israel with her husband and three children, finds that old habits die hard:

Part of living here is enjoying that freedom for your kids, feeling that they're safe among everyone. Here we feel totally confident letting our kids walk distances alone. But you don't feel the same there. We flew to the States, the girls were four and two, and we walked into a Barnes & Noble. My husband was in charge of looking after one of the girls. I came up to him and said, "Where is Ma'ayan?" He said, "Oh, I dunno, somewhere." I said, "What? You can't do that! You cannot know at all times where she is! It's not the same here!" In the States anyone can come along and scoop up your kid, and you'll never see them again. That's how I was raised to feel. In the United States you can't take your eyes off your kid in a public place for a second. In Israel you know that whoever finds them is going to find you and bring them to you. There's a sense of confidence in the people around you.

Miriam's trust and sense of security is especially remarkable when you remember that she lives in a country where an armed guard monitors the entrance to every elementary school.

There is also the litigious nature of our society. In other countries, lawsuits are relatively rare, but in ours, the common thinking is that when something goes wrong, someone should pay. And so we live in a cover-your-ass society, where people—and especially doctors, day-care workers, and other childcare professionals—feel obligated to take extreme precautionary measures to avoid being accused of impropriety or negligence. It's why our playgrounds are universally sanitized, static, and boring.

And then there's the Internet, that portal to the information age. The Internet sometimes makes my job extremely difficult. More than once, parents of children suffering headaches have tried to pressure me to order expensive and unnecessary tests to rule out a brain tumor, even though a neurological exam revealed nothing suspicious. I've known parents who found doctors willing to put their children through biopsies because they wanted to be absolutely sure that the tender, swollen lymph nodes that can remain after a head cold weren't signs of leukemia. These poor parents are convinced something is terribly wrong, and that doctors are being cavalier about their child's health. They are determined to be the kind of advocates they read about in their magazines.

I admire parents who ask questions and show a fierce devotion to their child. But they make me sad, too, because nine times out of ten, they have worked themselves up into a panic for nothing. And it's time they can't get back. In addition, there is strong evidence to suggest that children absorb our stress. In one study conducted by researchers at the University of California and New York University, it took only minutes for a child's body to mimic his or her mother's stress response—in the form of increased heart rate—on being placed in her arms. This suggests that when parents put themselves in a chronically anxious state, they're putting their kids there, too.

And all that information takes a psychological toll. You can't worry about what you don't know exists, yet today you have to practically live off the grid to enjoy any of the blissful ignorance of generations past. All that knowledge gives us the impression that we have control over our environment and our circumstances. No wonder parents blame themselves when things go wrong (which is supremely easy to do in a society that immediately points the finger at parents for their children's behavior and mistakes). As writer Erika Christakis said after raising this point in a 2012 Aspen Institute panel discussion on the goal of parenting, "It does create a lot of anxiety, I think, to live in a world where we feel so responsible . . . even though many studies show we have a lot less influence on our kids than we think."

Finally, some observers of American society suspect that parents are like canaries in a coal mine, reacting adversely to the effects of living in an intensely capitalistic and competitive society. Kate, an Australian who frequently visits her American mother's large extended family in the United States, thinks our weak social safety net may lead us to carry subconscious fears that affect the way we raise our kids. After all, she wonders, how can we ever relax when we know that even if we do everything right, there's no guarantee of security? For example, in her native Australia, "If you want to be a doctor, you know if you study hard and get good grades, you can do it. [Thanks to the country's system of student welfare payments and interest-free loans] it's not something that can be restricted by money. We may have more opportunity than you do that way." That opportunity is a source of hope and optimism in her country, which is something sorely lacking in ours. Our insecurity makes us feel like we have to shore up our kids' futures right away, which then compels us to push our children and ourselves too hard, leading to unhealthy levels of stress and anxiety that could risk spoiling some of the best years of our lives.

For Borgit, an American who lived in Guatemala and Venezuela before returning to Salt Lake City, the contrast between her family's calm life in South America and the busyness and pressure inherent in the United States proved to be too much:

> Life in the States is hard. You're busy from the time you wake up to the time you go to bed, and the time you get with your kids during the week is short. I felt exhausted every night. I

don't know how much quality there was with our two kids. People that haven't experienced living abroad think this is how life is. Part of why we moved abroad again was to get that time and quality back. . . . When we said we were moving to Saudi [Arabia] we got lots of looks, not very positive, but this place is a perfect environment for people with kids. Culturally and as a woman it's hard, but I can't imagine moving back to the States. I don't see us returning any time soon, not as long as the kids are in school.

IN SUM, MIRIAM, Kate, and Borgit are confirming something many of us hear and read all the time—it's just easier to raise kids abroad. But we can't all pick up and leave. And most of us love our country and don't want to. So what do we do when we can't unknow what we know, and neither the media nor our social policies nor our workaholic culture is likely to change? What can a parent do to fight the fear that can make parenting (and childhood) such a challenge in this country?

The first step? Get some perspective.

THE RISKS—THEY'RE NOT WHAT YOU THINK THEY ARE

In all my years as a pediatrician, neither my colleagues nor I have ever been confronted with a case in which a child patient drowned in a toilet, probably because it is so exceedingly rare. In fact, over a four-year period, the US Consumer Product Safety Commission received reports of only 16 children under the age of five years (out of a US birthrate of about 4 million births per year) who drowned in a toilet. They do sometimes drink toilet water, but so what? It won't kill them, so do we really need toilet bowl locks? Kids bump their heads while they're learning to walk. They get over it. Does anyone really need table bumpers? Kids get sick, but most of the time the illnesses they catch are minor, especially if they have had their immunizations. If they don't catch something from a grocery cart because you've protected them with a grocery cart cover, they'll catch it elsewhere. (What's next, portable elevator button covers?) The risk of sudden infant death syndrome (SIDS) has decreased in the United States by 50 percent since 1992, but it's because parents started putting their children to sleep on their backs, not because they could watch their child through a monitor or even track their heart rate and temperature through the Mimo, a onesie outfitted with a tracking device that feeds a constant stream of data about your sleeping child. Nor was it thanks to the Owlet, a $250 baby monitoring sock whose CEO sees a "wearable future" for children that "will include every single baby coming home from the hospital with a health monitor." Many parents know they're going a little overboard when they purchase these products, but they do it anyway because it makes them feel better. But if parents weren't already conditioned to be afraid, would they have to go to such lengths to find peace of mind? (Full disclosure: I developed an inexpensive beanie called the Tortle to prevent infants from developing flat head syndrome, which has increased by 600 percent in the United States. I created it as a last resort when I finally realized that even with extensive education, our modern lifestyle makes it difficult for parents to prevent the syndrome on their own. See chapter 3 for hard data about flat head syndrome.)

Do terrible, tragic things happen to children? Sadly, they do.

But not nearly as often as we have been convinced they do. In fact, one of the main predictors of unintentional injuries and fatalities in childhood in this country is poverty. But note that the makers of these safety products don't market to poor people. Rather, they target insecure new parents with disposable income.

FAQ: What Can I Do to Reduce the Chance That My Baby Dies of Sudden Infant Death Syndrome?

A number of babies in the United States continue to die of SIDS, about 5 per 10,000 births. There are a number of factors associated with SIDS that you cannot change, such as congenital brain abnormalities, low birth weight, family history of relatives who have died of SIDS, and race. These factors are likely the cause of many cases of SIDS, but there are environmental factors, which you can influence, that can significantly reduce the risks:

- Position your baby on her back to sleep.
- Provide a firm surface free of loose blankets and soft fluffy items.
- Don't sleep with your baby.
- Don't smoke or allow others to smoke around your baby.
- Try to provide some breast milk even if you can't fully breastfeed, to provide some protection from infections.
- Keep up to date with your baby's immunizations (for example, whooping cough).

A global cross-cultural perspective can help rid us of our fear. When you realize that an entire country feeds honey-spiked desserts to its infants, you won't tremble as you offer your baby his or her first spoonful of the stuff. When you realize that women have been leaving their children in other people's care for centuries, and that many still do and yet continue to share an unbreakable bond with their babies, you won't feel so guilty when you leave for work in the morning. When you learn that the happiest families in the world are the ones living in cultures that *don't* encourage them to jam their children's days with classes and activities, and that they still reliably produce new generations of smart, healthy, productive citizens, you won't worry so much that you're doing things "wrong." Perspective will allow you to recapture the joy and the fun of raising kids.

> Perspective will allow you to recapture the joy and the fun of raising kids.

WHAT'S "NATURAL" IS WHAT WORKS BEST FOR YOU

I am not the first to suggest that parents turn to other cultures for inspiration in child-rearing. For years, for example, childcare experts and anthropologists have encouraged parents to model some habits of primitive tribes. Unfortunately, in some cases, the message became that the primitive way was how we were supposed to raise kids all along, and that our troubles stem from having divorced ourselves from our natural environment. However, some of the methods we have been encouraged to adopt because they are supposedly more natural, like co-sleeping and baby wearing, can often make a modern-day parent's stress worse. Critics who judge parents for citing convenience or effi-cacy as a factor in their parenting choices ignore that the reason those "natural" techniques were adopted millennia ago is pre-cisely because they were convenient, allowing parents to do what they needed to do with the greatest ease possible. In other words, parents have always put themselves first out of necessity. It stands to reason, then, that as parents' needs and circumstances change, so should child-rearing strategies. Simply transplanting the techniques of another culture without adapting your lifestyle to match rarely works. The key to success is to be sure that we bor-row traditions and techniques that actually fit the lives we live now, not the ones we might have lived thousands of years ago.

We need to remember what much of the rest of the world never forgot: Parents are supposed to be guides, not guards; mentors, not monitors. In my experience, those who understand this are generally happier, healthier, and report greater life and marital satisfaction and stronger relationships with their chil-dren. Life is complicated and busy enough as it is, why add to it? Fight the fear, trust yourself, and regain some perspective so the time spent with your children is relaxed and happy. We are so lucky to live in an era when we have the luxury to enjoy our chil-dren. Let's not waste it. The years we get to spend with our little ones are short and precious—let's learn to model fearlessness, confidence, and optimism so that one day they are excited, not scared, to go out into this big, beautiful world in which we live.

2

Caring for Your Newborn—and Yourself

PARENTING WITHOUT ANXIETY takes practice and forethought. In fact, you'll probably have to start your resistance training far sooner than you imagined, for the inculcation of fear starts early. When Chris, a twenty-nine-year-old EMT, announced that she was pregnant, she enjoyed reveling in her friends' and family's delight but was taken aback at the number of cautionary asides that followed almost immediately on the heels of their congratulations. "Get all the sleep you can, because you are *not* going to sleep after this baby comes—maybe for years!" "Enjoy yourself now, you're about to lose all your free time." "Oh my, just wait till you feel the 'ring of fire.'" "You'll probably need a C-section."

So often—too often—even as they are feted with baby showers, good wishes, and Anne Geddes cards, expectant moms (and dads) are fed a deluge of warnings about how the arrival of their baby is going to ruin their bodies, rob them of personal time, and upend their lives. Women compete to provide the most harrowing birth story—the forty-eight-hour labor, the emergency C-section, the ineffective epidural—all laughed off with a remark about how the pain was worth it. There is cachet to suffering in labor.

This is markedly different from the way I saw new mothers welcomed to the fold when I lived in Kenya and South Africa. The congratulations, support, and encouragement the African mothers received from their friends and family were not delivered with a side order of cautionary tales. It was also simply taken for granted that the new mothers would figure out how to address their infants' needs and adjust to their new roles without much to-do. Consequently, new mothers in many parts of underdeveloped Africa rarely anticipated the arrival of their babies with the same anxiety and soul-searching as Americans. I noticed they were also much more matter-of-fact about labor, despite being aware that in the "natural environment," many things can go wrong for mother and child. Still, they discussed labor less as a miraculous though frightening cross to be borne and more as a natural, manageable rite of passage. Even today, I'm told, few mothers in underdeveloped Africa anticipate having a C-section or even receiving medicine during labor.

It is simply assumed that mothers will know what to do when the time comes, and though many African women have much less information than most American mothers regarding the health or positioning of the fetus, they approach labor with little fear. Many women are tended during their labor by their own mothers, mothers-in-law or even by friends, though increasingly babies are born in a hospital. Even then, however, though medical practitioners monitor their patients, they generally intervene only when it's time to push or when something raises their alarm. And while new mothers have often witnessed childbirth and know through other family members' experience the inherent risks of labor, they are generally calm and prepared for the event and go in optimistic they will have a successful outcome and a positive experience.

How can expectant mothers be so optimistic and calm in a country where childbirth can be one of the most dangerous things a woman will do in her life and infant mortality rates are high, while in a wealthy country like the United States, with one of the most advanced healthcare systems in the world, maternal stress is so prevalent it's been identified as one of the key causes for our frequent cases of low birth weight and prematurity? I suspect it's the same reason I don't fret if I forget to lock my doors—when you have lived with real danger, you know better than to wear yourself out imagining it. During the Kenyan Mau Mau uprising of the early 1950s, I awoke every day knowing that my family was a prime target for the anticolonial resentment that had fueled kidnappings and the murders of several white families in their homes as well as launched a spate of brutality against entire villages that did not immediately align themselves with the Mau Mau cause. It was also second nature for me to keep a constant lookout for the scorpions and poisonous snakes that were commonplace in the grass and along the paths near our home and that occasionally made themselves comfortable in our toy boxes, shoes, and beds.

War and venomous wildlife were the facts of my African existence. Moving to the States was like going on vacation. No scorpions scurrying around under the bed, no angry mobs threatening to hack my family to death, and central air-conditioning, too? Heaven. For a while, my biggest challenge was teaching my children, who had spent most of their lives scampering like little wildebeests in the South African desert, how to watch out for cars. Then my fourth child was born prematurely and we had to spend a month in the NICU. I was terrified for him, as any mother would be, but once the danger was over and we knew he would live, we left the hospital, along with my worries, behind. Of course my husband and I had to be extra careful to protect our son while he was still tiny and fragile, but there was no doubt in our minds that we were up to the task. Worrying about what might happen or could happen would only make us weak, and our little guy needed us to be strong and steady.

It is so much better to start your life with your child armed with confidence and optimism. This chapter identifies ways to help you develop these traits before and after the arrival of your new baby. Treat the advice herein as a virtual vitamin supplement for the soul. Like the real thing, it will make you stronger and more resistant to outside forces that are apt to wear you down.

IN THE BEGINNING

If you're just beginning to share your good news about your pregnancy, there are steps you can take right away to create a protective buffer zone around yourself so that you begin this marvelous new journey calmly and confidently.

Deflect the Negative

It can be extremely difficult to block out the unsolicited advice and warnings so many people feel compelled to share on hearing your baby is on the way, but I urge you to try. Life with a baby does not always smell like roses, it's true, but neither does it have to be an overwhelming struggle. Just because one baby screamed through the night for six weeks doesn't mean that yours will (especially if you follow the advice in this book—see chapter 5 for tips on setting sleep schedules). Just because your sister's toddler was a major handful doesn't mean that yours will be. You will probably experience a monumental shift in priorities, and you may be astounded at the emotional floodgates that open, but your life doesn't have to change in anything but the best of ways. You will go out to nice restaurants again. You will be able to continue work you love, or find time to read a book, or spend time alone with your partner. It simply takes preparation, planning, and remembering something that our culture tends to forget—that new parents need as much special attention and care as new babies. So when people try to tell you horror stories or start talking about how little sleep, sex, money, and free time you're about to have, try interrupting with a smile and say, "We're so excited, we prefer to concentrate on everything we're about to gain, not what we might or might not lose."

Use Social Media with Caution

It's become an exciting rite of passage to post baby news and even ultrasounds onto social media, but be careful about using it to solicit advice, and don't take your friends' newsfeeds too much to heart. Parents post loving tributes and adorable photos of their progeny, but often the most popular threads chronicle the wars they are raging with their three-year-olds or laments about the tantrums, incessant crying, allergic reactions, and trips to the emergency room. Remember, your friends are having their experience, and you will have yours. Social media can be like a drug; many people turn to it for a hit of gratification and validation. Parents post to show off, to garner sympathy, and to vent. Do not let other people's insecurities and negativity affect you. Once you have your child in your arms, social media can be a wonderful companion and resource, connecting you to friends and relatives all eager to know how you're doing and answer your questions. But there is a big difference between asking specific questions about the baby you have, and projecting about the baby you will have. Let your baby guide you, and don't try to predict ahead of time who he or she will be. You'll find out soon enough.

Avoid Watching Medical Procedural Dramas

Please. Television writers love to create plotlines in which a birth goes horribly wrong. You just don't need to see that, especially when the script often features the most unlikely scenarios possible.

Don't Just Hope for the Best Outcome—Expect It

Most OB/GYNs offer their pregnant patients a battery of tests to help screen for maternal health problems such as gestational diabetes as well as fetal anomalies and chromosomal abnormalities. In fact, tests are now available to screen for more than 800 genetic disorders. It can be nerve-racking for parents to face one test after another and then wait for the results, especially if they decide to poke around on the Internet to see what could happen should a test come back positive. OB/GYNs use those tests to help them manage your pregnancy, initiate the right conversations, and ensure your child gets the best start in life possible.

The real problem, as I see it, is that many doctors underestimate the amount of anxiety these screenings and tests can cause, despite the fact that complications and genetic abnormalities are exceedingly rare.

The problem is, they don't feel rare, because if you look on the Internet you will find thousands of stories about parents who were forced to contend with disappointing or even devastating news following an ultrasound or blood test. Their grief is real and their stories deserve to be told, but you don't need to be the one to listen. At least, not right now. There are millions more who did not get that bad news, and there is every reason to expect that you will be one of them.

Turn to Your Partner

So often expectant parents turn to their Facebook friends for support, encouragement, and answers to their questions and forget to give their partner a chance to fulfill that role for them. Now is the time to join forces and make sure all the communication channels and emotional connections are open and functioning well. The long-term benefits of these emotional investments are well understood, but the short-term benefits might surprise you. Studies show that mothers with higher-than-normal cortisol levels, which indicate elevated maternal stress, report fewer pregnancy or labor complications when they take a class emphasizing communication and conflict resolution with their partners *in addition to* a traditional prenatal class that focuses on the physical aspects of pregnancy and labor. In other words, the childbirths of women who feel emotionally supported and confident show a markedly better outcome. Do your prenatal education with your partner and plan to involve him or her in every step from pregnancy, labor, delivery, and infant care. Be in this together.

Stand up to Peer Pressure

Of all the advice Chris heard before she gave birth to her son, the one that took her aback the most was, "Double up on your classes, because once you have that baby, you're not going to be able to go to school." She had completed her EMT training and only had to be certified. But her family and peers made it clear that in their eyes, good moms didn't leave their children in day care to go to school. Responding to this advice, she dropped out and stayed at home for fifteen months. She adored looking after her child, but she quickly realized she had no future to give her son.

Whether to breastfeed, vaccinate, circumcise, cry it out, co-sleep, teach sign language, cook organic, use day care, hire a nanny, be a SAHM—one of our country's strengths is that we are a land that supposedly allows people and parents infinite choices. Unfortunately, many parents limit their options to appease their families or align with the demands of the peer group to which they want to belong. Sometimes it can seem like our children are walking billboards for our values and beliefs.

We are all vulnerable when our peers and families try to pressure us to live according to the standards they have set. The trick is to set our own, and stick to them. You need to feel good about the choices you make because that will make you a happy parent, which will result in a happy child. In ten years, when you're talking to your children about how to resist peer pressure, it will be helpful if you can point to yourself as a good role model.

AT THE HOSPITAL

I experienced one of the biggest surprises of my life the day that I was admitted to a hospital in Denver to give birth to my fourth child, David, my first to be born in the States. Minutes upon arrival I was put on a fetal monitor and given an IV. It floored me. "I'm not sick!" I said. "This isn't going to take long, it's my fourth!" The nurse replied, "This is what we do in America. We don't want you to get dehydrated." I've always been a strong advocate for preventative medicine and doing due diligence to avoid problems, but in the countries where I had delivered my previous three children, the role of medical practitioners was, and continues to be, far less interventional during hospital births.

In another book we might now segue into a critique of the overmedicalization of the birth industry in our country. But I am neither questioning nor condemning the use of tech and medicine, either in the OB/GYN's office or in the delivery room. There is no denying that our extreme caution and intense medical supervision before and during childbirth has ensured the health of millions of children and mothers, making the United States one of the safest places to give birth.* Japan, where pregnant women's health and even diet are strictly monitored by their doctors and ultrasounds are a routine part of every prenatal visit, needs only a quarter of the number of NICU beds we do in the United States, even correcting for their lower birth rate of about 1 million per year.

---

* If you are neither poor nor uninsured, that is. Most of the time, our country's troubling infant mortality rates are strongly linked to poverty and low education and are not based on the number of babies who survive hospital births but rather the number of babies who die a few weeks after going home.

Why? Because the mothers live in a culture that reveres authority figures, and they usually do exactly what their doctors tell them to do (some doctors have been known to call a woman's employer if they feel she needs "encouragement" to follow medical orders). By minimizing the number of variables and complications they might have to confront in the delivery room, doctors help ensure more predictable outcomes during childbirth.

In America—a nonconformist, ethnically and sociologically diverse society where no two mothers will have followed the same regimen during their pregnancies—physicians and hospitals use IVs and fetal monitors in their delivery rooms to implement a standardization of care in the one place where they have real control. Here, at least, they can make sure everyone gets what she needs.

Yet for some parents, all the equipment and wires and the constant comings and goings of nurses arriving to check their patients' vitals can make a very natural process seem like an imminent emergency and make them feel nervous and constrained. To address those concerns and offer a more individualized, empowering experience, many hospitals now offer "natural" birthing suites where women can choose to labor without medical intervention, yet with the reassurance that the hospital's medical team and sophisticated equipment is just minutes away. It's an excellent option and far safer than giving birth at home.* Unfortunately, I have met many new mothers a few days after giving birth who struggle to reconcile their idealized vision of what their child's

---

* Proponents of home births will cite statistics that show a home birth attended by a doula or midwife is as safe if not safer than having a baby in a hospital. That's just not the case. If everything goes perfectly, then yes, a home birth would be a great way to bring a baby into the world. But I have seen too many avoidable tragedies caused by unexpected complications during a home birth. Sometimes the difference between a happy or a tragic outcome can be measured in the time it took to get to the hospital.

birth was supposed to be like and the reality of what happened. If they ultimately requested an epidural or had to be transferred to a more traditional clinical setting to finish their labor, they sometimes feel like they have been betrayed by their body or regret that they weren't strong enough to hold out for a natural birth. It's like they failed to gain admittance to an elite club.

Do not do this to yourself. It's a wonderful thing to prepare for the birth of your child and to have the luxury of weighing your birthing options, so go ahead and make the choices that make you feel most comfortable. Draft the birthing plan that gives you the greatest sense of control. And then, once everything is in place and everyone around you knows what you want and what role they are to play when the big day arrives—relax and forget about it. Don't allow identity politics or idealism keep you from being open to improvisation and the unexpected. Once you're in labor, give yourself permission to do whatever it takes to make that labor a wonderful memory. If that means asking for an epidural so you can catch your breath, so be it. There is no glory and no prize given to those who suffer more than they need to. Asking for help or relief does not make you a failure or a weak link in the annals of strong womanhood. In fact, I'm positive that many Neanderthal mothers would have happily accepted epidurals if they could have.

> There is no glory and no prize given to those who suffer more than they need to.

There is little evidence that epidurals hamper a complication-free childbirth or have negative effects on the ability of a healthy newborn to breastfeed, especially with the newer lower-dose drug formulations. In addition, "a 2011 study published by nurses at the University of Illinois at Chicago reported that women who received epidurals had similar levels of the stress hormone cortisol in their umbilical cord blood immediately after birth as women who had no drugs. Since cord blood cortisol is a good proxy for newborn alertness, the findings suggest that epidurals probably have no effect." Opt for pain medication or don't, either choice is fine so long as it feels right to you.

FAQ: Will Having an Epidural Affect Breastfeeding?

There can be an effect during the first twenty-four hours; however, the difference is fairly small according to some studies evaluating this question. Epidural drugs are designed to stay compartmentalized within the spinal cord area so as not to affect the rest of your system.

Bring someone you really trust to the hospital—your spouse, your partner, your parent, your sister, your best friend—but not a whole cheerleading squad. This is a joyous occasion, but not a social one. Too many people in the delivery room can be problematic for the professionals trying to assist you in a safe delivery. Trust your medical staff will do their utmost to provide you and your baby with a perfect outcome. Be confident that you will know what to do, and follow the directions they give you. Remember that everyone in that room is trained to educate you, support you, and keep you and your baby safe. Everything they do, in particular putting in that IV, is about being proactively safe. I assure you nothing is done because it's convenient for the nurses and doctors. Contrary to what the natural labor movement would insist, doctors don't use technology to increase your hospital bill (all the doctors I've ever spoken to *hate* dealing with billing); they use the technology because it gives them immediate and accurate feedback on what's going on with you and your baby, allowing them to make quick adjustments to your care. Because in the birthing room, if something does go wrong, it can go wrong extremely fast.

The day your baby makes her way into the world will be just the first of many where you discover that despite all your efforts you can control only so much. The happiest, most confident parents are the ones who understand, accept, and even embrace that reality. In fact, they believe it's part of what makes the journey so much fun.

AFTER BIRTH

At last, you have your baby in your arms. Time to relax. In many other developed countries, even mothers with uncomplicated vaginal births stay in the hospital for a full week so nurses can observe the mothers with their infants and make sure everyone gets started on the right foot, whether by offering breastfeeding advice or watching for signs of common infant problems. Since that option isn't available to most women in the States, what can you do to ensure that you're rested and ready as possible to care for your newborn when you go home?

Stay in the Hospital as Long as You Can

Even if you have an army of attendants waiting to take care of you back home, try to make the most of what little time you have in the hospital, which will probably be two days for a vaginal birth and three or four if you had a C-section. Many of your friends will tell you they left the hospital earlier because they wanted to get started being a family. I urge you to stay put. You will be tired. Take advantage of the time you get in the hospital where you have literally nothing to do but get to know your new little one while everyone waits on you hand and foot. Once they're home most people feel obligated to get up and about as soon as possible, especially if there are other children who need attention. In the hospital there is no obligation to anyone but yourself and your baby. It's a rare moment. Enjoy it.

Another reason to stay in the hospital is that there are certain cardiac conditions that can be masked for a day or so while the baby's body adjusts to living outside the womb. Physicians often cannot detect these ahead of time, but they can put your baby in distress extraordinarily quickly. In addition, there are infections for which a mother might test negative but could be present in the baby. The stress of fighting the infection might take a day or so to register in the baby's blood. It's better to remain where the doctors have easy access to you and your child so that when you do leave, everyone is assured that you're both in the best state of health possible.

Accept Pain Medicine Only If You Really Need It

In a normal low-risk delivery it's your call whether to ask for an epidural, but even if you do, sometimes you have to wait a long time before you get it. And yet nurses freely offer pain medication, usually Percocet or Vicodin, after labor, usually before you even ask for it. It is at this point when you might think twice before you accept, however, especially if you intend to exclusively breastfeed.

If you're hurting and you can't rest or enjoy your time with your baby because of it, you should definitely accept something to take the edge off. But if you aren't actually in enough pain to complain, consider passing it up. First of all, if you aren't in enough pain to ask for it, do you really need it? Second, and more important for nursing mothers, once the narcotics travel through your system and into your breast milk, they then go straight to the baby, making him tired and lethargic, which can often complicate those first breastfeeding attempts. If the new mother continues the drugs at home, it can affect breastfeeding for days. For women who have their heart set on exclusively breastfeeding, it's really important that those early breastfeeding sessions not only go well in the hospital but that the practice is not hampered once they are on their own with their infants at home. It's not as though you live in the UK, where a community midwife will come visit you at home every day for up to ten days to check on you and your child and make sure everything, including breast feeding, is going smoothly. In America, once you're home, it's going to be six weeks before your postpartum checkup with your obstetrician. This means you will have to depend on your pediatrician for breastfeeding advice, who may or may not be totally comfortable with helping you breastfeed. She may refer you to a lactation specialist, but all the while your infant may lose excessive weight or become jaundiced, which could stress you out.

And there's a third reason to think before taking narcotics after childbirth, a reason few people will ever mention: They can make you extremely constipated. As if you needed to add another discomfort to that area of your body!

Consider Using the Well-Baby Nursery

The baby nursery used to be the heart of the maternity ward, a room lined with bassinets filled with little mewling peanuts wrapped in pink-and-blue blankets, but full-term healthy new-borns are spending increasingly less time in them. Many new mothers take it for granted that they will room in, meaning their baby will sleep in a bassinet next to their hospital bed at all times, and more and more hospitals are encouraging the prac-tice. It wasn't long ago when the nursing staff took care of the infants at night, bottle feeding them formula while new moth-ers got some much-needed rest. For the most part, those days disappeared once breastfeeding became the new gold standard for infant nutrition and care. In fact, some hospitals are insist-ing on rooming in, leaving the baby nursery only for high-needs infants or for administering tests. Rooming in, the theory goes, promotes better bonding, allows new mothers to learn to read their babies' hunger cues, and allows more frequent nursing, thus speeding up mothers' milk production.

There are many excellent reasons to breastfeed, but the con-troversy and strongly held views surrounding breastfeeding on demand has made it so that many women don't even realize they have a choice about whether to use the baby nursery or not. In addition, some nurses are being trained to dissuade mothers from sending their children to the nursery, even when they are ill or are recovering from a C-section. This can leave new moth-ers who might feel sore, weak, or woozy feeling utterly aban-doned when they don't have a partner or family member who can stay in the room with them to ensure they're able to maneu-ver the baby in and out of the bassinet safely. Ironically, it also increases the risk of the mother falling asleep with the baby tucked in the bed with her, a practice that most hospitals ada-mantly discourage due to the risk of smothering the infant (more on co-sleeping at home later).

It is a marvelous thing that as a society we are recognizing the value of promoting strong infant–parent bonding through skin-to-skin contact and breastfeeding from the first day of life. But let's get some perspective.

Allowing your baby to spend a few hours in the baby nursery if you are sick or just plain exhausted will not hurt your ability to bond properly. If that were true, few people over the age of twenty-five, who were born before rooming-in became popular, would have a close, loving relationship with their mothers. In rural Africa, when a mother is too tired or unwell to care for her baby herself, it's expected that her mother, sister, or friends will take the baby for a little while to allow her to recover. Those who could would very likely even breastfeed the baby for her!

A healthy mother who chooses to use the baby nursery so she can rest for a few hours is neither selfish nor lazy—she's smart. A well-rested, refreshed mother is much better able to devote all her energy to her newborn than one bordering on psychosis for lack of sleep. Some first-time mothers who take advantage of the break a nursery represents get the hang of breastfeeding, diapering, and other infant care much faster and more easily than their exhausted counterparts.

Rooming in can be a wonderful experience, but it does not have to be your only option. Take advantage of the nursery for a short time—guilt-free—if you feel you need to.

Ask to Meet with a Lactation Consultant

Even if this isn't your first child, ask to see a lactation consultant on your first day in the hospital. Most hospitals have them on staff, though many do not make them a standard part of postpartum hospital care. Your nurses can be wonderful resources, but they're not specially trained to look for any of the subtle but significant factors that can impede successful breastfeeding. They'll see that the baby is sucking, for example, and reassure you that all is well, but they won't be able to tell that in fact he's tongue tied and therefore compensating with his lips in such a way that's going to cause you unnecessary pain.

If there is any question about breastfeeding or if I find a baby's weight is lower than it should be, I've made it a standard part of many of my patients' first pediatric appointments to ask mothers to nurse their babies in front of me. I could usually see in seconds when the baby was improperly latched or that the trouble was in the way the mother was holding her infant. Many times I could improve the situation quickly by gently pressing my hands down on the mother's shoulders while saying in a soothing tone, "Relax." Almost immediately I'd usually see the tension leave the woman's face and hear the wonderful sound of milk letting down and the baby swallowing.

 FAQ: How Do I Know If My Baby Is Tongue Tied?

A tongue-tied baby is one suffering from ankyloglossia, which is a condition that occurs when the frenulum, the membrane that attaches the tongue to the bottom of the mouth, is too short and tight. The condition can affect a baby's ability to latch properly to the breast and is sometimes the cause of a mother's breastfeeding discomfort. If left untreated, it can later cause speech and dental problems. Often doctors will look in a baby's mouth and notice it, but other times the condition is drawn to a pediatrician's attention only when a mother complains that it hurts to latch her baby. Once your doctor has evaluated your baby and made a diagnosis, she should be able to clip the frenulum very easily in the first days or weeks of life and fix the problem.

In the beginning, when it can take four hands to get a baby latched on properly (yes, really!), you need someone who can take the time to sit with you, observe your technique and make adjustments. Don't wait until you're struggling to ask for help. Request a visit with a lactation consultant while you're in the hospital so you can be sure you have an enjoyable breastfeeding experience. At the very least, have the phone number of a lactation consultant on hand before you give birth, so that if you decide you need help when you get home you can make an appointment quickly if necessary.

FAQ: My Baby Keeps Falling Asleep When She Nurses. How Do I Know She's Getting Enough?

If your baby is falling asleep while feeding, particularly within the first ten minutes, she has not had enough and is just snacking! Try to stimulate her by stroking her cheek to keep her awake and actively feeding. After ten minutes take her off, burp her, and put her back on the other breast. Similarly try to keep her awake for another eight to ten minutes. Your baby should then be able to sleep for two to two and a half hours. If she is waking sooner, it is another indication that she is not drinking enough at a feed.

AT HOME

The biggest difference between how new mothers are treated here and in other countries occurs not in the hospital, but when the happy family goes home to start their new lives together.

For example, in China, when a mother brings her baby home, she begins a month-long lying-in period called *zuo yuezi*, following strict rules about what to eat, drink, and wear; rarely if ever leaving the house; and not infrequently hiring help to allow her to sleep. Most Iranian women give birth in a hospital, but when a new mother is discharged she and her whole family moves into her mother's home for forty days, where traditionally the new mother stays in bed nurturing and feeding her child while the other family members tend to her and her other children. After seven to ten days, a period during which she is not allowed to bathe, the mother and her infant participate in a ceremonial public shower. In Bali, new mothers are expected to stay out of the kitchen until the umbilical cord falls off, and they and their baby can expect daily massages. Miriam raved about her experience in Israel:

I had no family here when I gave birth to my kids, not my family and no in-laws, and I still felt hugely supported. I can't even tell you how amazing the hospital staff is. They fawn over you and your child. They have lactation consultants come in, breast pumps in the maternity ward. If your milk's not coming in and you need help, they're ready to sit with you and help. And it's all free. Then across the board, any time anyone has a baby, you have at least three weeks of meals delivered by the community, from friends and strangers alike. If you're not religious, it's through your children's school, if you are, it's the synagogue. Messages go out, and it's just expected that everyone is going to help. It's the best feeling to know you don't have to cook or prepare food for your other kids. There's a lot of taking care of each other. I don't know how I would have done it anywhere else.

Miriam's experience is not unusual outside the United States. In other countries, during those first few weeks and months after a baby is born, a new mother is given leave to check out of the real world for a while. Borgit, who gave birth to her first child in Guatemala, described the days after giving birth as "stress free." Most middle- and upper-class Guatemalan families hire live-in nannies, so "once you give birth you come home and you're showered with gifts, your nanny is there to take care of the hard parts of a life with a newborn, which includes night feedings, and your job is to relax and get back to normal. It was nice and quiet and peaceful." Whether it's with the assistance of family or paid help, in most other countries it's understood that upon the birth of a child, everyone's attention should turn to caring for the baby *and* the new mother. In this way, the mother is able to rest, recover, get to know her infant, and benefit from the advice of others who have raised children of their own.

The picture couldn't look more different in the United States. If there's one thing new mothers in America are not supposed to do, it's retreat from the real world. I find that that's true for both working and stay-at-home mothers. There's a cultural expectation that after a few days of rest, new mothers will be ready to start participating in family life, caring for older children, preparing meals, running errands, and visiting with friends eager to meet the new baby. If they're lucky, a mother, sister, or mother-in-law will come in for a week or two and help out. But after that, moms are on their own. And with only 12 percent of US workers having access to paid family leave, as many as a quarter of the 71 percent of mothers who work outside the home are actually back on the job within two weeks of giving birth.

Many experts have written books decrying the state of our family leave policies and how we care for families with young children, and I will leave the discussion of what we should demand from our legislators and employers to them. But there is a reason almost every other country in the world pampers new mothers and grants them generous time off from the regular routine of family life, not just from paid work: It makes for happier mothers. Happy mothers—usually women who have had time to heal, to rest, to hormonally recalibrate, and to focus on incorporating their new babies into their families—especially when their other children may need reassurance that Mom doesn't have a new favorite—are more patient, more relaxed mothers.

This is a good place to address an accusation that gets tossed out whenever the debate over family paid leave or society's responsibility toward new mothers comes to the fore—that women who demand family policy changes are soft, even derelict in maternal instinct and responsibility. Critics will question why American women (or any women) should get special treatment after child-birth when there are plenty of women in the undeveloped coun-tries who pop babies out and head straight back out into the rice paddies or the fields. While it is unlikely that this scenario is either the ideal or the norm in any country, it does happen.

When I was expecting my third child in the South African desert, as was expected of anyone who could afford to offer work to others in the area, I had a young woman, Rachina, helping me in the home. She was also expecting. She lived in a small house on our property, and when she went into labor slightly early, I helped. After the baby was born I left her to rest and went back to my house. Within an hour, she surprised me by appearing in my kitchen with her baby strapped on her back. In response to my shock and dismayed reaction upon seeing her, she said, "You're expecting a baby, you let me do my job."

In every culture, lying-in traditions and rituals developed to protect new mothers and their infants and give them time to bond. Even new mothers in colonial America were given three to four weeks to recuperate and were excused from their daily chores and childcare, which were taken over by other women with the understanding that the favor would be reciprocated when it was their turn to birth a child. But there is no lying-in in societies where survival is hand to mouth. Not coincidentally, citizens of these societies, especially nomadic ones, live in groups. Even if it is their tradition to leave the camp to labor alone, when they return with their newborn, they know they will have their sisters and their mother there to help them by taking on their share of the work, even nursing the baby. A new mother is never alone. The whole village—mothers, brothers, elders—considers it their responsibility to help that human life.

But Rachina was alone. She came from a nomadic tribe, so for her it was perfectly natural to get on her feet as quickly as possible and keep moving after childbirth. In the desert, new mothers and babies are vulnerable to predators; the longer you stay on the ground or isolated from your family, the more of a target you become. My family was able to provide a little house for Rachina to live in and regular meals, but she was still separated from her people, so for her work meant survival. But she was in an artificial environment. If she had been with her own tribe, I'm reasonably certain she would have gladly accepted any help or rest she could get.

It's not that women in the developed world are soft or incapacitated after having children; mothers can handle anything they need to when they feel secure and can properly plan. For all my belief in lying-in, I wasn't able to do it the last time I gave birth. Only hours after my prematurely born fourth child was transported on a ventilator to the intensive care unit, I shocked my OB by calling him at 6:00 A.M. and asking to be released from the hospital. My son had chosen to be born the day before I was to sit my pre-med finals; I needed to get to the school to take them. My OB called me crazy, but I explained that I now knew I was going to spend months with my baby in the NICU; I needed to reserve my time for my child. If I didn't take the tests now, I'd have to prepare all over again later, this time with a preemie on my hands. My sick infant had already been transferred to the Children's Hospital on a ventilator, so I went to school, took my tests, and a few hours later headed downtown to the intensive care nursery where my husband was sitting with our tiny baby. One stressor that I could control was now out of the way.

There's another reason that older cultures established lying-in traditions—to increase the infant's chances of survival, which depended entirely on being shielded from germs and especially having easy access to his mother's breast milk. Even until recently, if a baby were admitted to the NICU, his mother would move in with him for the whole time. But in this country, healthy babies will not die if we can't breastfeed. Even the poor have ready access to formula through the Special Supplemental Nutrition Program for Women, Infants, and Children (WIC program) and food stamps. So do new mothers really need a prolonged lie-in period?

Only if they want one. There are some who don't. After giving birth, Marissa Mayer famously took only two weeks of maternity leave from her new role as CEO of Yahoo!, building a nursery directly next to her office so she could still be close to her son. Three years later she announced she would take only a minimal amount of time away from the office after the birth of her twin daughters and would work throughout her leave. However, most women would benefit emotionally, psychologically, and physically if they got not only paid maternity leave but also more than the culturally sanctioned week or two of caretaking we generally allow ourselves. If we could build in the expectation that new mothers should get help, whether paid, or from friends, family, and partners, and should be absolved from doing any housework, cleaning, cooking, or rigorous childcare of older children for several weeks, we would be setting mothers up for a calmer, more confident return to the real world. Every woman deserves to have the best experience with her new child. That's valuable to everyone in the family.

Let me emphasize that it's not just working mothers who should receive better care after giving birth—it's all mothers. Becoming confident parents is not always an overnight process; it takes more time and patience than our society is willing to acknowledge. But if more parents took the following steps to re-create the support systems that benefited previous generations, they might get their sea legs a lot faster and with a lot less angst, worry, and fatigue. Society would definitely benefit in the long run.

So what to do?

Create Your Own Lie-In

Americans love babies, and as soon as there's a new one they can't wait to meet it. In China, however, no one except immediate family lays eyes on the baby until at least four, sometimes even six weeks after the birth. Friends are not expected to visit. It's understood that the weeks immediately following a baby's birth are to be as quiet and restful as possible as well as a time to shelter the new infant from community illness, something that can't happen if the mother has to make herself presentable every day for visitors. I've had many new moms tell me how tiring and even anxiety provoking it is to entertain friends and well-wishers who want to hold and cuddle their newborns. Their instincts are screaming at them to protect their children, but society insists that a new baby is practically public property. My advice? Keep all visitors away and blame it on your pediatrician. I always advise my patients that infection is a real possibility and at certain times of the year respiratory syncytial virus (RSV) is a serious concern, so it would be in the mother's and baby's best interest to keep exposure to anyone other than immediate family to a minimum. Most of the moms I've worked with have been happy to blame me for discouraging visitors during those first few weeks. I'm sure most pediatricians feel the same.

I'm Going Stir-Crazy! Can I Go Out with My Baby a Little Every Day?

You can go anywhere you want. Just keep a light blanket over your child to discourage people from leaning over or touching him.

Take as Much Time as You Can

While many new mothers in other countries are often waited on hand and foot for over a month, and many governments cover the cost of healthcare professionals visiting a new family's home every day, here the average amount of time a woman can often reasonably hope for in-home help from family seems to be about two weeks. One possible reason is that many grandmothers are still in the workforce and two weeks is how long they can take off to help out with a new grandbaby. But even when grandparents or other family volunteer caretakers don't have to get back to a job, there's often an understanding that two weeks is pretty much how much time any self-respecting mother should expect to get daily help. And yet, that's often just not enough time for a woman to physically recuperate from the strain of labor. For example, it can take up to four weeks just to recover from an episiotomy or a moderate vaginal tear, and some women still feel perineal pain and pressure months after giving birth.

There's no way to know how you're going to feel after you leave the hospital, so the most prudent thing to do is prepare yourself and your partner for a long recovery time and then be pleasantly surprised at how fast you bounce back. Parents must find the courage to ask for the amount of help they need, as well as for the amount of time they need it—not the amount society thinks they need. Take as much time as you can get from any family member who offers to help you. Ask your best options—mother, mother-in-law, and any other family who you really like and trust—to stay with you and tag team so they can stretch out the amount of time you're accompanied in the home.

Of course, for some women following a forty-day tradition of resting in the house with the constant attention from one's mother or mother-in-law might sound like a nightmare. Plus, many women have to go back to work far sooner than they would like. And some women really are ready to put the responsibilities of work and families back on their shoulders two weeks after giving birth. That's fine. The important thing is to take advantage of whatever time you can get. The more time you build into your leave from the normal routines of life, the more flexibility you'll have to make that time work best for you. It's the resentment and anxiety many women experience when they feel the weight of outside pressure or expectations and lack the freedom to do what feels right that hurts their recovery and robs them of the sense of competence and calm so important for new mothers. Even if you don't or can't take three months of maternity leave, gather whatever troops you can muster, accept their offers of help and keep them close to make your life easier so that your first days with your new child are as stress-free smooth as possible.

Accept as Much Help as You Can

When the help arrives, let them help. Don't try to cook or entertain. If it's your sister's first time to your city, don't set up an itinerary or promise to act as a tour guide. Focus on yourself, your partner, your other children, and your baby, and let everything else go. If you must, offer instructions for how things are generally done around your home, and then accept that it's not the end of the world if your laundry isn't put away exactly the way you would do it yourself. You can always put everything back the way you like it once you're ready to take on the world again. But for now, let your family be your world. You've got your whole life to do laundry.

If you decide or are obliged to go back to work quickly, let your family and friends make the transition as easy as possible for you. Even if you put your baby in day care, let your family members stay home and keep your house tidy and well stocked. Allow them to cook for you so that neither you nor your spouse have to think about the logistics of shopping, prepping, and cooking, and can simply bond when you're home together. If anyone says, "Let me know if you need anything," don't just smile and nod—let them know! Tell them you'd really appreciate it if they set up an online calendar and asked your friends, neighbors, and colleagues to sign up to help with meals, childcare, carpool obligations, or errands on various days of the week. Anything to take the pressure off while you heal and adjust to the needs of your new family.

Give Up the Night Shift

Most of the time when family members come to stay, they expect to spend most of the day helping out around the house and running errands. Few would think of offering to take your baby for you during the night. But they should, and you should consider letting them, because if there's one thing that drags new parents down and can make the early days with a newborn more difficult than they need to be, it's exhaustion. Yet as a society we react viscerally to the idea of anyone other than the new parents—and especially the mother—rousing themselves in the night to feed a baby. In fact, an article in the *Washington Post* in 2014 about a couple who hired a baby nurse agency to help them care for their set of premature twins generated more negative comments than a piece running simultaneously about a young girl who sold her virginity over the Internet.

This type of outrage is . . . outrageous. I can't think of anything that would be better for an overtired, bleeding, sore mother than to get a good night's sleep. You're giving your baby all your attention during the day, wouldn't it make sense to allow a close friend or relative to take one feed during the night (using your expressed breast milk if you like) so that you can get six straight hours of sleep and feel refreshed, relaxed, and energized when you start the next day? Of course it does. The problem is that such an act of self-preservation would require new mothers to let someone else feed their child, and with a bottle no less. And unfortunately, a lot of mothers have absorbed the message spread by militant breastfeeding advocates that to let others feed their children will weaken their bond or their baby's ability to breastfeed. They also fear being judged as selfish. I will explain at length in chapter 6 why it's highly unlikely for the former to happen in any circumstance. As for the latter, if we could each make a promise to stop judging women, and mothers in particular, and concentrate on offering them support, kindness, and compassion, we'd immediately put women in a better position to make empowering decisions for themselves and their families.

Let Dad Step Up

Even if you won't allow a family member to take over nighttime feedings, I strongly urge new mothers to allow their partners to help out with at least one feed, especially the last feed before midnight. When the exclusively breastfed baby cries, a father has no option but to hand the baby over. It can make him feel inept and left out. This arrangement also categorizes the mother as the only one who can provide nourishment and comfort, which can lead to an all too familiar cycle where eventually the mother is handling everything from meal preparation and camp registrations to doctors' appointments, leaving Dad with plenty of leisure time and flexibility and Mom with very little. You will eliminate a ton of potential stress from your life by setting up good patterns of equal involvement early on.

Many studies show that fathers bond better and faster with their babies when they are allowed to feed them. Even better, fathers who are allowed to participate in feeding their children are more proactive around the house, as well. The end result? Happier, better-rested moms, more capable, confident fathers, and a baby who knows he or she will be safe and cared for no matter which parent is in charge. The combination makes for an ideal stress-free starting point for any new family. Whether you choose to pump or give formula should be completely your choice. Just give your partner the opportunity to feel special, and for your child to connect with his or her other parent. Such an arrangement is therapeutic for moms, dads, kids, and marriages.

Banish the Image of the Selfish Mom

You might fear that you're acting entitled or spoiled to arrange for the kind of special treatment outlined in this chapter. You're not. And if it helps, you can always pay these kindnesses forward. In fact, you absolutely should. When your friends or your sisters give birth, encourage them to ask for the same kind of help, and offer as much as you can. I hope that as more women feel brave enough to ask for what they need, instead of accepting what society tells them they should need, we'll be able to move the cultural needle in the right direction, benefiting families and children in the generations to come.

Raising the expectations of all new families will be the first promising step we can make toward getting us all started on the right track.

Simple Ways to Boost Baby's Brain

BACK IN THE days when most parents raised large families in which the older children helped raise the younger ones, babies weren't much of a mystery because most people had one or two in the house while they were growing up. What was there to know? They cried, they slept, they ate, they pooped, they learned to crawl, then walk, and they became part of the family. Before long they were helping out around the house and trying to prove they could keep up with or even outperform their older siblings. Some did it sooner, others did it later, and no one worried about it. Often, only when certain milestones didn't happen at all would parents think to raise a red flag. It wasn't that they weren't paying attention or didn't care about catching problems early like we do now; it was they had been exposed to so many children in their lifetimes they knew that babies ran the gamut on the developmental spectrum, and that most turned out all right.

With smaller families of two or three children more the norm today, many of the new parents whom I meet have had little exposure to and experience with babies by the time they give birth to their own. They have absolutely no idea what to expect, what to look out for, or what to do, so for reassurance they turn to the milestone checklists that appear in most baby books or the Internet or Facebook. But instead of reassurance, these resources often just cause more anxiety. In a competitive culture like ours, milestone charts can give parents yet another reason to fret when their children don't fall right in line with the developmental timeline listed in their baby books, or worse, lag behind other children in their social circles (although some have told me they'd prefer their child walk as late as possible because it is easier for them to keep the baby safe). They don't realize that many milestones can be cultural constructs.

> Many milestones can be cultural constructs.

The range of normal infant development is actually far broader than most Americans realize because the majority of the social and behavioral scientific research that we read about is conducted on WEIRD populations just like ours. That is, Western, educated, industrialized, rich, and democratic populations. Expand those studies into populations across the globe, however, and the results show that developmental milestones are often shaped by what a culture decides is most important. For example, infants raised in traditional Kenyan villages frequently sit up and walk several months sooner than most American children, and in Papua, New Guinea, babies born to the Au, an indigenous tribe, skip the crawling stage altogether. In a nomadic society or one at risk from predators or parasites on the ground, it's better for babies to be carried around in their mothers' arms until the very day they're strong enough to walk on their own. There are practical reasons to get children moving quickly, and parents therefore grant them freedom and encourage their movement and independence at a very early age. Western parents can generally afford to allow their babies the time to learn to crawl and walk more gradually.

While some American parents often seem quite satisfied with slower motor development than parents in other cultures, and frequently get concerned only when their child falls well outside the "normal" range, many do want evidence that their child is smarter than average. Increasingly, I see signs that everyone—not just the achievement-obsessed upper-middle-class parents but also middle- and lower-socioeconomic families—is looking for ways to give their children an edge. Like every generation before, they want their children to do better than they, and most believe that path is through academic success. When jobs are hard to come by and education is expensive, the desire to identify and cultivate their children's intellectual or physical gifts becomes even stronger. Some parents will ask me what they can do to stimulate their children's cognition, usually sometime around their first birthday. Play classical music? Download some baby apps? Show them the newest digital educational game for the preschool set?

Some of these can be beneficial to a baby within reason, but if you really want to enhance your child's cognitive capabilities, you have to focus your attention on enhancing both her motor skills as well as her cognitive skills. Motor function drives cognitive function; it is the stimulation of all the sense organs that actually develops the human infant brain. So to enhance cognitive development, you have to start with the five senses. And you should be doing it during infancy, long before your child is even able to walk.

> To enhance cognitive development, you have to start with the five senses.

That's where we get things backward. As our children get

older, we often ramp up our involvement in their activities, guide their play, get extremely hands-on, introduce musical instruments and start drilling them in math and teaching them to read. But we tend to leave our infants to their own devices. They're with us, they're even attached to us, and they get abundant love, cuddles, and attention, but it's rare for parents to take the time to teach and even actively play with infants the same way they do with toddlers and older children. I'd love to see that reversed. Some milestones differ across cultures, but sensory development is biologically programmed. It can, however, be enhanced or slowed down. Parents often start thinking about actively developing their babies' cognition around one year old, but cognition starts being shaped long before that. In fact, it's the time you and other loving adults spend with your child during her entire first three years of life that will most effectively and dramatically encourage her intellectual development. Infants don't need classes or new toys or digital media. They need to feel someone stroking them and hear people talking to them. These casual, relaxed interactions are far more valuable than anything you can buy.

Enhancing children's sensory capabilities during the first year of life is crucial. All it takes is making a special yet small effort to regularly expose infants to different smells; pleasant sounds; and new shapes, textures, and colors. Especially important, it requires giving them plenty of freedom to move. Incredibly, that last part is sometimes more difficult than it seems. Though in our society children are rarely given a moment to slow down (more on overstimulation later), we actively discourage parents from allowing babies to move freely. Yet when we restrict free movement in infancy, we also run the risk of restricting a baby's cognitive (and physical) potential.

WHY WE IMMOBILIZE OUR INFANTS

Ask any parent how they're doing, and whether they stay at home or are in the workforce, you'll often get the same one-word answer: "Busy!" We don't need to read any of the published studies on stress and parenting to know that this busyness is having a negative effect on parents' physical and mental health. But there's another side effect. We're so used to seeing babies with slightly flattened heads that it doesn't take us aback anymore, but it's not supposed to happen. The only time doctors used to see abnormal head shapes was in premature or sick infants who were required to spend weeks to months in incubators or bassinets with their heads turned to the side. Premature infants can develop what medical professionals call dolichocephaly, a narrowing of the skull. Dolichocephaly is still common in NICUs, but now pediatricians are reporting high rates of two other skull abnormalities: plagiocephaly and brachycephaly, two forms of what is known as flat head syndrome. We're seeing it in up to 50 percent of babies aged two to three months, even in those born healthy and full-term. Why so many?

Before the Back to Sleep campaign launched in 1992, when parents were first instructed to put their children to sleep on their backs to prevent the risk of SIDS, the rates of flat head syndrome were exceedingly low (2 to 3 percent) and reserved mostly for sick or premature infants who had to remain hospitalized in a NICU or pediatric intensive care unit (PICU) during the first few months of their lives. By the time the Back to Sleep movement took hold, however, child passenger safety regulations had also been enacted in all fifty states requiring parents to put their infants in car seats when traveling by vehicle. It didn't take long to confirm that both of these safety precautions were a good idea—rates of SIDS and infant motor vehicle deaths did indeed go down. But at the same time, for various social and cultural reasons, life started speeding up, which meant kids started spending more time in their car seats and other restraints designed to keep them still and safe while allowing parents to keep up with standards, responsibilities, and a pace never imagined by previous generations.

At home, babies were placed in bouncers, Pack 'n Plays, and swings to keep them content and out of the way as their parents did their best to keep up with the house and prepare the nutritious, from-scratch meals that became one of the main hallmarks of good parenting. Outside the home, parents on the go buckled their babies into various carriers, strollers, and seats designed for optimal safety standards with the sturdiest, most rigid construction. If the children fell asleep, or even if they were simply content and quiet, parents often left them in their detachable seat and carried them indoors rather than disturb them. All in all, children started spending a significant amount of time with their heads resting against firm surfaces.

Many parents also started binding their babies to their bodies in carriers like the Maya Wrap or the BabyBjörn, which gained popularity as parents started practicing attachment parenting, the philosophy that encourages parents to wear their babies and limit the amount of time they are separated. Attachment parenting, originally popular with the granola set, quickly went mainstream. But their babies developed flat head, too, albeit to a lesser degree, disproving the belief that flat head can't ever occur when babies are worn. Why? Because many parents tend to use the same arm every time they load their children into these carriers, so the children get placed in the same position again and again, their heads resting on the same side against their parents' chest or back.

THE COGNITIVE CONSEQUENCES OF FLAT HEAD

In the two decades since the adoption of Back to Sleep, child restraint seats, and attachment parenting, this country has seen a 600 percent increase in the rates of flat head syndrome. (The incidence has risen sharply in scattered areas around the world that have adopted the busy Western lifestyle and can afford the comforts of modern life; a Canadian study found that almost 50 percent of infants aged seven to twelve weeks are affected.) Up to half of these children also suffer from torticollis, a tightening of the neck muscle that limits infants' ability to turn their neck or move their head from side to side. Torticollis usually requires treatment with physical therapy, and severe cases of flat head syndrome sometimes require correction with a helmet. Yet contrary to many people's belief, these conditions aren't always a mere cosmetic problem whose effects go away after treatment. Infants with flat head syndrome are at risk for increased short- and long-term developmental delays. In addition, it's being documented that babies with flat head can develop problems with their vision and hearing.

I have been at the forefront of the effort to eliminate this largely preventable problem, increasing the time I take with new parents to teach them how to avoid it, and I even developed the Tortle—a beanie that promotes turning a baby's head from side to side when she's resting on a firm surface. But the Tortle fixes only the physical symptom of the real problem, which is that our babies, whether at home or in childcare, are not being given enough freedom and time to move. In fact, my conclusion is that the developmental delays being seen in the research data have less to do with the children's head shape than with their being restrained and their general lack of movement and exercise. *The New England Journal of Medicine* released statistics that showed children's tendency toward obesity might be set by the time they are five years old; researchers hoping to turn the tide of public health may want to start looking at how a chronic lack of free movement affects children even before they can walk.

Yet even as the medical community's awareness of this dilemma grows, parents are getting worse about limiting their children's movement, not better. As we've discussed, part of the problem is that the market is saturated with products meant to instill fear. For example, I was recently informed about a harness being developed meant to secure a baby in its crib so that it could never roll over. But once babies are capable of rolling over, we're supposed to let them. That's how babies develop. Unfortunately, while we've absorbed the lessons of the Back to Sleep movement, we've ignored "tummy to play" and thus have taken our mandate to protect our children to such an absurd degree that, in the interest of safety, we're causing a whole new danger.

A few years ago, a colleague sent an eight-month-old boy and his parents, young professionals in their thirties, to my clinic for evaluation because he was starting to suspect the boy was cognitively disabled. He couldn't sit up. He couldn't even hold his head up. And yet when I met him I didn't believe he was cognitively disabled. His eyes were alert and followed me. He had normal muscle tone and although weak, his body wasn't floppy. None of this was typical of an infant with a neurological problem. What he did have was a weirdly shaped head, and some developmental delay. After spending some time with the child I told the parents that I really didn't think there was anything wrong with him other than he needed to move more and build some strength. Both parents began to cry with relief. I arranged for the baby to start therapy for motor development, and we got him fitted for a helmet to fix the shape of his head. As soon as his father knew for sure there was nothing wrong with his child, he took all of my advice and began working with the boy to make him active and build up his strength. The mother, however, took a lot longer to come around. Whenever she brought him in, I could see how uncomfortable it made her to watch me maneuver her child on the examining table. Her face would tighten every time I rolled him over or pulled him up.

As it turns out, before she brought her baby to me, she never put him down. If he wasn't sleeping, he was in her arms. He got no stimulation and no play. "He's just a baby!" she told me weakly when I tried to explain that he needed time on the floor, "He could get hurt."

I showed her how I could pull her little boy into a sitting position by his arms. "See, he's not crying. He doesn't mind." But she just shook her head. "I don't feel comfortable doing that."

Fortunately, the mother eventually came around, and her child started to move about on his own within a couple of months. I monitored the family until I moved to another state when the child was about five years old. By that time he was running around like any other little boy and even showing signs of mental precocity.

BUILDING A BETTER BRAIN

It was only because this child started treatment for his inactivity well before he was a year old that he grew out of his induced lethargy and suffered no permanent side effects. Babies' cognitive and motor development is directly related to their environment in infancy, especially before their first birthday. For example, when a baby's head is severely flattened between the back and the ear on one side, the eye and the ear on that same side often move forward. When that happens, the baby starts to shift his eyes, looking first with one eye then the other; he may be unable to look at an object with both eyes together at the same time. If this continues without correction, after a year babies lose the ability to develop normal binocular vision, or the ability to use both eyes together in a coordinated fashion. A lack of normal binocular vision affects depth perception and can make it hard for the eyes to track, which can make reading difficult. Often when these children reach school age they have problems learning to read along a line, which can lead to academic struggles and even dyslexia.

The human brain sees its fastest rate of growth immediately after birth, with the head circumference increasing by ½ to 1 inch per month, until about three months of age, with the cerebellum, which controls motor function, more than doubling in volume. Flat head syndrome usually starts to show between four and eight weeks of life, so pediatricians don't become aware of the problem until they see the infant at her two-month well-baby checkup. At that point they will usually try to help by recommending repositioning the baby's head from side to side. The problem is that by then the infant often doesn't want to turn the other way because it's less comfortable. As brain growth slows down, the skull bones become firmer, and by six months old the skull is fairly firm and almost fully formed. At this point just repositioning is no longer a good treatment option, and babies with severe flat head are sometimes fitted for a helmet. Some get fitted even later. Unfortunately, it takes several months for the skull to reshape itself, and the longer the baby waits to get into the helmet, the longer it takes to fix the problem. And if you wait too long, some problems, such as binocular vision, cannot simply be corrected by reshaping the baby's head with a helmet.

There's a reason new mothers around the world routinely use traditional methods to ensure a round skull and build their babies' strength, stamina, and flexibility as soon as possible. Kenyan mothers massage their babies' heads daily to keep them beautifully round. It's common for a grandmother to inspect the baby's head to make sure it is perfect. Jamaican mothers use bath time to stretch and massage their babies' limbs. Mothers in the Mithila region of India and Nepal have been known to hold their babies from their ankles and swing them gently upside down or toss them several inches into the air to instill fearlessness, which they believe promotes good health. I'm not at all advocating that we should go this far, but we have become so consumed with keeping our infants still—because in our minds, stillness equals safety—that even after introducing tummy time to counter the effects of Back to Sleep, we still have a generation of flat-headed babies.

Recently, fitness professionals and child advocates have developed and implemented programs geared toward helping school-aged children incorporate exercise into their lives. But these habits need to be developed from infancy so children have the building blocks in place to develop more strength and skills to enjoy an active life. In fact, a combination of sensory development with plenty of supervised free play is perhaps the most valuable thing you can do to encourage exceptionally strong cognitive *and* motor skills in your child both during infancy and later life.

We can't change the way we put our babies to bed—all the data show that putting a baby to sleep on his back on a firm mattress in a crib cleared of all bedding except a fitted mattress sheet is the most effective way to prevent SIDS—and it would be unreasonable to instruct parents to restrain their activities and travel so that children no longer spend time in carriers and car seats. We have to find a solution that balances our need for a grown-up life and our babies' biological needs for mobility and the freedom to experience new sensations and the great big world.

TUMMY TIME

One of the first things you can do is make it a priority for your child to spend time every day flat on her stomach. Pediatricians started encouraging tummy time a few years after doctors and physical therapists realized that the uptick of children in their care experiencing motor delays could be traced to a combination of Back to Sleep plus car seats doubling as infant carriers. Many people know that tummy time is necessary to help babies build strength in their neck and learn to crawl, but they don't realize that it's also a wonderful chance to work on stimulating the senses. There is so much happening when babies are on their tummies. Their lips are touching the blanket; they can smell the blanket and your hand; they can hear your voice; they use their eyesight as they reach out to touch the patterns or toys on the blanket underneath them or they watch the family pet that is either trying to snuffle them or keeping a wary distance. All of these stimulations work to develop a baby's brain. Tummy time is the umbrella activity that makes all other functions—sensory, motor, and cognitive—fall into place. Make sure your baby does it early and frequently, starting immediately after coming home from the hospital. If you wait too late or do it too infrequently your child might object to the newness of it or be too weak to push herself up and feel safe. You cannot begin this exercise too soon. When the American Academy of Pediatrics encourages Back to Sleep and supervised Tummy to Play, they mean it should start from the first days of life!

Tummy time takes very little time or effort on your part, and it's a wonderful way to slow down and enjoy yourself for just a few minutes several times a day and really revel in how much your life has changed with the arrival of this new little one.

FAQ: My Baby Cries Every Time I Put Him on the Floor for Tummy Time. How Can I Make It More Enjoyable for Him?

He's not crying because he's in pain, but because it's an unfamiliar experience. Babies don't cry during tummy time if someone is down on the floor with them. Start them on their back and chat with them, show them toys and get them comfortable before rolling them onto their tummy. It's only when they're in an unfamiliar position, or feel isolated and helpless like a beached whale, that they cry.

If your child is in other people's care, talk to them and make sure that they commit to this exercise during your baby's waking hours several times every day, and then add one longer session—twenty to thirty minutes if possible—when you get home after work. This is also a great activity that your partner can enjoy. Encourage your partner to lie on the floor facing the baby and then make playful noises and stroke the baby's back, arms, and legs. It's hard not to delight in a baby's response to his or her parent's touch and voice. Have fun. These moments are priceless! The time your baby spends on that blanket or play pad on the floor could be the most exciting part of baby's day, and the most relaxing and enjoyable part of yours.

 FAQ: What If My Child Already Has Flat Head Syndrome?

- Start holding your baby with the opposite arm from the one you predominantly use. For example, if you are right handed, you will most likely hold your baby in your left arm. Switch to using your right arm. Yes, it will feel awkward at first.
- Change the direction in which you lay your baby down in his bed so that every time he goes to sleep you reverse the direction his head and feet are facing.
- When your baby is lying on his back on a blanket, on the floor, or in a car seat, stroller, or bouncer, place his toys, mobiles, and even yourself on the opposite side from the one where he usually prefers to look. This will encourage

him to turn his head in a different direction from the one he is accustomed to and ease the constant pressure on the flattened side.

- Encourage lots of tummy time (as discussed in this chapter). Ensure that you or your child's caretaker sits on the baby's less-preferred side or directly in front of him so when he lifts his chin off the ground he doesn't turn his head in the same direction each time.
- Turn the crib around so the wall is now on the other side.
- Exercise your baby by helping him push up on your knee or reach out for objects.

DEVELOPING THE FIVE SENSES

As we discussed earlier, developing a baby's five senses is the key to developing a baby's cognitive potential to the fullest. And there's no better way to help develop those senses than when you are interacting with your baby during tummy time. You can use this sensory developmental timeline as a guide.

What Can Baby See?

Your baby will be fascinated by faces, especially yours. Since a baby's survival depends entirely on his caregivers, his sight develops in relation to how far away they are likely to be. A newborn can see between eight and twelve inches, which just happens to be the general distance between a baby's face and his mother's when he is nursing at the breast. At four months, when he's bigger and his mother might put him on her knee, his focal length is the distance between where he sits on her knee and her face. By the time a baby is six months old and should be able to sit up alone, he should be able to see far enough that he can recognize his mother across the room. And when that baby is mobile, somewhere between nine and twelve months, he'll have complete adult visual acuity.

Most baby toys and nursery decor come in sweet pastel colors, but that's because the designers' target audience is the parents and other adults buying the gear, not babies. Infants actually prefer strong colors and patterns like red, white, and black combinations. Some research suggests bold contrasts are restful to infants because they don't have to work hard to see it as their brains process all the other new stimuli in their environment. They're also attracted to things in motion, which is why mobiles are such a popular nursery staple. Their eyes are acutely sensitive to light, so dim the lights a little in whatever room you happen to be in, or pull down the shades if you have them in your car. The more babies' eyes remain open, the more opportunities they have to practice tracking. Tracking with their eyes eventually leads to improved eye–hand coordination as they start to reach out for the objects they see.

You can help your baby practice tracking during your tummy time sessions or just while you're waiting for dinner to finish in the oven. Place yourself about arm's length from your baby and hold a medium-size contrasting colored toy or object in your hand about one foot away from his eyes. Then move the object slowly in front of your baby's face, just a few times, from side to side. Do this for about thirty seconds, one time per day. Most babies will be able to track the object with their eyes by the time they are about two months old. Most babies learn this skill whether or not their parents practice with them, but those who practice early on generally see more rapid gains in eye–hand coordination and later on may have an easier time with reading skills.

What Else Can You Do?

Install a baby-proof mirror in your baby's crib; she will stare endlessly at the interesting face she sees there. Just make sure to switch the mirror around in the crib so that your baby is encouraged to turn her head in different directions.

Consider placing the crib in the center of the room so your baby can have a 360-degree view, and put up large brightly colored pictures on the wall to draw her attention. Don't bother with a mobile unless it, too, is in strongly contrasted primary colors, or even in black and white.

What Can Baby Hear?

Newborns arrive into the world with fully developed hearing. Studies have shown that exposing a baby to gentle music, especially classical, might help develop the synaptic pathways that also correspond with spatial reasoning, but in general scientists are still debating whether listening to music at an early age really translates into improved cognitive function later in life. Music classes geared toward six-month-olds probably just provide nice opportunities for parents or caretakers to get out of the house. Still, there's no doubt that babies like music and respond emotionally to it, so for that reason alone it will be wonderful if you can make music a part of your and their daily life.

The real music to babies' ears, however, is the sound of their parents' voice, especially when they speak "motherese," that slow, repetitive, high-pitched way of speaking most people use when communicating with infants. Babies as young as three to five days old are already mimicking the tones of their native language when they cry, suggesting they are listening to their parents from inside the womb, and in one study newborns only hours old showed a greater interest in the sounds of their native tongues than in foreign ones, solidifying the argument for introducing bilingualism as early as possible.

Not only can babies hear their parents' voices but they can interpret them, too. As early as three months old, babies can differentiate between sad tones of voice and happy or neutral sounds. They will sometimes become fussy or stop feeding well when they hear anxiety or stress in their mothers' voice. This helps explain how nursing and bedtimes can become major battlegrounds. If a mother gets stressed or frustrated with breastfeeding and allows those emotions to creep into her body and voice, the baby can absorb them, which can then cause her to struggle at the breast even more, slowing down feeding and putting a wrench in even the most carefully timed schedules. A baby gauges her safety by the sounds she hears nearby, so it's important to do our best to try to speak in gentle, reassuring tones when we're around our little one.

What Else Can You Do?

Sing. Around the world, lullabies are remarkably similar in tone and structure. Babies love to hear their parents sing to them. Choose a classic or make up your own. Babies don't care if you don't have a great voice; they just want to hear you sing in a loving way!

Provide many opportunities for babies, once they are a few months old, to make their own music, either with baby-size musical instruments or just a pot and wooden spoon.

If you speak a foreign language, use it! Babies usually have no trouble learning more than one language at one time, and there is evidence that bilingual children sometimes develop high reading and problem-solving skills.

What Can Baby Smell?

The most developed sense at birth is our sense of smell. A baby's favorite scent is her mother's, and within a couple of weeks babies are able to recognize their mothers by scent alone. Their sense of smell continues to develop until about the age of eight, after which it plateaus and then diminishes in old age.

Why would we want to pay particular attention to developing our babies' sense of smell? Well, for one we connect memories to scents. In addition, it allows us to enjoy our food! In fact, the human nose is the main organ of taste as well as smell. The so-called taste buds on our tongues can distinguish only four qualities—sweet, sour, bitter, and salt. All other tastes are detected by the olfactory receptors high up in our nasal passages.

What Else Can You Do?

Try to avoid wearing perfume. Not only can perfumes trigger allergies in some children but they mask the natural scent your baby loves.

Use unscented laundry products, which otherwise can interfere with babies' ability to smell the world around them.

Take time to get outside, even if it's just to take a walk around
the block or sit out on the stoop. Create opportunities for
your baby to smell different things: flowers; aromatic foods
from a food cart, restaurant, or backyard grill; fruit; grass;
and anything else you come across when you're out together.
Ask your child's other caretakers to do the same (preferably
with the phone silenced).

What Does Baby like to Touch?

For months, babies in the womb are rocked by their mothers'
body movements and soothed by the sound of their mothers'
voices. Then suddenly, labor begins, and they're thrust from the
warm, watery cocoon into a world of bright light and sound
where they need to inflate their lungs and breathe on their own
for the first time. This is why they cry! But babies are quickly
calmed and comforted when they are laid naked upon their
mothers' bare chests immediately after birth. This skin-to-skin
contact helps trigger the mother's maternal instincts, and her
body heat, heartbeat, and the rise and fall of her chest as she
breathes help the baby regulate his own cardiovascular function, glucose levels, and breathing. Babies who spend the first
hour or so on their mothers' chests tend to easily make their
way to their mothers' breast and have more successful first feeds
than babies who don't or who are unable to because of immediate health problems. The practice of "kangaroo care" is encouraged in many hospitals. Even tiny premature infants spend

hours on their parents' bare chests once they're stable enough, carefully covered to keep warm. As often seems to be our tendency, however, many people have taken good information—babies love to touch their mothers—and taken it to the extreme.

FAQ: If My Baby Needs Intervention Immediately after Birth, Will She Still Be Able to Breastfeed and Bond with Me?

Absolutely. If your baby needs help right after birth, her medical needs must take priority. But once she is well, you will have time to teach her how to breastfeed and bonding will come quite naturally as you work together.

THE PROS AND CONS OF BABY WEARING

While it is true that in some cultures mothers carry their babies like baby koalas close to their bodies for months, once those kids can stand on their own two feet, and especially once they can walk, they don't generally get a free ride unless the mother is traveling a great distance. Baby wearing was born out of necessity. Tribes needed to keep moving and women needed to gather food and collect water, so they strapped their babies onto their bodies. But as soon as they could put their children down, they did. Mary Martini, a professor at the University of Hawaii, studied the Marquesans, inhabitants of a remote group of islands in French Polynesia, and took note that while adults "held, coddled, entertained and slept with their children when they were babies . . . as soon as a child learned to walk, his mother turned him over to the care of other children." Of course she did! It's hard to get anything done or go anywhere quickly and efficiently with a toddler around. Now, there's no way in our society we would condone putting our babies in the care of their slightly older siblings. However, the other solutions we have devised aren't ideal either and can actually be harmful.

Some researchers are starting to think that our overreliance on strollers when children are of walking age is contributing to later tendencies toward low physical activity and weight gain. And increasingly, mothers are carrying their children from infancy on through toddlerhood, not on their hips or in their arms, which would give them plenty of freedom to move, especially as the mother shifts the baby's weight around, but in packs, carriers, and wraps that aren't appropriate for children over a few months of age. More than once when out and about, such as at the supermarket, I've had to point out to a mother that her baby's leg was turning blue because the leg opening of her carrier constricted the blood circulation. Some carriers can also unnaturally position a child's pelvis and hips. Baby wearing for short periods of time is a nice option, but once children are strong enough they need to walk and explore. As one Nairobian woman said in response to the first attempt to market strollers in Africa, "In Africa, we just carry our children or let them roam. They can't sit like lumps."

It's wonderful to carry your baby close to your body, and strollers and car seats are necessities for busy parents. Just make sure to carry your baby as much as you can if you are not in a vehicle. Ideally, whenever possible, your baby should be balanced on your hip if you're standing or on your knee if you're sitting. Don't keep your child in his car seat while you're waiting for an older sibling to get out of gymnastics class, even if he is perfectly content in it. Don't leave him in his stroller. Pull him out and let him see his surroundings, feel your hands around his waist, and let him squeeze your fingers in his chubby fists. Not only will this help strengthen your baby's back, improve his balance, and avoid flat head but it's an easy opportunity to fit some bonding and play time into a busy schedule.

OTHER WAYS TO ENHANCE BABY'S SENSES

Babies love caresses and kisses, so indulge in every impulse to touch them. It's a global practice. In African tribes, it is standard for grandmothers to teach new moms massage techniques. It is a consistently social, emotional, and cognitive experience for parents and infants. Touch helps babies bond and interpret emotions. Studies have shown that touch stimulates physical and emotional health; without it, children wither. In fact, the interaction is critical during the first year of life. That's why it is so hard to socialize or rehabilitate children who spent their first year in Russian or Chinese orphanages, notorious for being stingy with physical affection, or even children who spent the majority of their first year in the exclusive care of a severely depressed postpartum mother.

Toys

What are the best baby toys you can offer children to help develop their senses, motor skills, and cognition? While there are some good ones on the shelves of your local toy store, switch those out every other day or so and make toys out of regular household objects. Young children love to open and close boxes, put things into them and take them out. Or head right out in your own backyard or neighborhood park, where you can pick up toys for free. Manufactured toys are colorful, but they have no scent and their textures tend to be homogenous. A plastic ring stays the same shape and texture no matter how much you play around with it, as does a soft tabbed blanket. Put sand in children's hands, though, and watch them delight in the crumby feel of the grains, then giggle as their drool turns it into mud. They also enjoy feeling smooth stones and other items found in nature. A nontoxic flower, a branch, a shell—nature makes the best children's toys in the world.

A Word on Electronic Media

It would be impossible not to mention the effects of electronics on the developing senses of an infant. Nature is definitely a child's best teacher and the outdoors her best schoolroom, but technology does not have to be the enemy of a healthy childhood. The questions are, When is the best time to introduce it, and how much at a time? The answers are, later than most parents probably wish, and less than they probably want.

There's a deluge of information available about how electronic media are turning our children into a generation of housebound couch potatoes, but most people don't think their children are using tech enough to put them in that category. The problem is, they are. Add up all those minutes of iPhone and tablet time and many young children are spending an hour or more per day in front of a screen. Many of the same arguments against tech are the same ones that have been used for years to discourage parents from letting their kids watch TV. And most people will say, "I watched TV and I turned out okay." The difference is that when you watched TV, that was the only screen in the house, so once it was off, you did something else. Now, kids could conceivably go from a TV to a tablet to a smartphone to a handheld game, and they can take some of these screens outside! It has to be kept in check, and most parents don't do as good a job about that as they think they do. Most of us can barely control our own media addictions, so it stands to reason that it's extremely easy to lose track of how much time our kids are using it. The circuitry in a baby's brain doesn't develop well when stimulated by an array of short bursts of light and sound. While some people consider the recommendations from the American Academy of Pediatrics a bit overcautious, it is correct to recommend only two hours of screen time per day for children ages three to eighteen years, and none for children two years old and younger.

None? That's tough for most parents to accept. Most families will admit that they sometimes stick an iPhone into their children's hands when they go out to eat or turn on the television for an hour so they can get dinner made or have a little quiet time to themselves. When pressed to explain, they almost always say it's the only thing that works. But parents were distracting their children to keep them quiet long before the advent of TV or electronics, so we know children don't need screens to entertain themselves. If anything, those screens just rev them up even more, making it harder to put them down to bed at night. Tablets and smartphones are great for keeping children quiet, but they are not good for the developing mind or for developing conversation skills. The constant motion and flashing lights affect how a child's brain processes information and sustains attention. Add in the hyperkinetic music that usually accompanies children's shows and digital games, and you've got a recipe for an overstimulated brain. Our babies' brains don't process disjointed, abrupt sights and sounds very well. Research shows that the connections in the nervous pathways develop better when exposed to fluid, coordinated input, such as classical music. When the developing brain is exposed to flashes and disconnected sounds with no continuity, it tends to become a somewhat disorderly brain with limited attention span.

I see a lot of chronically overstimulated children. We live in a culture that prizes busyness and productivity, and these tendencies have trickled all the way down to the way we interact with our infants. We tend to think that if one hour of engagement and interaction with a person, toy, or digital device is beneficial to children, then several hours must be even better. But everyone needs downtime to dream and relax, especially babies. Make it a habit when your child is very young to put him on the floor with some interesting items and things to chew, and leave him be. You'll have happier, easier children if you don't resort to stimulating games and screens to keep them occupied most of their waking hours. Allow them to develop their sense of touch, taste, and smell, not just their sight, until their central nervous system is well developed at around age two. After that, you can introduce some small, carefully monitored media. Even better, watch their shows or play their games with them now and again so they can enjoy your being part of their entertainment.

> Everyone needs downtime to dream and relax, especially babies.

Many parents worry that by holding back on introducing electronic media, especially educational games, they'll short-change their children. "What if the other kids are counting and mine is still chewing on sticks?" First, the vast majority of kids over the age of four aren't actually playing educational games. And if you do meet a precocious child who plays on an iPad and can count to ten by the age of three, most likely it's not the iPad program that is teaching the child to count, but a parent using the media with the child. No child left alone in front of a digital device is going to learn more than a child who interacts with another human being.

> No child left alone in front of a digital device is going to learn more than a child who interacts with another human being.

Once children are of school age, some tech in limited quantities is appropriate, but early exposure won't make children any smarter. If anything, it hurts their social development. Studies have shown that young children who spend time in front of media at young ages have difficulty learning empathy. All it does is rob them of time they could have spent observing and exploring the world around them and learning to socialize with family and friends.

Where Do I Find the Time?

I see a lot of chronically overstimulated parents—working and stay-at-home—too, who are often frustrated by admonitions to spend more one-on-one time with their children. "I'm busy and tired. Can't I just take some time to myself?" Absolutely. In fact, you should make personal downtime a priority. But consider that it is not just in your child's best interest to make that one-on-one time happen now; it's in *your* best interest as well.

Babies who get focused one-on-one attention are happier and not driving everyone around them nuts. They're easier to manage, sleep better, eat better, and are generally more pleasant to be around. You're going to do the time somewhere. Enjoy spending the time here, now, while it's easy. That said, knowing that the first three years of a baby's life are crucial for cognitive and motor growth shouldn't compel you to consider quitting your job or worry about how to clear big blocks of time in your schedule. The motor and cognition exercises I've suggested should not be done for hours at a time, and the responsibility can be shared with a partner, family member, or caregiver if necessary.

Keep Things Simple

Think small and easy. You don't have to spend every minute interacting with your children or turn every experience into a sensory teaching moment to give them a head start during those first three years, nor do you need to enroll your kids in structured classes. They don't need to take baby Mandarin or viola—unless they love it, you love it, and it's a completely stress-free activity for both of you. The problem with these kinds of classes isn't with the classes themselves, it's with the pressure that often accompanies them, whether it's in the form of pushing a child to perform, racing to get to the activity on time, or the strain on the family budget. Your children will not be at a disadvantage if they don't have these things. Filling the kitchen sink with bubbles and letting your children make a splashy, watery mess is enrichment enough. You don't have to do more and spend more. Include your kids in your activities and what you do around the home. They are constantly learning when they are just doing their own thing by your side, like counting the carrot pieces as you make salad or filling and emptying a laundry basket again and again. If you really want to give your child a head start in life, don't buy him a million toys. Toys won't alter the trajectory of your child's life. Getting him moving and stimulating his senses will. You don't need much for that. In fact, the list of items your baby really needs is small. A safe car seat, but nothing unnecessarily expensive. A blanket for the floor. A lightweight stroller for occasional use. Diapers. Often one of the reasons people work their tails off is to earn enough to provide the trappings of the expensive life they think will benefit their children. And yet, it's doing the things that cost nothing and don't take a lot of time that will have the most positive, long-lasting impact on a child.

> Toys won't alter the trajectory of your child's life. Getting him moving and stimulating his senses will

A woman I will call Anh, a Vietnamese mother who has lived in the United States for three years, told me that no one in her immigrant community spends a lot of money on their babies. They can't afford it, for one, but more important, they don't see the need. It doesn't cost much to lotion a baby up after a bath or play peek-a-boo on the floor. She asked me, "Do you think these American babies really need all that stuff?"

They don't, and I believe most parents know it. But marketers know what they're doing, and it's hard to resist the beautiful things made for children or the safety gear that play off parents' fears and insecurities. In addition, when we see other parents with these things, we can worry we're short-changing our children if we don't buy them. But we're not. One of the best ways to relieve your stress is to take stock and recognize that you rarely have to shower your baby with anything but love.

SPEAKING OF SHOWERS . . .

Baby showers are fun and give friends and family a way to show their love and excitement for the expecting couple and their new child. People want to buy baby things. But what if we changed some of the focus of baby showers away from the baby, who doesn't give a hoot about socks or diaper wipe warmers, to the parents? If it's true that once a baby arrives it becomes difficult for moms to get time to themselves or couples to get time together, maybe we could consider shower gifts that will support mothers and strengthen families so that they are the best parents they can be when they are with their child. If you are a close friend or relative, the next time you're invited to a baby shower, offer a pack of free babysitting coupons, or if you don't feel up to that, buy gift cards to a local restaurant or movie theater, or splurge for a couple's spa package. Consider chipping in with friends and family to pay for a weekly cleaning or meal delivery service for six months.

Of course you can indulge in a precious baby outfit or help stock the child's library, but try to add it to something that makes the parents' life simpler, reduces their stress, and takes a little work off their shoulders. These types of gifts make adults happy, but in the long run the baby will benefit from them, too, by learning to feel safe even when in other people's care, and by growing up surrounded by relaxed, happy, connected parents. You don't have to reserve these kinds of gifts for baby showers, either. They're perfectly appropriate for birthdays and holidays, as well. And, of course, I hope you will feel free to request any one of these ideas or anything else you think might accomplish the same thing, should anyone ask you what you would like for a baby shower gift or any special occasion.

IT'S NOT ALL ON YOU

Now is your chance to develop your child's senses, establish a strong cognitive foundation, and set your child up to be excited about learning and open to new experiences. Enjoy this special time of close interaction when you can; it's the one time when you'll have your child's undivided attention. Later in life, children turn to their friends and teachers and start exploring on their own. At that point it will be your job to get out of the way and let them run, learn to build relationships, interact with others, and problem solve. But for now, you and the other loving adults contributing to their care are all they've got, and you are pretty much all they want.

4

Gather Your Village

IN CHAPTER 2 we met Chris, who was surprised at how many people wanted to give her cautionary parenting advice even before her baby had arrived. The most disturbing thing she heard, however, was the repeated admonition to hurry up and finish school, because once the baby came she'd have to quit. A college student nearing the completion of her EMT training, Chris planned to finish her degree and get her professional certification after the baby was born. But most of her friends and family frowned on her decision, implying she was being naive, even selfish for considering leaving her child in day care while she finished her education. Concerned that she was overestimating her ability to juggle work and motherhood and determined to give her child the best start in life, she dropped out of school and moved in with her family after the birth of her son, Bradley. She stayed home for fifteen months, and while she loved the time she spent with her baby, she couldn't stop thinking about the education she had abandoned and the opportunities and advantages she and her son might miss if she didn't find a way to go back. Finally, unbeknown to her family, she registered for classes at her local community college, registered her child in the college day care, and took a part-time job in a nursing home. Once the child's grandparents also started pitching in with childcare, she was able to make it to the gym a few times a week, which kept her physically and mentally at her best. Life was still busy, but she believed she could make it all work for her little boy.

I'm happy for and supportive of any mother who is able to make the choice to stay home full-time with her child. Who wouldn't want to spend as much time as possible getting to know the precious small person she just created? And what a gift to be the one able to incorporate those crucial sensory, muscular, and cognitive experiences we discussed in the last chapter over the span of your day with your child. But I find that many mothers in my practice are quick to seek my approval when they decide to stay home with their babies. Their need for validation pains me, just as it pains me that many mothers in my practice who work full-time are often equally quick to apologize for it or to make clear they're doing it for economic reasons because they are well aware, they assure me, that a baby is better off with its mother at home.

Their guilt is misplaced and their apologies unnecessary. Whenever I find myself cheerily reassuring these mothers that their babies won't suffer any negative consequences for not having a stay-at-home parent, I remember a conversation I once had with Anh, the Vietnamese mother who had moved to the United States. I had asked her whether she had had a lying-in period after giving birth in Vietnam. Consistent with many Asian cultures, she said that her mother and her sister had temporarily moved in following the birth of her now five-year-old daughter. But the lying-in period was short. As she told me unapologetically, "Most of us have to work to provide for our families. We arrange for a babysitter." Her response and attitude echoed a practicality I've heard from many mothers around the world, who rarely apologize for doing what they must to support their families or express guilt for accepting help. Unfortunately, in many parenting circles guilt is rampant. Getting help is often considered a luxury at best. At worst, I've seen it twisted into a sign of unworthiness for the job.

A child is supposed to represent the addition of something new and wonderful to our lives, not the end of everything we were before it. Yet for the last few decades our culture has fed parents two ideals that essentially demand they completely upend their lives: good parents should be able to handle raising their children all on their own, and young children belong with their mothers as much as possible. Chris may have felt unduly pressured to become a full-time stay-at-home mother, but at least her family was willing to support her so she could meet their expectations. When you consider what it takes physically and economically for most people to meet these two standards, it's no wonder that millennial mothers with children under the age of 18, followed closely by Gen Xers, are the most stressed-out people in the nation, and maybe even in the Western world.

As we've discussed, parents in many other countries, Western and otherwise, often get a tremendous amount of help from their extended family and even other members of their community after they bring a new baby into the world. In many cases, that kind of communal care doesn't ebb after a few weeks the way it often does here. Rather, it's a given that when a child is brought into a community, it is the community's responsibility to help the parents raise that child and watch out for each other every day. In her book *Welcoming Spirit Home*, Sobonfu E. Somé, author and community leader from Burkina Faso in West Africa, explains her Dagara tribe's philosophy on child-rearing and family: "It is not enough to want to be a good parent; we need help and community—it takes community to keep a couple sane." I remember seeing women in the South African desert walking uphill carrying enormous buckets on their heads with newborns strapped to their backs (there is no lying-in when you have to get food and water to survive). These women were models of toughness, self-reliance, and devotion, but they probably had the energy to be so because when they got back to their villages, they knew they weren't alone—the childcare, cleaning, cooking, and all other household obligations would be shared by many. Unfortunately, much of what makes America great, such as our independent spirit and relatively easy geographic mobility, puts parents at a global disadvantage in this regard. As a country we are unmatched in generosity and compassion when we find out one of our own is sick or struggling after an event like a natural disaster. But when it comes to raising children and keeping a home running every day, parents are expected to tough it out on their own. Yet while we do owe it to our children to provide unconditional love, a safe, nurturing, play-filled environment, and to advocate for them when necessary, historically, it has never exclusively been a parent's job to make a child successful. Until very recently, it was considered a shared responsibility.

CHILD-REARING IS BETTER AS A GROUP EFFORT

Siblings, grandparents, teachers, friends—everyone can and should play a role in shaping our children. Day-care programs and pre-schools, too. Much of the rest of the world knows this. In Denmark, whose citizens repeatedly land at the top of polls ranking the world's happiest people, almost all one-year-olds are enrolled in publicly supported early education programs, and 80 percent of mothers with children aged fifteen years and under are in the workforce. In Belgium, most kids start preschool by the time they're about two-and-a-half, and in Japan, by the time they're three. But in America, where a lack of publicly funded subsidies means the burden of paying for childcare or preschool falls squarely on parents' backs, not even 50 percent of three-year-olds are enrolled in preschool, and the percentage goes up to only 69 percent once they turn four. And that helps explain why, in my experience, stay-at-home moms—who are often trying hardest to live up to the almost impossible American parenting ideal—are just as stressed out as their working peers. No matter how much you love your children, their constant companionship and demands for attention can be exhausting. And yet our society is set up to encourage mothers to spend the vast majority of their time alone with their young kids. Is it really any wonder moms are worn out? Danish moms—most of whom work—routinely get about ninety minutes of child-free time to themselves per day. An American mother gets around thirty-six minutes.

The really sad thing is that even when moms can afford a few hours of childcare, they often feel guilty about using it. You can see the evidence of this pressure in mother-centric chat rooms. Whenever women bother to explain why they need recommendations for Mother's Day Out programs, they often say that they need a little time alone to do the shopping or run errands. Almost inevitably, however, they'll add something like, "Or get a pedicure!" often accompanied by an emoji. Why must a mother's desire to take care of her needs and even indulge in some fun be reduced to a joke? Why should women be embarrassed to admit that they just want some time to themselves?

There's no need to feel bad about leaving your children in someone else's care, even in day care, whether it's to work, go to school, or pursue an interest for pure personal satisfaction. A study published in the April 2014 issue of the *Journal of American Marriage and Family*—the first large-scale longitudinal study of its kind—reported that the amount of time spent with parents makes far less difference in the behavioral, emotional, or academic outcomes for children between the ages of three and eleven years than a mother's income and level of education. The quality of the activities and emotional bonding that occurs between parents and children matters far more than the quantity of time they spend together, with one exception. It's during adolescence, right when many parents start to loosen the reins and step out of their children's lives, that the amount of "engaged time" parents spend with their kids makes a big difference. The results of this study, combined with the evidence from around the world, shows that many young children who receive plenty of nurturing one-on-one time do not suffer ill effects from attending a quality day-care program or preschool or being with a trusted babysitter. In fact such time away from a parent helps these kids develop great social skills.

FAQ: How Do I Choose a Great Day-Care Program?

The best way to find a good day care is to talk to other parents for recommendations, check the program's references and licensure, and pay them a visit. I got my best information by spending time observing the ebb and flow of the day care and its routines, as well as observing the interaction between caregivers and children. Always try to check out a few day-care facilities before making a final decision, and once you've narrowed your choices down, ask if you can bring your child in for a visit. No matter what day care you choose, make sure they have an open-door policy that allows you to visit your child at any time.

The key word, of course, is *quality*. Quality can be expensive, which is why Scandinavian countries and others that offer universal childcare put caps on the percentage of income any family has to pay for it. Research shows that a child under the age of six whose time with a parent is mostly spent "watching TV or doing nothing" can actually have a "detrimental" effect on them. That has to be true for time spent with any adult, not just a parent, which means people who can't afford high-quality childcare have good reason to be concerned about how their children's time away from them will affect their development and outcome. More should be done to help these parents and secure their children's futures, but that is a subject for another book. For most middle- and upper-middle-class families, however, the guilt and worry we expend over leaving our young children is simply unwarranted and even harmful. And not just to us adults.

FEELINGS ARE CONTAGIOUS

Most people intuitively know that depression can severely affect the way parents interact with their children, but many assume that our stress and guilt is merely our own cross to bear, a consequence of modern-day parenting that may not be great for parents' mental or physical health but is tolerable so long as it doesn't affect our kids. Except it does. All that stress, fatigue, or guilt you might be carrying bleeds into your interactions with your children. A mother who is tired of being "on" is not going to be as attentive, patient, or even as much fun as one who regularly gets time to herself to rest, exercise, pursue her own interests or have an adults-only lunch with friends. If you resent work as a necessary evil separating you from your child, your children will eventually feel that way about work too, and once they are old enough they will do everything they can to keep you away from it for as long as possible. Anyone who has ever started the day off trying to wrench his or her leg from a screaming child's grip knows what I'm talking about. Children can sense when Mom and Dad feel bad about the choices they are making. Working and nonworking moms who fret every time they leave their child in someone else's care are sending a subliminal message to their children that they really aren't safe unless their mothers are right by their side.

It would be more useful to teach children from the beginning that work is a natural part of adult life, and something that in the best of cases is to be enjoyed, not dreaded or resented. Ideally, all working mothers would have the same attitude as Kate in Australia, who works as an EMT: "Working makes me a better parent. I make a lot more of the time I do get with [my daughter] and make sure we do a lot of fun things together. I think the time apart is good for us." How empowering to give your child the confidence to know that she can have a good time without you, and that you will always come back for her. Infants who learn these lessons early become toddlers who aren't plagued with fear and worry whenever their parents aren't around.

So having a life beyond your kids is good for you, and it's good for your kids. It's also good for your relationship with your partner. You have to take the time to focus exclusively on each other, and not just occasionally, or you risk forgetting what it was that drew you together in the first place before kids. Just as children respond negatively when stress and anxiety pervade a home, they react positively when it's filled with happiness and harmony. A home that's run by parents who are still in love, who enjoy being together whether alone or with their children, is a great incubator for happy kids. And it's a great incubator for parents, too, preparing them for the time when once again it'll be just the two of them. For it's not just our parenting standards that have risen; our expectations for what we should expect and achieve in all chapters of our lives has increased.

In a *New York Times* article on why couples over the age of fifty are divorcing at higher rates than at any other time in our country's history, author and director of research and public education for the Council on Contemporary Families Stephanie Coontz said, "We expect to find equality, intimacy, friendship,

> Having a life beyond your kids is good for you, and it's good for kids.

fun, and even passion right into what people used to see as the 'twilight years.'" But meeting those expectations takes effort. "It's not something you can put on the back burner while you raise your kids, for example, and think it won't scorch somewhere along the way." Whether you're spending time alone or with your partner, think of the moments you take for yourself as preventative medicine for a happy marriage that wards off the harmful effects of empty nest syndrome.

How to Ease Your Stress and Guilt

1. Acknowledge What You Do, and Don't Knock Yourself for What You Don't

Instead of berating yourself when you feel like you're not living up to society's image of the ideal parent, make a list of all the wonderful things you do for your children. Singing lullabies, playing Itsy Bitsy Spider, turning up the music and dancing around with your child in your arms . . . these activities are all free, they take very little time, and they all have a huge positive influence on your child.

2. Pursue Your Own Needs and Interests

Be a good role model and show your kids that it's possible to be a wonderful, loving parent and still work or be active in your community. You want your children to grow up seeing you as a whole individual, not just a parent whose entire life revolves around them. Children often experience a lot of pressure when they feel like they are their parent's reason for being. It's okay to think about yourself. Indeed, put yourself first every now and then. And do it soon. The earlier you teach your children that they are safe and capable of having fun without you, the better chance you have of sparing your child from developing separation anxiety. Eliminate or avoid separation anxiety altogether, and you also eliminate or avoid one of the most guilt-inducing stressors in a parent's life.

3. Prevent Separation Anxiety

Separation anxiety is caused by a fear of the unknown. It can start quite early. The most common cases I see are in infants who have been exclusively breastfed and had the majority of their care provided by one parent, usually the mother. I hear about this situation all too often: A mothers tries to leave the child with his dad just for an hour or two so she can go out, get her hair cut, run an errand, or attend a dental appointment, and the infant screams hysterically the whole time she is gone. The father, equally distressed at being unable to comfort his child, is usually reluctant to try the experiment again.

This sad scenario is completely preventable when a child's father participates in all of a baby's caretaking from the beginning, and if the mother is willing to regularly take a little time off from mothering and leave her partner to enjoy some one-on-one time with his child. Better yet, parents should help their children become secure with other caretakers, too. Introduce other friends and family to baby's world, let them hold him and play with him, and even better, allow a select few to babysit so you and your partner can go out on dates together. If you socialize as a family in friends' homes, put your child to bed in their guest bedroom or let him bunk with your friends' children. It's all about well-planned exposure to different environments that enables a child to feel safe with different caretakers and even enjoy the opportunity to spend time with others free of your intervention.

FAQ: My Child Already Has Separation Anxiety. Help!

The answer is not to avoid situations that will trigger your child's reaction, but to give him more frequent exposure. If your child is terrified when you leave him, start setting up lots of playdates and occasions to spend time with a grandmother or close friend. Try not to be the one who leaves. Wait until your child is happily involved with a friend or loved one and moves away from you before exiting the room. This may take a number of attempts, but keep trying until your child gets comfortable. Talk up these playdates excitedly, and don't ever put a negative spin on or apologize for leaving.

Whatever you do, don't wait until the first day of school or preschool to try this exercise. It might be very scary for a child to have to deal with two completely new experiences at the same time. It is much better to ensure that your child is already comfortable spending time with other children and without you long before he needs to start school. You want your child to make only positive associations with these new settings, so make sure to give him plenty of chances to practice his independence in loving environments where there's no pressure and nothing at stake for either of you. Around the time your child will be preparing to attend day care or school, start talking very positively about the new experience so he looks forward to the opportunity. These places have lots of other kids around, a new playground, and other fun group activities, and most children who are used to being without their parents warm up to the change fairly quickly, especially if they already have friends attending the same day care or school.

PRIORITIZE

There is, of course, a big difference between leaving a child for a few hours while you take a photography class or attend a volunteer board meeting, and leaving the house in the morning knowing you won't see your child again until the end of the day. How can you help but feel like you're missing out, and that maybe your child is, too? How can you keep from feeling crazed and stretched too thin as you try to do your paying job and your parental job equally well? Assuming once again that the quality of the childcare you're able to provide is not in question, the solution is to become a master at prioritizing.

When we were living in Idaho, I was the only neonatologist for 120 miles. Sometimes I'd stay up working all night in the

NICU, go home, take a shower, and then work all day in the clinic. There was very little respite because, by definition, my job was to deal with a constant stream of life-and-death situations. Out of necessity I learned very, very quickly to differentiate between what was important and truly made a difference to me and my family and what didn't. And what didn't, I put aside without a single regretful or guilt-ridden glance.

People are terribly busy, but they're often compounding their busyness by doing things that aren't necessarily good for their quality of life or their children's. Starting your evening at home angry or frustrated because you see the laundry still isn't done doesn't do anyone any good. If a clean home helps you feel rested and relaxed, and your partner can't help you and you can't have someone to come in and spruce the place up once or twice a month, give yourself ten minutes after the kids are in bed to tidy up one part of the house—just one—and then drop it. The dust in the corner, chores, social media, catching up on the news . . . for some people those things are very important, but they can and will wait. The real human beings right in front of you should not. If you try to block the time you spend with your children from any other distractions, so you aren't feeling pulled in several directions, your stress levels will go down. And then you'll see your child's stress levels go down. When he knows the time he spends with you is sacrosanct, he won't feel like a low priority when you go away.

Try to remember that the time you'll get with your child while he is still young will be very short. Singing, reading, talking, cooking (even a toddler can chop avocado with a dull dinner knife), giving a relaxing bath, being silly . . . it's not just what you do with children that counts, but *how* you do it. The quality of and

> It's not just what you do with children that counts, but *how* you do it.

especially the mood infusing the time you're with your children matters more than the number of hours you are with them. You won't evoke positive feelings in your children if you're in the house with them but your eyes are on your phone or you're racing around trying to get things done, or you make it clear that you cannot wait for them to go to bed so you can get some down time. That's not time that any of you will look back on and reminisce about. It's a missed opportunity that could have been turned around with a bit of intention and attention.

Deborah, a pediatric nurse who also works as a babysitter, has seen firsthand what an unnecessary strain parents put on themselves and their kids when they don't prioritize and they don't trust anyone else to care for their children. She was once hired to watch two children, Ainsley, aged eighteen months, and Brett, aged eight, while their parents took a six-day trip to the Caribbean. Like any responsible parent considering putting her children in someone else's care, the mother, whom we'll call Judy, put Deborah through a rigorous interview and double-checked her references, who all confirmed that she was an excellent and trustworthy babysitter. What was amazing, says Deborah, was that despite knowing that she had fourteen years of experience looking after children and despite the glowing references, Judy acted as though there was no way Deborah could possibly know what to do with the kids. Over a series of many phone calls and visits to the home, Judy explained every detail of the children's routines and repeatedly told her what she would need to do. Then, just to be sure Deborah got it right, Judy typed out all the instructions from start to finish. By all accounts Deborah was a good cook, and she and Judy discussed various dishes the children would enjoy while the parents were gone. Yet when Deborah showed up for her first day on the job, she found a freezer full of food Judy had cooked ahead of time. During her first visit to the home just to get the lay of the land, Judy had shown Deborah the children's closet and told her to dress them appropriately for the weather, which shouldn't have been a problem since it was summer and it was a safe bet the weather would be consistently mild and sunny. But when Deborah arrived, she found six days' worth of matching outfits laid out in each child's room.

Deborah spent one night with the family before the trip to get a sense of the children's routine. The atmosphere was tense; nothing felt quite right. Judy kept interrupting the dinner conversation to nag the eight-year-old to get his elbows off the table, and once the meal was done she spent another twenty minutes racing around the living room picking up every toy off the floor, emptying the recycling bin, turning over the compost, and several other small chores around the house, while the father retreated to his study. Bath time was quick and efficient; Judy bathed the baby girl, her husband came out long enough to help with the boy. After the children were in bed, Judy came downstairs and flopped into a chair, smiling ruefully, and said, "I'm exhausted!" She seemed to be looking for Deborah to express some sympathy, but Deborah couldn't. Not when all that exhaustion was so clearly self-imposed.

The parents finally left for their trip, and Deborah spent six days looking after the children and getting everything on the to-do list accomplished exactly as Judy had asked her to. Well, not exactly. She did it without driving herself or the kids crazy. For six days, she went to work while the kids were in school, but otherwise she played and talked with the kids, got them to their respective schools, put them to bed on time, made sure they were fed and bathed every day, and took care of all the household chores as well. Granted, there was no one emailing her after hours to get her approval on a project, no late-night correspondence or last-minute spreadsheet to create for a presentation the next day, so it was easy to focus all her attention on the kids. But in her observation, in an attempt to create the "perfect" environment for their children, the couple was generating so many responsibilities for themselves that the quality of the time they spent together was compromised.

What about the kids? Was the stress, anxiety, and the pressure these parents put on themselves theirs to bear alone? Two things Deborah told me makes me suspect this wasn't the case. Whenever she'd play games with the eight-year-old, he couldn't just play and enjoy the fun. Everything was a competition, and he was a terrible sore loser. The girl whined incessantly around her mother, but this bad habit mostly cleared up as soon as Deborah started spending time in the house. It sounded to me that perhaps the children were learning that anxiety and stress were a necessary byproduct of doing well, a sign that the family was succeeding at the game of life. What an unfortunate lesson to pass on to one's children. What an exhausting life. Even with all the resources she had available to ease her strain and introduce calm back into the home, Judy couldn't accept help for fear of relinquishing control over her role and subjecting her children to anything less than her standards of perfection, while actually achieving the opposite.

HOW TO BUILD YOUR VILLAGE

Other societies where mothers (and fathers) report greater life satisfaction than in the States understand that a strong country needs strong families, and have put support structures in place, whether through government-funded programs or via tight family and community ties, to make sure parents can balance their needs with those of their children. Sobonfu E. Somé, who spends half her time in her native Africa and half her time in California, explains why the village is important for children, too. "If a child grows up with the idea that only mom and dad are her community, then when she has a problem, if the parents cannot fix it, the child doesn't have anybody else to turn to." Then she adds an utterly simple yet, to American ears, utterly radical thought: "The parents alone are responsible for whoever the child becomes, and this is just too much to ask of just two people—or, many times, just one person." Indeed.

However, because it's unlikely the relief will be coming from our legislators any time soon, parents need to create their own villages to help them raise their children so their quality of life stays high even after they have kids; so they don't feel like everything got turned upside down and they're constantly behind; and so they are able to focus on their partners, their friends, and all the other people who matter to them. This should go a long way toward alleviating the rampant stress that wears so many parents down and whose negative effects spill over onto their children and home lives.

START AT HOME

First, turn to your partner. Though men have increased the amount of work they do around the house in impressive numbers, they still on average don't do as much as women. (Same-sex couples seem to be better about sustaining egalitarian labor arrangements during child-rearing years.) For some reason, men often don't seem to see the unwashed dishes, the unfolded laundry, the unmade bed that drive their wives crazy, or if they do, it doesn't bother them enough to do something about it. And, unfortunately, many don't even realize how much silent, behind-the-scenes work their wives are carrying on their shoulders. They don't recognize how much mental effort it takes to schedule pediatrician appointments, research childcare or preschools, arrange play dates, and choose summer camps. Yet planning small people's lives on top of one's own takes a lot of forethought and energy and cuts deep into what little free time mothers have, whether they're working outside the home or not. In fact, despite increasing the number of hours they help out around the house and spend with their children, fathers in general reportedly get about three hours more leisure time than mothers per week. Unless parents establish a routine early on that fairly distributes the work of running a family, fathers are generally going to take their me time when they want it and assume that if the mother wants some, she'll take it, too. But many mothers don't, because they don't believe they can take leisure time until everything they think needs to get done gets done. And in a world where there is always more to do, mothers can spend much of their lives bouncing back and forth between responsibilities and obligations like a careening pinball if they're not careful.

Ideally, couples should establish a sustainable division of labor before they become parents. But even the most egalitarian couple can unintentionally create an imbalanced situation. It happens slowly. Perhaps a baby comes along and both parents initially find it easier and faster for the mother to be the point person on all things baby related. Then as the child gets older, the number of child-related responsibilities slowly accumulates without anyone noticing, until the mother explodes in a furious fit or retreats in seething anger. Either way, it can lead to a couple looking at each other in dismay, wondering how they got to this tense and overwhelmed place.

Often mothers have to hit the reset button after having kids and demand change. One suggestion is to follow the advice offered by Alexandra Bradner in a 2013 article she wrote for *Atlantic Monthly* called "Some Theories on Why Men Don't Do as Many Household Tasks." She suggests mothers draw up a list of "invisible work" categories that make up running a home and raising a family, such as remembering to send birthday cards out to family members and planning weekly meals. Fathers who want to improve their relationships with their wives, not to mention the atmosphere in their home, might look at this list and question how much of it they've ever taken on themselves. Then the couple can work together to find ways to communicate better so the father takes ownership of more on the to-do list. Fifty-fifty fairness may be difficult to achieve or even be unnecessary. What's more important than absolute parity is that mothers feel they are being taken care of too, and that their partners don't take their labor for granted. This advice might sound more appropriate for a relationship-therapy book, not a parenting book. But keeping your relationship happy and healthy keeps you happy and mentally healthy, which makes you a happier, healthier parent. Taking care of yourself and getting the help you need are two of the best ways you can ensure your child's future success.

> Taking care of yourself and getting the help you need are two of the best ways you can ensure your child's future success.

And once children are older, they can help as well. A three-year-old might really enjoy the responsibility of putting a scoop of dry dog food into the pet bowl every morning, although she will likely need a daily reminder; a five-year-old can help clear the table. These small tasks won't take a huge load off your shoulders, and they would probably get done faster if you did it yourself, but asking children to participate in keeping their home running will set a good precedent for when they're older and can take on more responsibilities. One mother told me the final item on her two boys' daily chore chart was, "Ask 'How can I help?'" It's her way of teaching her kids to notice what other people are doing around them, and raising them to recognize that all the members of a household can work together to make it a home.

TURN TO YOUR COMMUNITY

Two years after I arrived in the States, I divorced. For a while I was a single mom with three children, largely isolated from all my family, who still lived on the other side of the world. I got a job at a local bank, and I sought out community where I could. I later married my husband, Jim. He had been a university professor and was then working as an athletic director. We had another child together. I had never abandoned my dream of being a doctor, and I felt that if I didn't try now I would not have another chance. Could I do it? Should I do it? Jim and I talked a lot and finally decided we would work together to make my dream happen. He helped me in every way he could, and I was accepted to the University of Colorado Health Sciences Center. Once I completed medical school, we moved to North Carolina so I could accept a position in a pediatric residency program there. Before the move my routine was to leave the baby at an excellent day care while the other three children caught the bus to their schools. In our new surroundings in North Carolina, the morning supervision fell to me. My husband would leave for work in the very early hours of the morning so that he could be back in the afternoon to help with the kids. However, I was now required to be on call every third night for work as well, which meant I couldn't always be home first thing in the morning. My husband, however, still had to leave for work before any children's day care was even open. What were we going to do?

Determined to find a solution, I went down to the local swimming pool. I knew no one there, but I seated myself near a group of women and started to chat. Soon enough, I told them my problem. I needed someone to be at my house every third morning at about 4:30 to cover those few hours before day care opened. The women smiled sympathetically and said, "Well, yes, that is a problem." But they had no solutions. They did, however, say they'd ask their friends if they knew anyone who might be able to help. To my surprise, a few days later one of the women called me back and told me that her husband was a Duke football coach who had to get up at the crack of dawn, which meant she did, too. If my husband could drop our kids off at her house on his way to work, she could take my little one to day care once it opened and the older children could catch the school bus from her house. She said it would make her feel good to know she was helping another family out. Over time I found her to be an extraordinarily kind and wonderful human being. The children loved the mornings when they got to go to her house!

There should be no shame in asking for help. There should be no shame in admitting that

> There should be no shame in asking for help.

we may not be able to do everything ourselves. If American families would reach out more toward each other instead of hiding when they are struggling, they could create the kind of support networks that parents in other countries enjoy, so that even if they are on a limited budget their quality of life could stay high after they have kids. Embrace good-quality day care, rely on your friendships, and delegate tasks whenever you can if that's what it takes to keep you from feeling put-upon and overwhelmed. Some communities have started childcare co-ops that work well for parents who work part-time. Others have created babysitting co-ops so that parents can get a night out together at least once a week or month and nurture their relationship. Where there's a will there's a way.

It's important to teach our children that we are not their sole source of security. They need to see us as whole people, with interests and passions and, yes, obligations other than them. It's good for them to know that you can do all the things you want to do, whether it's volunteer, work, go to school, or pursue a hobby, and still have plenty of love and time left to give them. And the way to ensure that's true is to make sure you don't feel like the weight of the world is on your shoulders. Which means you have to move some of it from your shoulders to someone else's. You have to get creative. You have to ask for help. And when you do, you have to actually let the help . . . help. You cannot do it all, and you should not try.

5

Sleep Through the Night—Really!

THE YOUNG MOTHER paced the nursery, bouncing her baby gently in her arms for what seemed like hours. Finally, when the only sound she could hear was that of the ocean waves crashing onto the beach just a few hundred yards away, through the window she had left open to catch a bit of the cool sea air, she slowly, carefully slipped her little bundle back into his crib, holding her breath lest the slightest noise disturb the hard-won silence. She quickly tiptoed out of the room, almost stumbling over the big golden Labrador that had parked himself directly outside. He followed her like a shadow into her bedroom where her husband lay, his head hidden by the pillow strategically placed over his ears. She crumpled into the bed, breathing a long sigh, and fell asleep almost before her head hit the pillow. But her peace didn't last long. Not two hours later, she awoke to the sound of her baby crying in the next room. She listened to him through the walls, willing him to go back to sleep. But his distress only grew louder as he choked on his tears. Resigned, exhausted, praying that if she just remained patient and kind this would all stop, she dragged herself back out of the bed and padded down the hall, the Labrador following silently behind.

The young mother pacing the floor through the night was me, of course. I was twenty-five years old and living in Australia. After giving birth to my first child, Cameron, I did not get one single uninterrupted night of sleep for four years. I read every book on infant sleep I could get my hands on, and tried everything I could think of including all of my well-meaning friends' suggestions and my pediatrician's suggestions, but nothing worked. And I had no one but myself to blame.

In the first days after I brought my son home, like many new mothers I had enjoyed rocking him in my arms while he drifted off to sleep. It was a beautiful, peaceful, relaxing routine. I loved watching him. Unfortunately, he, of course, also enjoyed that routine, and after that nothing else would do. I'd put him in his crib sound asleep, and an hour or so later he'd be up, wailing, until I took him back in my arms. My husband would try to soothe him but he met with the same result. Daytime wasn't much better; thanks to the restless nights, he was often tired and feisty. We were beyond exhausted. Every day I would pray for just two or three hours of sleep.

I learned my lesson. A year and a half later I had my second son, Brendan, and another year and a half later, my daughter, Julianne. With each additional infant, we started a new routine that did not include the endless rocking or letting them fall asleep in our arms. Although still sweet and cozy and filled with kisses and lullabies, the routine did not require my assistance once the babies were in bed. I'd gently lay them in their cribs calm, clean, and well fed, with their eyes still open, and after one last kiss I would quietly leave. Instead of associating safety and sleep with constant motion and Mommy's and Daddy's arms, they learned it was safe and comfortable to sleep in their own beds until the next feed or the sun came up the next day— or until their big brother's screams woke them up.

Years later when I went to medical school, the literature on infant sleep confirmed what I had figured out on my own in Australia: Babies are creatures of habit, and how a baby learns to fall asleep in her first few days is how she will always want to fall asleep. Unfortunately, it has proven an uphill battle to pass that hard-won knowledge on. A recent study from the University of Michigan found that only about 30 percent of parents consistently comply with their pediatrician's advice, and only 18 percent follow their pediatrician's instructions when it comes to sleep training! I didn't need a study to tell me this, though. I see the proof every day.

> How a baby learns to fall asleep in her first few days is how she will always want to fall asleep.

When I ran my pediatric clinic, I met a lot of babies for the first time on or before their three-day checkup. At these meetings I tried to keep things simple. I checked the newborn for weight, and I would ask if the baby was wetting his diapers. I would ask questions about feeding and sleep. And when we were done, I would send the family home with only a short list of basic guidelines regarding the mom's and baby's needs for sleep and food. Even before they left my office, though, I could usually tell who was going to take my advice and who was not. I knew whether I was right when these parents—usually the mothers— came back for their two-week visit. The moms who listened and followed my basic instructions usually looked calm and put-together. The ones who didn't were often exhausted, emotional, and even bedraggled. I could see my twenty-five-year-old self in them. Too many parents just don't believe me when I tell them that aside from keeping their babies well fed and cleanly diapered, the best thing they could do in the first month is teach their babies how to go to sleep without their interventions so that they will sleep well and stay in their own beds.

Why is it so hard for new parents to accept that their babies don't need their constant presence to sleep through the night? Because in many circles, such a statement is heresy. We've come a long way from the misguided admonishments from nineteenth- and even twentieth-century pediatricians who discouraged mothers from showing too much affection or picking their children up when they cried in the night for fear of spoiling them. Now we've got the opposite problem—parenting experts who insist it's unnatural for infants and even young children to sleep anywhere but within arms' reach, especially if their mothers are to successfully breastfeed on demand. It's advice that might be appropriate if most of us were still living in unheated cottages or sleeping on the dirt-packed floor of a hut, where food was scarce and the night filled with predators. It might also be more reasonable if many of those trying to follow this advice didn't have to get up at dawn for ten-hour workdays topped off by a few hours of pre-bedtime emails or didn't have to face long days alone taking care of multiple children while running errands, preparing meals, and volunteering at older siblings' schools. But as it stands, many parents are attempting to follow the parenting practices of our ancestors while also trying to be productive twenty-first-century citizens, model employees, and engaged romantic partners. And the strain of trying to do all of it well brings many to the brink of exhaustion. As it is, our lifestyles make it exceedingly difficult to get the rest we need. But we'd get a lot closer to being the best version of our parenting selves (not to mention citizen, employee, and romantic partner) if we made getting that rest a priority. But is it actually possible for new parents, or is sleep-deprivation inevitable?

It's not, of course. In her best seller *Bringing Up Bébé*, Pamela Druckerman expressed amazement that most of the French babies she met slept through the night no later than six months, and some as early as six weeks. By the age of six months, Dutch babies are generally getting two hours more sleep per day than American babies. Why? How? The answer, according to Kay Hymowitz, a Manhattan Institute scholar, is partly cultural. She suggests that from the beginning new parents teach their children how to adapt to their social environment, using "the materials of their culture, the shared beliefs and the related repertoire of behaviors that will eventually turn their children into Japanese, Italian, or American adults." The influence can be seen in children's behavior and development as early as infancy. For example, she points to a comparative study between Dutch and American mothers and their infants that found that, whereas Dutch mothers believed their children needed to be kept "calm, cheerful, and well regulated" and structured their routines accordingly, American parents believed their children needed to be "stimulated." Consequently, the authors of the study observed that Dutch babies tend to remain in a state of "quiet alert," while American babies are far more active. It's not surprising that the Dutch babies also get more sleep. In other words, you reap what you sow.

Whether they realize it or not, parents tend to have culturally conditioned goals for their children in mind from day one. Americans tend to value busyness, independence, and productivity, so a typical American child's day is often filled with stimulating activities and outings, even during infancy, making it all the more important for her to get a lot of sleep. That stimulation, however, can also potentially make it harder for her to sleep or stick to a sleep schedule. And therein often lies the conflict.

HOW WE SLEEP-TRAIN OUR BABIES

There are two especially popular sleep-training methods in the United States, and though diametrically opposed, both work. Unfortunately, they usually also require a painful trade-off. Too often, babies who regularly enjoy a full night's sleep have parents who have compromised their own. An examination of both practices reveals why.

Crying It Out

Many people think Crying It Out (CIO) is synonymous with the Ferber method, named after Dr. Richard Ferber, the pediatrician who popularized his sleep training technique that teaches babies to fall asleep on their own and in their own beds. But CIO was only one strategy out of many that Dr. Ferber suggested to help combat infant sleep issues. Ideally, you'd use Dr. Ferber's advice to prevent those issues in the first place. Dr. Ferber correctly asserted that babies who rouse briefly throughout the night—as all humans do—in the same environment as that in which they fell asleep will easily go back to sleep until morning. So theoretically, a baby who falls asleep alone in his crib won't be frightened when he wakes up to find himself alone in his crib. He'll just roll over and settle back down, resulting in a long, peaceful night's sleep for everyone—no CIO or any other tactic necessary. But remember, babies are creatures of habit. So parents who have spent weeks or months rocking their child to sleep or nursing him every time he whimpers have trained him to believe that in order to sleep, he needs to be rocked or nursed. Naturally, when babies accustomed to their parents' presence upon falling asleep wake up to find themselves alone in their cribs, they cry and may even panic. Now, if the parent races to the child's side to soothe and comfort him, the baby learns that when he cries, Mom or Dad comes to soothe and comfort. And maybe there's milk, too! So the next time he wakes up, rather than going back to sleep, he cries again, even if he's not hungry. And if Mom or Dad doesn't come running, he'll cry harder and louder. He's not being spoiled or manipulative. He's scared. Eventually, he's probably angry. He can't imagine what could possibly have gone wrong. Everything was so nice before, and now it's not.

> Babies are creatures of habit.

The thing is, Ferber insists that CIO as interpreted by many parents—and often used as a last resort after they've already trained their babies to expect help in going back to sleep—"suggests a misunderstanding of what I've been teaching for so long." He "never encouraged parents to let their babies cry it out." Rather, one of several sleep training techniques he recommended was called "gradual extinction," which, as the name suggests, was meant to help a baby slowly but surely become accustomed to his new surroundings. On the first night, the baby is put down in his own bed to sleep and the parents leave. Predictably, he will either fight going to sleep alone right away, or he'll go to sleep only to wake up and cry. Parents are supposed to wait a bit to make sure the infant doesn't go back to sleep on his own, then calmly enter the room and soothe the child with a few gentle words, just to let him know someone is nearby. According to the method, under no circumstances is the parent to pick the child up. Then, even if the baby hasn't stopped crying, the parent leaves. Eventually the child will fall asleep for a while, probably only to reawaken. Over and over, the baby is going to wake up and cry, and each time the parent is to wait a longer and longer time before entering the room to calm the baby down. Over the course of a few days, the child figures out that this is the new sleeping arrangement and that no amount of screaming is going to change it. At the same time, as the situation becomes familiar and his fear subsides, he will start to fall asleep quickly and develop a comfort sleeping on his own. Usually, it takes only a few days before he learns to self-soothe when he wakes up or enters a light sleeping period in the middle of the night and to go back to sleep.

CIO is uncomfortable for both parents and babies, but it is not immoral. Long bouts of crying, even a few hours' worth, will not cause lasting psychological damage or hurt a child's ability to bond with his parents, as some critics claim. In fact, the authors of several of the studies cited by some detractors have come forward to denounce the conclusions drawn from their science, particularly since their research concentrated on children born into abusive environments. One author, Dr. Alicia Lieberman of the University of California, San Francisco, insisted that her research was "not relevant to the argument . . . because my work involves babies and young children whose parents are in the pathological range of neglect and maltreatment . . . not children with normative, 'good-enough' parenting." Another, Dr. Joan Kaufman of the Yale School of Medicine, claimed, "It is a mis-citation of our work to support a non-scientifically justified idea."

It is not cruel to let your child cry while learning to sleep on his or her own. CIO is not, however, and as Ferber has repeatedly insisted, appropriate for every child. A child suffering from reflux or feeding intolerance is in pain and can't self-soothe. It would be wrong to expect a baby who is sick to go back to sleep without being comforted. So before trying the gradual extinction method, you must make an effort to consider and, if possible, eliminate any reasons why your baby may be crying every night. Regardless, even successful CIO can feel like pure hell for everyone involved for the amount of time it lasts. If you don't have to put yourself or your child through it, why would you?

Co-Sleeping

Over the past two decades or so, a growing and increasingly vocal camp has asserted that the mistake most sleep-deprived parents are making is not that they aren't adequately training their babies to sleep alone, but that they are trying to train them to sleep alone in the first place. They point out that until very recently, humans slept in groups. Why would we think that those biological imperatives would change all of a sudden? Co-sleeping makes sense—the baby feels safe, the mother doesn't have to make a big production to change a diaper or nurse (the vast majority of co-sleeping promoters are also strong breastfeeding advocates). In many countries such as Japan, Iraq, and India, children sleep in their parents' bedrooms well into their tween years. So what's the problem?

Technically, co-sleeping refers to the practice of parents and children sharing a room, usually in close proximity, commonly by attaching a co-sleeper, which is like a mini-crib except one side can drop down so mothers can attach it to their side of the mattress, making it easy to scoot the baby toward them to nurse during the night. The thing is, when most people talk about co-sleeping, they're actually talking about bed sharing. And many proponents of bed sharing in this country overlook one extremely important and problematic detail: the parental bed itself.

In those countries where bed sharing is common, and the rates of SIDS are low, people sleep on thin, hard mattresses, or even on the floor, with thin blankets and pillows. People in Western countries, however, sleep on puffy pillows, big plush pillow-top mattresses, with multiple sheets and blankets. And that's why babies who share a bed with their mothers are up to five times as likely to die than babies who sleep in their own crib, whether from SIDS, suffocation, or overheating. Even if families traded in their beds for harder mattresses it wouldn't make enough of a difference because it's not just the beds, but also everything about our lifestyles that has changed. Bed sharing is simply not a sensible alternative, and the research is clear: It's not worth the risk. One report that drew together the results of five studies and examined nearly 1,500 cases of SIDS in Britain concluded that 88 percent of the infant deaths examined would not have happened if the infant hadn't been sharing a bed with her parents. Out of over 8,000 cases of unexplained infant deaths over an eight-year period, researchers in the United States reported in the journal *Pediatrics* that 74 percent of babies under the age of four months died as a result of bed sharing.

With a few exceptions, most co-sleeping families become that way out of desperation. People will do anything to get the sleep they need, and if a baby's nighttime wakings become too much to bear, especially if a mother has to return to a job and resume the rhythms and pace of the work world, she'll bring the baby into the bed. And for a while bed sharing usually does work and everybody sleeps a lot better than before. But whoever coined the phrase "sleeping like a baby" to describe someone as a sound, quiet, and calm sleeper never actually slept with a baby. They wiggle. They kick. They whimper and cry out in their sleep. And as they get bigger their limbs get longer, their kicks get harder, and their knees and elbows get pointier. The child sleeps very well. The parents, not so much. But of course, after only a day or so the habit is set. The child likes the new arrangement and any attempt to put him to sleep in his own bed will likely be met with massive, vocal, sleep-denying resistance. It's easier for most parents in this situation to just let the child stay in the bed and resolve to deal with the problem when they're better able to cope with lack of sleep the transition will surely entail. Which for most families is pretty much never.

Of course, some mothers love bed sharing, especially those who want to nurse for more than a few months. They enjoy having their babies close, and as anyone can attest who has gone more than a day or two without more than three hours of sleep in a row, any sleep, even slightly interrupted sleep, is better than none. But I cannot tell you how many men I meet at my clinic who have been sharing their bed with their children for years, and beg me to encourage their wives and partners to start transitioning their children to their own beds. Co-sleeping in any form for long periods of time can have a disruptive effect on a couple's intimacy, if not their sleep. And that disruption can often have far more negative and long-lasting effects on a relationship than a few rough nights of sleep training.

CIO can be heart wrenching and guilt inducing. Bed sharing

is risky and can be disruptive. For years, however, I've been sharing a gentle sleep training method with the new parents in my practice that can have the whole family sleeping safe and sound within just a matter of weeks.

Dr. Jane's Really Simple Steps to Easy Sleep

1. Start Early

I'm asked all the time, "When should I start sleep training my baby?" Right away. Whatever routine you use to put your baby to sleep when she is just a few days old is the same routine that baby will expect every single time night or day. You can't suddenly change your mind one day and decide you're going to use a different method, then expect children to be okay with it. They usually won't be, because they like what you taught them, so when you suddenly try to change it, most children will fight you. You can surely see their point of view.

> "When should I start sleep training my baby?" Right away.

2. Set a Goal

Successful sleep training requires commitment. You have to decide, preferably even before your baby is born, what you want your sleeping arrangements for the next few years to be.

It's certainly common for parents and children to share a room, sometimes for years, in many countries around the world.

But I suspect these cultural traditions are grounded more in the cost of real estate, space limitations, safety in numbers, and efficiency, than exclusively in personal preference. And if they are preferred, it may be because it works for people's lifestyle and it's what they're used to. In countries where co-sleeping is the norm, any other sleep arrangement might seem bizarre.

But that doesn't mean sleeping alone actually is bizarre. It sure seemed like an enticing proposition to all those American families fleeing cramped city apartments in the 1950s for the suburbs. It seems reasonable to consider the possibility that if given the option and a chance to get accustomed to it, parents in other countries might find some benefits to reclaiming a little personal space, and sleeping apart from their children.

The beauty of living in this country, of course, is that you can choose to buck the cultural norm if you wish. I treated a well-educated Indian family in Colorado in which the parents had set up mattresses on the floor of their bedroom to include their twelve-year-old. And I once knew an American physician and his wife who shared their room with their infants and school-age children and were in no hurry to change the sleeping dynamics. They didn't care what other people thought. But I had to wonder, did their children? Were they equally comfortable with the arrangement, or was it something they felt they had to keep secret? Often, social norms do eventually matter to children, even if their parents have chosen to reject them. You might consider this as you set your goal.

So now is the time to decide: Do you want to be sharing your room or your bed with a child five years from now? (It may seem a long way away, but time has a tendency to speed by once you have kids.) Where do you think you'll be living in five years' time? Will you be working? Will you have more children by then? Given your answers, will you mind tending to a small child several times during the night or sharing your bed? Will your partner? If so, you should practice putting your child to sleep in her own bed (though not necessarily in her own room) the first day you come home from the hospital. Otherwise, you will likely consign yourself and your child to an eventual bout of sleep-training hell once you decide you want to make a change.

However, if your baby is healthy and full-term, with no feeding or other medical problems, and you adhere to my suggestions from the day your infant is born, you will likely have to neither share your bed nor listen to your baby scream for you through the day or night. In fact, my method should allow your child to sleep about four to five hours per night within two to three weeks, and up to seven or eight hours per night by the age of eight to ten weeks. All it takes is a little planning, patience, and perseverance. Many parents think it all depends on their baby's temperament or stubborn behavior, but it doesn't. It's almost always related to *your* behavior. What Mom and Dad do gives baby the cues for how sleep will happen.

FAQ: What Are the Ideal Bedtimes for Babies, Toddlers, Preschoolers, and School-Age Children?

Babies: During the first weeks of life, there is no such thing as a formal bedtime. However, as feedings become larger in volume, if you keep breastfeeding sessions close together while you're awake, the baby will be able to start dropping nighttime feedings, giving you and your baby a block of time to sleep between 11:00 P.M. and 5:00 A.M. As the night feedings get fewer, the nighttime sleep will often start around 7:00, and eventually baby will usually sleep about twelve hours.

Toddlers: These children often sleep about the same as babies at night but will want to keep a one- to two-hour morning nap as well as an afternoon nap of about an hour, depending on the child.

Preschoolers: Preschoolers keep similar hours to toddlers, but they usually have only an afternoon nap and sleep ten to twelve hours at night. I like to keep an early bedtime, like 7:00, so parents can have some quiet time.

School-age children: These kids still need eight to ten hours of sleep. They often have activities and homework, and often need to catch early morning buses to school. I think 8:00 to 8:30 is late enough for them to go to bed once they have a full-time job at school to handle. Kids tend to perform better when they are well rested.

3. Buy a Bassinet before You Bring Baby Home

It's perfectly fine to share your room with an infant if you create a setup that allows you to gradually move your child out of your room without causing the child distress, usually after the age of six months. The way to do that is to invest in a bassinet. As I mentioned earlier, a lot of families purchase co-sleepers. The problem with a co-sleeper is it puts your baby in such close proximity it's really an extension of the bed (it's a far safer but not completely risk-free option than actual bed sharing). Your baby will feel safe and secure in his own completely contained little space if he starts his life in your home sleeping in one. That's why a bassinet is a better choice than a co-sleeper. Yes, you do have to actually sit up (if it is right alongside your bed) or get up to nurse, but you don't have to go far, and then when you're ready to move your infant into his own room, somewhere between six and twelve months, you can do so guilt-free, and it is usually a change your infant is largely unaware of. Not having been accustomed to feeling you right next to him in the night, your baby won't notice the difference and won't get upset.

4. Be Consistent

Consistency, above all, is the key to starting a smooth sleep routine with your baby. It should be exactly the same every time he goes to bed. In the evening, however, it is really nice to add a gentle massage or, once the umbilical cord has fallen off, a warm bath in the evening, before you feed him and put him down. Keep him wrapped in his warm little towel or a soft blanket for now—you'll dress him later—and enjoy a cuddle. Make sure the lights in his bedroom are low. There's nothing nicer than snuggling with your baby right before his evening bedtime, so enjoy this quiet moment. By all means settle into the rocking chair you bought just for this moment. As your baby takes his last bottle or nurses, you could sing to him or recite poetry—he loves to hear your voice—or even pull out a few books and get into the habit right away of reading quietly to him.

5. Watch for the Moment

The practice you need to perfect is this: After each feeding, watch for the moment when your baby has had his fill and appears to be ready to close his eyes and go to sleep. This is how he will communicate that it is time to stop everything and be put to bed. Don't wait to let him fall asleep in your arms! Burp him if he has not been burped, then gently lift him up and go to the changing table, change his diaper, dress him in his sleep sac, or onesie plus a swaddle, and gently lay him quietly in his bed. If all of his needs are met, he should settle down and go to sleep. When he enters his light sleep cycle about an hour or so later, he'll know that he is right where you left him, he will feel safe, and he will go back to sleep. He may need a few practice runs to get this down, but it usually takes only a few times or certainly no more than a few days.

If your baby starts to cry shortly after being put to bed, wait a minute before picking him up to see if he's just grumbling a little while he soothes himself. If the crying continues, respond so he doesn't get used to practicing prolonged crying. Go ahead and pick him up. Babies don't usually cry unless something isn't quite right. Maybe he has a bubble in his tummy. Maybe he's not quite full. Try to fix the problem, then lay him back in the bed *while he is still awake and not crying.*

IT'S NOT WORKING. WHAT'S WRONG?

If you've followed these instructions exactly, and your baby still won't settle for four or five hours overnight within three to four weeks, there are a few things that could be going on.

Hunger

The most common problem is usually that the baby's intake of milk hasn't increased enough to allow her to sleep longer. Infants need to be able to increase their intake over the first few weeks. Once they eat enough they can skip a feed and sleep for a longer period at night. Nature supports this by increasing the amount of milk a mother makes per nursing over the weeks and months. At the same time, the baby's stomach keeps getting larger and her appetite should increase.

Most babies require about eight feeds per day—that is, they should eat once every two and a half to three hours when they first come home. The number of feeds should slowly decrease over time until they finally sleep through the night, ten to twelve hours. They will nap throughout the day, but do not allow your infant to take long four- or five-hour naps because that means she misses a feeding, which then means she will have to feed in the middle of the night to catch up. You don't want that. It's better to try to keep feedings about three hours apart during the daytime to ensure your baby gets enough to be adequately nourished and grow. Wake her up during the day if she sleeps longer and set the routine. It takes about 24 ounces per day to provide enough calories for a baby fully sustained on milk to grow during the first few months of life. Though the feedings will increase in size as the baby grows and sleeps longer at night, the overall daily amount will stay the same.

Reflux

We'll talk more about the causes of reflux in the next chapter, but it is a common problem that can make it painful for a baby to lie flat on his back. Frequently the sphincter between a young baby's esophagus and stomach does not work effectively. When the baby lies down after feeding, it has the same effect as laying a soda bottle on its side—the milk in the baby's stomach sloshes out and up to the esophagus. When it functions correctly, the esophageal sphincter keeps a tight seal over the entrance to the stomach, but if the sphincter is still immature, milk mixed with the natural stomach acids can seep up from the stomach into the esophagus and burn it. One solution is to allow the baby to sleep more upright in a car seat or, even better, in a bassinet with the upper part of the mattress raised. The car seat is not ideal—it's much preferable for a baby to be able to move freely in his bed, and the quality of his sleep will be higher if he's in a bassinet. But if reflux is hurting him, and the car seat is your only option, the upright position fixes the problem for many infants and should allow him—and you—to get some rest. A baby's reflux problem usually resolves by about four months. As we'll discuss in chapter 6, there are many other ways to treat reflux medically if needed.

Too Much or Too Little Sleep

Naps are crucial to babies and young children's health and development—young kids usually need more sleep than they can get in one stretch overnight. A baby's rhythms are dictated by normal chemical surges, and babies who are allowed to follow these natural rhythms are calmer and happier. If their routine is disrupted and they're faced with inconsistent bedtimes or lack of sleep, they get tired, which affects their behavior, and dysfunction can set in. Even in countries where young children are often found up late at night, there is an underlying routine. Children in Spain and some Latin American countries are often found up very late by US standards and even go to bars with their families. But there, where homes are small, most socializing happens in public places that act as substitute living rooms where family and friends can gather. In addition, the work and school days tend to start and end later than they do in the United States, so even though the children go to bed late, they routinely get the number of hours of sleep they need. And although many modern-day Spanish and Latin American companies have given up the tradition of the siesta to keep up with the global market, the nap is still the norm for children. In each of these cases, the cultures are structured to meet their children's needs.

How different from the United States, where babies frequently nap in cars or pressed against their parents' chest. They are sleeping, sure, but they are not getting the same quality sleep they would get in their own beds. Our busyness makes it tough for some kids to enjoy a routine, but it is worth arranging our days around a child's nap times and treating them with the same consideration we would an appointment with an electrician or plumber. Of course, for parents who stay at home with their children, it means organizing your days around these naps, which can be frustrating sometimes. But instead of getting irritated, it would be better to figure out how to be productive and use these quiet times for yourself. If you establish a routine, you will be rewarded with a happier child, which will make your time together easier and much more pleasant. On the upside, the day-time nap routine should be simple and short compared to the nightly bedtime routine. A quick lullaby, or a very short story, and down they go, giving you an hour and sometimes more to rest yourself or get a few things done.

Sometimes families put their children down for late-afternoon naps, at 3:00 or 4:00, or let them sleep too long. Morning naps tend to be much easier; older infants and toddlers will often wake up between 6:00 and 7:00 A.M., eat breakfast, and then want to take a nap at about 9:00. After this nap, they will often play and enjoy themselves before their lunch and again seem to be ready to nap at 1:00 or 2:00 in the afternoon. Try to put your baby to rest in the early afternoon so she is awake for at least three hours before going down for the night.

FAQ: If My Toddler Refuses to Nap, Does It Mean He Doesn't Actually Need One?

Children don't necessarily know if they need a nap. Some toddlers will fight their nap and then get tired in the early evening, which is unfortunate because this is usually the one time when everyone is home and can spend time together. If your child just won't sleep during the day, my suggestion is to at least require some quiet time. Put your child to bed or on a blanket or mat on the floor. He doesn't have to sleep, but he does have to lie still. It's fine if he wants to rest there with a picture book if he likes. This is the norm for many day-care programs. Start this habit of taking a daily break as early as possible, even if your child doesn't seem to want to sleep. The rest is valuable, even if it's just for an hour.

While we're on the subject of naps, I have to emphasize that we'd all be better off, if every one of us, young and old alike, took one in the afternoon. Aside from improving your concentration and ability to work after a break, taking a nap removes the effects of gravity on your heart and vascular system for a little while and provides a much needed break for your vertebral discs and joints. That can translate to a happier, healthier, more patient parent—the kind who maybe even remains unfazed by sleep-resistant children!

OTHER WAYS TO HELP YOUR BABY SLEEP

Swaddling

There are many videos you can turn to online for swaddling instructions (select one that has been reviewed by medical professionals). When done correctly, swaddling—the practice of wrapping a baby from the collarbone down in a thin blanket like an immobilized baby burrito—can effectively calm children and promote sleep. Once again, *when done correctly*. Many parents find that swaddling doesn't work, but it's usually because of one of the following reasons.

The Swaddle Is Too Loose

The whole point of a swaddle is to contain a baby's movements and give him the same sense of immobility and security he might have felt in the womb. If the swaddle is loose, the baby can start to feel unsafe and start to flail. In addition, loose swaddles pose a SIDS risk. The American Academy of Pediatrics (AAP) strongly advises against covering a baby in his crib with a sheet or blanket because of the chance the child could wrap himself in it or under it; blankets increase babies' risk of SIDS and suffocation, especially when they start being able to roll over. A loose swaddle becomes the equivalent of a blanket, which can be dangerous.

The Swaddle Is Too Tight

If drawn too tightly, swaddling can restrict a baby's breathing, cause a hip dislocation, or cause him to overheat. Swaddling isn't about wrapping a baby as tightly as you can, but about re-creating the position the baby enjoyed in utero. There, he was almost cross-legged, and he had a little room to move. You wouldn't want to be strapped down in bed. Your baby doesn't either.

Place the baby on his back in a completely empty crib—no toys, no pillow. It may look stark, but the baby doesn't care, I promise. To check that you're not tying the swaddle too tightly, make sure you can easily insert three fingers between the blanket and your baby's chest.

The other thing you don't want to do is swaddle your baby for too long. The AAP suggests discontinuing swaddling at the age of two months because it keeps babies from learning to roll and can be a suffocation risk if the baby winds up on his side, which is a common occurrence. Babies can fall forward, and without their arms free to push themselves up from the mattress, they cannot protect themselves. Unfortunately, babies have died of suffocation this way. In addition, pediatricians suspect swaddling can make babies overheat and help put babies in such a deep sleep that it decreases their arousal, which can increase the risk of SIDS.

As your baby grows, you need to start reducing the amount of time he spends in a swaddle. Babies should not be in it if they are wide awake—too many parents leave their child in the swaddle because they want to keep him calm. But if your baby is awake and looking around, he's ready to play or eat. As the weeks go by, he should be encouraged to move around and touch things. Babies learn about the world through their mouths, so they need to be free to bring their arms up and suck on their fingers. You want them to sleep, of course, but when they're awake you want them to have new experiences. For example, even this early you should be giving your baby tummy time, allowing him to practice pushing himself up from the floor, turning his head from side to side, and indulging his senses.

Pacifiers

Some lactation consultants strongly advise against introducing pacifiers because they fear it will confuse the baby and interfere with breastfeeding or because they can become one more habit you'll have to work to help your child drop later. But I don't necessarily agree, nor does the American Academy of Pediatrics (AAP). From a physiological standpoint, at least for the first year of life, non-nutritive sucking is quite important—babies have a sucking need that goes beyond what's provided by modern breastfeeding practices—and pacifiers help satisfy that suck reflex. The trick is to time their introduction correctly, within one to two weeks of life, and only after the baby is comfortably and successfully breastfeeding and her latch is good, usually after the first week or so.

Pacifiers shouldn't be babysitters, and ideally they shouldn't be sleep aids, either, for the simple reason that they fall out. And then the baby wakes up and something is different from when she fell asleep. And then she screams until you come in and put it back in her mouth. In addition, you'll want to encourage your child to give up the pacifier permanently before she's about two years old because it can impact the development of speech and alter the alignment of the teeth and gums. I actually suggest the pacifier remains in the bed once the child is up walking around, usually by ten to fourteen months, to keep the pacifier clean and limit the amount it is used. Getting a child to give up her pacifier doesn't have to be as difficult as getting her to sleep alone. One lovely tradition some parents follow is to give their child the opportunity to donate the pacifier to a new baby. Some pediatric dentists have a pacifier exchange program in which they allow children to come to the office and trade in their pacifiers for a small toy. Or you could take your cue from the Danes and Swedes: In their countries, you'll find pacifier trees in the parks— live trees colorfully festooned with the abandoned pacifiers of the city's children. Regardless of how you get rid of the pacifier, once it's gone, it's gone. If your child regrets her decision and starts to beg to have it back, do not give in. It might be hard, but

I promise you the crying will stop after only a day or two, and then your child won't give the pacifier a second thought.

> ### FAQ: I Can't Get My Baby to Stop Sucking His Thumb. What Do I Do?
>
> A thumb sucking habit can often be harder to kick than the pacifier, but you really want to try to help your child stop before the age of two. Thumb sucking can cause terrible dental problems when the child is older. There are a few tricks that help. Some pharmacies sell a product that can be painted on the child's thumb. It tastes terrible but it is perfectly safe. You can also buy a thumb guard, a plastic cover that's worn over the thumb and held on with a tie around the wrist. It's bulky and spoils the pleasurable sensation the child derives from putting his thumb in his mouth, making it easier to stop. Don't shame your child by calling him a baby, but you can gently suggest that he's very grown up now, and if he doesn't stop soon his friends might comment on it. Children usually suck their thumb when they're nervous, anxious, or tired. If you catch him sucking his thumb, just gently point it out so he can remove it from his mouth; he probably isn't even aware that he's doing it.

Music

Playing music at bedtime is a lovely idea so long as it's not highly stimulating, and so long as you turn it off, if possible, before your baby falls fully asleep. Gentle lullabies or, even better, classical music without singing is perfect. Remember, if children go to sleep listening to music, it will become part of the "going to sleep" routine, and the music will have to still be playing when they move into a light sleep phase or they may not be able to put themselves back to sleep.

Gentle music in the bedroom is fine, but most other noises can be disruptive to good rest. It's a common thing for American children to have televisions in their room or for parents to leave it on while their children nap nearby. Studies indicate, however, that a child who sleeps with a television on even at low volume doesn't get the same quality of sleep as the child resting in a silent room or in one where there is only soft music playing. This does not mean, however, that street noise negatively affects a baby's sleep. Street noise is more like white noise, a hum in the background. There is a difference between street noise and TV noise. Television programs and especially commercials are designed to catch your attention and stimulate you. The nearby sound of human voices and conversations all through the night are disruptive.

YOU'RE READY TO SLEEP ALONE. YOUR BABY ISN'T INTERESTED. NOW WHAT?

If you're getting to this chapter after you already have a problem and you desperately need to change the sleeping dynamics in your home, strict CIO is not your only option (though it is probably the option that will work the fastest). If you can handle just a few more weeks of compromised sleep, you can teach your child to sleep without you. The key is to provide support and go slowly and gently. One thing that might help you resolve the problem is to acknowledge your role in creating this situation. If you helped contribute to the problem, it's only proper that you help fix it, right? If you approach this as just one of the first battles you will wage on behalf of your child, you may find the strength you need to see it through. Again, though, you absolutely must be consistent. Don't start this process only to cave three days later, or you'll be dealing with this problem for another year. And that would be detrimental for both of you. I should know, having done this myself!

Really, what you're asking your baby to do is change his need to sleep with you, so give him ample opportunity to see that he doesn't actually need you right by his side. Make sure your infant has had enough to eat throughout the day and early evening. Then, if he's sleeping in your bed or in a co-sleeper, start by transferring him into a bassinet, Pack 'n Play, or crib positioned right next to your mattress. Maybe you can keep your hand resting on the mattress beside him so he can still smell you and feel your touch. After a few days, when your child is comfortable with this arrangement, move the bassinet farther away from your bed. And then a little farther, and a little farther, until finally there is a doorway separating you. The whole process could take as long as a month. If you're still nursing, position a chair near the bassinet so all you have to do is pick the child up, feed him, change him and immediately lay him back down in his bed so you can quickly crawl into yours. Better yet, ask your partner to get up and start bottle feeding, which will move the process forward more quickly.

If your baby is still unhappy and you have no choice but to let him cry it out, get help from others. Switch places with your partner in the bed so you're no longer the one lying next to the child. If you can't take his cries, move to another room and let your partner handle it from there. You'll know your child is safe without having to torture yourself. Ask your mother, mother-in-law, sister, or friend to come in and give you a break. Have her check on your baby periodically if he is crying and, if he's still getting a night feed, perhaps offer him a bottle. Make sure your helper understands the importance of sticking to the plan and being consistent. While having another person do the job might not necessarily be the most comfortable for your baby, sometimes a mom can get so worn out it may truly be necessary, at least for a night or so, to allow her to catch up on her sleep and be able to work through this.

Often good sleepers suddenly regress, especially after a period of illness or a break in the routine when you've been traveling or having visitors. They may want to sleep with you and start crying for you or, if they're old enough, start getting into bed with you in the middle of the night and refusing to budge. It can happen at any time, but I've found it's especially common after another child is born. My suggestion is to break the new habit as soon as possible. Better yet, try to not let it start. Take your child back to his own bed and comfort him through his illness or insecurity in his own room. If a new baby has joined your home, make sure your older child understands that the new situation is permanent but that he is absolutely still important and that nothing has changed between you.

RECLAIMING YOURSELF

There's another benefit to teaching your children to sleep in their own space: you can start to reclaim your own. It's easy to become consumed by the massive love we feel for our kids, to the point that we start to neglect the other relationships in our lives, and even ourselves. There is the rest you get from a good night's sleep, and there is the rest you get from getting away from children and reconnecting with a partner, friends, or just being alone for a little while. Both are vital to helping you be the best parent, and the best person, you can be. Right now your baby has no way of understanding that you have an identity apart from being a parent, but by teaching her that you don't have to be her sole source of comfort and safety, you're setting the groundwork for later. This period will not last forever, and it will be in the best interest of your child's health, of your relationship with your partner, and of your own sanity to remember to set aside time for yourself and to sometimes make your own needs for silence, or rest, or fun a priority. Keep building your village and use this time to help your child get comfortable being with your partner and other caretakers. Everyone needs downtime, every couple needs date time, and getting both decreases the levels of stress and even resentment that can build when people don't get time to themselves or time to remember who they were before they had children. At all times, you want to strive to feel a sense of calm and well-being. In the end, planned hours away from your children will make the time you spend *with* your children infinitely more enjoyable, fun, and relaxing for you both.

Breastfeed (or Don't)
the Worry-Free Way

IF WE CAN accept that every family's circumstances, lifestyles, and needs are different (and many of us say we can), then we should also be willing to withhold judgment when parents find that our "rules" simply don't work for them or their children. For years, perhaps one of the most ironclad rules has been Breast Is Best. Though as recently as the 1950s American obstetricians and pediatricians thought it was healthier and more sanitary to bottle-feed babies with formula, and hospital nurses gave new mothers pills or estrogen injections to dry up their milk, today women have taken to the streets—as well as restaurants, airports, and department stores—to assert their right to breastfeed wherever and whenever they choose. Yet while I applaud the efforts that have been made to encourage women to feed their babies the way Mother Nature intended, I often see evidence that our well-intentioned fervor has gone too far.

More than once, new mothers would arrive in my clinic crying because their babies wouldn't stop screaming every time they tried to feed. If after examining her it appeared to be a simple problem of the mother's breast being so engorged the baby was having a hard time latching, there were a few easy things I could do to help. One was to teach the mom some positioning techniques. Other times a little gentle massage worked well to express a bit of milk and reduce the pressure around the nipple so the breast was softer. But if neither of those attempts made enough of a difference, sometimes I would go over to a cabinet and grab a bottle nipple, or if available, a thin, pliable plastic breast shield. I would place it over the mother's own nipple to give the baby something a little easier to grab onto. The baby would latch quickly on the bottle nipple, mom's nipple would follow, and the baby would usually be able to start feeding. The silence that would come over the room the second that baby was drinking could be jarring. One of my moms, Kelly, told me that she and her baby, Joshua, loved this technique so much that for months she carried a nipple with her everywhere she went. She confessed that she had nearly given up breastfeeding until we hit upon this alternative.

Infrequently, however, the problem was not as easily solved. The mother might not have much milk, or I would notice that despite the poor infant's frantic efforts, little milk was being swallowed. When this happened, I would ask the mother if we could try giving the baby a little formula. Usually she was so anxious to help her baby she would acquiesce, albeit occasionally reluctantly. But as she saw her baby relax and heard him filling his tummy with food, an enormous smile would usually spread across her face. It was heartbreaking when I thought of all the hours she suffered hearing her child cry. As the baby fed contentedly, often falling asleep soon after in his mother's arms, we would discuss what we could do to give her and the baby a chance to rest and start over with more successful breastfeeding attempts. I was always struck and saddened by the huge relief I saw on these women's faces when they were given permission to combine some bottle-feeding with their breastfeeding.

For some of my patients the notion of supplementing with formula was unacceptable. Some mothers would even object to the introduction of a nipple or a bottle, even one filled with pumped breast milk, because they had been warned that bottle nipples confused babies and could cause them to reject the breast. Their babies were suffering and so were they, but too many had heard that only negligent, less-than-committed mothers would let formula or a bottle nipple pass their baby's lips. I've seen moms willing to sacrifice their own health and even their marriages to breastfeed. All around them, in parenting books, magazines, and hospital pamphlets, mothers are told that Breast Is Best, but the literature doesn't bother to explain what can happen when breastfeeding is failing. The result is that some mothers become so indoctrinated, they don't see warning signs and refuse to recognize that they as well as their baby need help. When this mind-set takes hold and breastfeeding is not successful, these infants often end up dehydrated and lose a dangerous amount of weight. They are sometimes admitted to the hospital within the first week of life, frequently with severe jaundice, which can also be extremely dangerous. It is important to understand that these are babies who are otherwise perfectly normal and who would have eventually been able to breastfeed just fine if their mothers had been open to doing things a little differently from what they had first planned.

I wish this would not happen. We do not live in an underdeveloped country and there are good alternatives to breastfeeding when it becomes problematic. It is horribly unfair that parents are made to believe there is one way, and only one way, for a baby to get the best start in life or for a mother to bond with her infant. We need to broaden the conversation and let parents know that as important as breastfeeding is, it does not outweigh all other health concerns. And, for the sake of all those mothers and babies for whom breastfeeding does not come easily, let's get some perspective, some compassion, and reality.

To facilitate this discussion, we first have to recognize that pumped breast milk and the act of breastfeeding are two separate topics. Putting them together under the simplistic slogan Breast Is Best does both mothers and babies a disservice by limiting their options. Very few things in this world are ever purely black and white, even something as revered as breastfeeding. By analyzing the benefits of breast milk compared to formula separately from the act of breastfeeding compared to bottle feeding, I hope I can offer some calming reason and reassurance into what for some mothers can be an unnecessarily emotional conversation.

IS BREAST *MILK* REALLY BEST?

Yes. All the research indicates that breast milk is undeniably the most nutritious option for your baby. Yet many cultures around the world supplement breastfeeding with formula or other fluids. In fact, for millennia it was tradition for many cultures across the globe—from the nomadic Swedes in sixth-century B.C.E., who fed their babies water mixed with bone marrow to ancient Middle Eastern civilizations who gave infants diluted honey to traditional cultures in Africa, Asia, Australia, America, and the

Yucatan—to restrict breastfeeding in the few days after birth. Native populations of Guatemala, Korea, and Sierra Leone, for example, once believed colostrum to be inferior milk; women who blog about their experiences giving birth in Japan note that many hospitals there continue to formula feed babies (a practice that clearly hasn't hurt their children's cognitive abilities, given the country's international test scores). While global health organizations have worked tirelessly to educate families around the world to the incredible benefits of nutrient packed colostrum, many populations continue to feed their infants supplemental fluids until mature mother's milk comes in.

This is unfortunate since breast milk and colostrum is quite literally custom made for your child. The ratio of nutrients found in breast milk, including proteins, whey, and casein, is important for a baby's digestion. Some of the beneficial proteins found in breast milk play a role in balancing the bowel by providing good bacteria that help fight infection. Breast milk also includes fats that are essential for brain, vision, and nervous system development and help with the absorption of the fat-soluble vitamins (A, D, E, and K). Of note, a mother's diet directly affects the nutrient makeup of her breast milk. Therefore, while any breast milk is good for babies, in order for them to get the full benefit, moms need to be extremely attentive to their diets as well as follow their doctor's guidelines for supplementing with prenatal vitamins. If breastfeeding can be established, mothers should consider breastfeeding for six to twelve months.

However, there is some evidence that some of the long-term health benefits previously attributed to breast milk, such as reducing rates of health problems like diabetes, obesity, and asthma, may have been overstated. I was surprised to discover how much brand-new data indicate that breastfeeding's positive effects on children other than newborns in the United States may be statistically negligible. One study on childhood obesity revealed that increasing the duration and exclusivity of breast-feeding did nothing to prevent children from becoming over-weight or obese, while a 2014 study analyzed siblings aged four to fourteen years—some breastfed, some bottle-fed—and con-cluded prolonged breastfeeding beyond infancy does not in fact result in any different outcome in a child's health, behavior, or academic performance than bottle-feeding, with one exception: asthma. But even then, some research results are not what might be expected; breastfed children appear to be at higher risk for asthma than formula-fed kids.

It's possible the heightened risk of asthma can be explained by the hygiene hypothesis—the idea that our immune systems are strengthened when we're exposed to pathogens and dirt at an early age, which happens less frequently in wealthy, educated communities, especially ones with stay-at-home mothers or mothers with the luxury of flexible schedules that allow them to breastfeed. The same reasoning also provides a likely explana-tion as to why earlier studies overwhelmingly showed a long-term benefit to breastfeeding. According to Cynthia Colen, associate professor of sociology at Ohio State University and the lead researcher of the 2014 sibling study, "Many previous stud-ies suffer from selection bias. They either do not or cannot sta-tistically control for factors such as race, age, family income, mother's employment—things we know that can affect both breast-feeding and health outcomes." In other words, the advan-tages breastfed babies enjoyed in previous studies may really have been products of the children's environment because most breastfed babies at the time came from wealthier, more privileged families with more flexible lifestyles.

A 2005 study of siblings (to help reduce selection bias) showed that babies who had been breastfed, even briefly, had a slightly higher IQ, by 1.68 percentile points, than siblings who were never breastfed at all. The researchers, however, did not report why some of the children in the study weren't breastfed. It seems possible that any medical condition that would preclude a baby from being breastfed might also cause a slightly lower IQ than his sibling. In addition, the study doesn't specify that the non-breastfed children's IQs were low; they were just lower than that of their brothers and sisters. Surely there can't be that much of a difference between the predicted successes of a child with an IQ of 131 and one with an IQ of 133.

Taken together, the current research seems to indicate that ideally every baby should be breastfed, especially during the initial six months of life. It's possible, however, that many of the health or cognitive advantages seen in children who are breastfed compared to those who are not are multifactorial and a result of a combination of nature and nurture, not just the breast milk itself.

What this means, too, is that the pressure we put on mothers to breastfeed for a full year, no matter what, is misplaced. When breastfeeding goes well it's a wonderful experience, but sometimes babies experience medical problems that preclude mothers from breastfeeding the way they anticipated. My second son, Brendan, started having such terrible reflux at six months I had to pump breast milk or use formula and thicken his feeds with rice until he was a year old. My daughter, Julianne, became so dangerously jaundiced after her first week of life I had to pump while feeding her with formula for three days until her bilirubin levels came down. And my preemie, David, was so weak he stayed in the hospital for five weeks. I had to pump my milk eight times a day for five weeks (while trying to keep up with the three other children at home) until he could feed directly off the breast.

Any number of problems, even minor ones, can make breast-feeding difficult. Not all mothers produce adequate supplies of milk. Many need to work and not all employers provide lactation rooms or even privacy to pump. Some women have health problems that require medicines or procedures that preclude breast-feeding. Some women adopt. And many moms simply don't have the resources or support systems to exclusively breastfeed their infants for prolonged periods of time. They are exhausted trying to reconcile what's best for their babies with the extremely busy lifestyles that have evolved in this country, and with no help. Although the infant mortality rates of many countries plagued with poor sanitary conditions and low nutrition would decrease if more women initiated breastfeeding immediately after birth, in many cases their long-term breastfeeding rates are actually quite high, likely because in small traditional villages there are always other women around to help care for and even breastfeed their neighbors' babies if necessary. Mothers in industrialized nations, especially the United States, often live in relative isolation from their own families and often don't have sisters and friends who can provide daily assistance. There's no one who can take over so a mother can catch her breath and rest, which can often lead her to decide it would be easier to quit breastfeeding.

I have seen many Western women become overwhelmed with trying to breastfeed on top of all their other home, work, and childcare obligations. They can get terribly emotional about breastfeeding, worried that if they can't keep it up they will be short-changing their child or failing their first test as a mother. It's not fair. As important and beneficial as breastfeeding is, no woman should ever feel that if she does not exclusively breastfeed she is failing her child. Individual circumstances and comfort levels, not cultural pressure, should dictate a woman's choice about whether and how long to nurse.

> No woman should ever feel that if she does not exclusively breastfeed she is failing her child.

WHY BREASTFEEDING CAN BE A CHALLENGE

Though breastfeeding is usually portrayed as the most natural thing in the world, it's not always easy, at least not in the beginning. Both moms and babies have to learn what to do first! There are many common reasons why mom and baby may have difficulty when trying to breastfeed, such as flat or inverted nipples and extremely large breasts. One woman I knew spent days wrapping her breasts in cabbage leaves to help ease her engorgement (cabbage has properties that can help dilate capillaries and move fluid); another needed no fewer than four hands, hers and her husband's, to get her baby positioned and latched properly; another spent all day and night pumping her breasts and then feeding it to her baby with a bottle, so neither she nor her husband got any sleep. In many cases, the only thing keeping mother and child from successfully breastfeeding is inexperience, a problem a few minutes with a pediatrician or a couple of sessions with a lactation consultant can usually fix.

If I see that merely getting milk into a baby isn't enough to calm him or makes his misery worse, that's a tip-off that there's something else medically that is going on.

Colic

People still commonly think there is no identifiable cause for colic, but old wives' tales have a habit of sticking around long after the medical community figures things out. As of ten or even fifteen years ago, we learned that in the vast majority of cases colic is actually gastroesophageal reflux, a condition in which stomach acid rises into the esophagus. In adults it's commonly known as heartburn.

The pain of reflux usually starts when a baby is five or six weeks old. The medical physiology is straightforward. Many babies are born without an effective sphincter between the esophagus and the stomach. To revisit an analogy I used earlier, a baby placed flat on her back or nearly so, whether to feed or sleep, is like a large soda bottle laying on its side—the liquid in the stomach is going to flow toward the esophagus. The sphincter should keep the contents of the stomach from rising too far up, but if it's not working properly it won't create a perfect seal. This isn't a problem at first because newborns' stomachs have a neutral pH, meaning their stomach fluid is neither alkaline nor acidic. Thus these babies may initially have no trouble drinking breast milk or formula; their stomach contents are so neutral that even if they have a bout of reflux, they feel no pain. By about six weeks of age, however, babies start to develop acidic stomach fluids in preparation for aiding digestion. At this point there can be a problem, and it usually catches parents off guard. It's right about this age that the baby is increasing the volume of milk in each feed, and parents are ecstatic because their baby is starting to feed less frequently and sleep more. But that increased volume of acidic liquid puts pressure on that still developing sphincter. Because the esophagus doesn't have the same protecting, mucosal lining as the stomach, any acid that seeps up, even just an inch or so, is going to burn like crazy.

If a baby vomits every time she eats, that's a pretty clear sign she is experiencing reflux, and parents usually know they need to contact their pediatrician for help. But many children experience silent reflux, which affects only the lower esophagus and doesn't cause them to vomit. It can cause a horrible cycle. The baby is hungry so she gets on the nipple and swallows the milk. But then the milk causes a burning sensation, so naturally she arches her back and comes off the nipple. The mother, not understanding what's going on, will try to latch the baby back on. The baby is hungry and eager to be at the breast, but as soon as that milk hits the esophagus again she will scream and push away.

The cycle turns what is supposed to be a nurturing bonding ritual into a battle zone. When mothers are already tired, their stress levels can go through the roof, especially if their partner isn't supportive or feels equally distraught. Most people expect some crying and imperfect sleep when they bring home a newborn, but these babies don't sleep at all because they're hungry and in pain, and that can take a terrible toll on any couple. There's nothing worse than feeling like you can't comfort your child, and many times mothers feel their child is rejecting them, causing them to feel incredibly insecure and even depressed, which can put them and their children in a precarious position if they don't get help quickly.

One way to make feeding easier, even for a child who isn't predisposed to reflux, is to make sure the baby is sitting in a somewhat upright position, thus using gravity to keep the milk down in the stomach. This also prevents gravity from increasing the letdown from the breast, which can make babies sound as if they were drowning. There are several alternate positions from which you can choose. The female human body has evolved to be perfect for feeding children. If you sit in a chair and seat a baby on your knee, with her bottom on your leg, lo and behold the distance between your leg and your elbow is just perfect for allowing the baby's neck to rest in your elbow. And guess what? From that angle, the baby is also in the perfect position to reach your breast. If you take the opposite hand, which is not holding your baby, and hold your breast in a more horizontal position, as if you were using a bottle, you can control the feeding nicely. With the milk letting down at an even pace, the baby won't gulp (introducing air into the stomach), the milk will go down to fill the bottom of the stomach, and you can significantly decrease the chance of your baby will suffer from reflux. And if your elbow, breast, and the baby's neck are properly aligned, you should be easily able to comfortably hold that position for the ten minutes or so on either side that it takes your baby to finish a feed.

The football hold is also good for babies susceptible to colic or reflux. Hold your baby against your side with her head resting in the palm of your hand. Let her bottom fall close to your hip until her face is directly in front of your breast. In either of these holds, if the baby is vertical, and the stomach is vertical, the baby will be comfortable as she eats.

Fortunately, if the problem really is gastroesophageal reflux and repositioning alone doesn't help, your pediatrician can treat reflux with a proton pump inhibitor (like Prevacid), which decreases the amount and therefore the effect of acid in the stomach. Most babies outgrow reflux by about four months, when the sphincter has matured enough to retain the milk in the stomach, after which you can discontinue treatments.

Lactose Intolerance

Some babies who suffer from colic actually have a lactose, or milk sugar, intolerance. The symptoms may be similar, but these children also have a lot of gas and many times loose stools as well. Mothers can reduce the amount of lactose produced in their breast milk by reducing their dairy intake. Another option if diet alone is not successful is getting the baby on a combination of breast milk and a lactose-free formula, which will help ease the baby's discomfort, allowing mom to successfully breastfeed while easing the symptoms.

Milk Protein Intolerance

The number of babies struggling with breastfeeding who don't fall into one of the previous two categories is minimal. A very small number of children, however, are actually allergic to the proteins in cow's milk. When a women ingests dairy products and soy proteins, they will transfer through to her breast milk. Thus moms can sometimes improve the situation through dietary restrictions. Many times babies suffering from this problem have blood in their stool and a great deal of difficulty with feedings. Fortunately, they do well on designer formulas.

Are There Any Foods I Should Avoid When Breastfeeding?

There are a number of foods that may cause a baby discomfort. Some babies get gassy and uncomfortable if their mom ingests lots of dairy. Other babies react when their mother eats spicy foods or drinks coffee. Leafy green vegetables can also be a culprit. If you notice a problem, eliminate these foods from your diet and then try reintroducing them one at a time. If the problems do not return, then by all means enjoy a wider diet. Always continue taking prenatal vitamins to ensure your health.

Anxiety

There have been times when a distraught mother has come in with her baby and told me that nothing is working right. The baby doesn't eat, doesn't sleep, and cries all the time. She's ready to collapse. Her tension fills the room. To help calm her down I will offer to hold her baby for a little while. Sometimes, shortly afterward, while I'm listening to her story for clues, the baby will fall asleep in my arms. That tells me a lot. The baby's problem isn't medical; it's mom's anxiety that is upsetting him. This isn't a surprise. It is well known that babies pick up on their mothers' excess tension, and it can affect how they eat, sleep, and generally behave.

This problem can develop from many causes. Perhaps the mother contracts mastitis, or her baby has reflux. She takes the struggle personally, sometimes seeing it as a sign that the baby doesn't like her. This can easily trigger some dysfunctional behaviors between her and her child. When pediatricians recognize this cycle of behavior, they get very concerned. Even if they can resolve the baby's problem, unless the mom's problem is addressed, she will be unable to successfully parent her baby. These issues can be as detrimental to the baby as postpartum depression or mental illness. Occasionally I am able to help a mom by pointing out the problem and supporting her with suggestions of spending time with seasoned or at least experienced parents, but sometimes mothers refuse these options and choose to stay in a state of denial. I have witnessed extreme cases in which children have eventually wound up in the hospital with failure to thrive. It's unfortunate because the baby would otherwise be a perfectly healthy child if his mother could just accept that getting help, perhaps in the form of some counseling, perhaps in the form of medication, doesn't make her any less of a wonderful mother. Once in the hospital, these babies usually rebound beautifully, and as long as they stay there, they eat well and put on weight. But this doesn't solve the underlying problem that exists in the home.

It's crucial for parents to recognize when their anxiety and stress are becoming chronic and toxic and take steps to mitigate these feelings, because otherwise the whole situation can snowball into one big unhappy mess. What many parents don't realize is that modeling good behavior has to start as soon as their baby is born. It's not only toddlers and young children who observe and absorb everything going on around them but infants, too.

> What many parents don't realize is that modeling good behavior has to start as soon as their baby is born.

FAQ: My Baby Doesn't Ever Seem to Burp. Is This Okay, or Am I Doing Something Wrong?

Some babies have minimal gas and don't seem to need to burp much; however, if the child is passing a lot of gas, it is possible you are not effectively assisting baby with the process. I notice that parents are sometimes so scared of hurting their babies they tend to be too gentle when they try to burp them. On the flip side, some spend too much time trying to get a burp out, which is exhausting for the baby. The only reason to pat the baby at all is to gently shake her enough to help move the bubble. Hold your baby in a perfectly vertical position so that the stomach is lined up with the esophagus and gently pat her bottom where she's diapered and nicely padded. That should be enough to help the air move up. Stop if your baby doesn't produce anything after three or four minutes, and don't worry about it.

IT DOES HAPPEN occasionally that doctors will meet a chronically crying baby and be unable to get to the root of the problem fairly quickly. Such situations are few and far between, but they are sometimes complicated cases and usually require a specialist evaluation. The majority of the time, however, there is a remedy to a baby's unhappiness at feeding time. It's the parents we often have a harder time bringing around. There is simply no reason for anyone to suffer without help.

LET GO OF THE GUILT

I asked Anh, whom we met earlier, whether working mothers in Vietnam pump to provide breast milk for their infants when they're left in the care of babysitters. She looked at me as if I'd asked a stupid question before replying, "Of course not." And then she repeated, "We have to work." Only women in very special circumstances can retreat during the workday to pump and then store enough breast milk to provide their children with enough to eat every day. While some women still may not understand the benefits of breastfeeding, many like Anh are wholly aware, but they take a practical approach to the problem. Their baby needs to eat. They need to work. Pumping isn't practical and formula feeding is. End of story. Anh refuses to feel bad about the choices she made, and that is a far healthier alternative than the angst I see so many Western mothers place on themselves.

If for any reason you were to find that breastfeeding is harder than you thought it would be, I urge you to be kind to yourself. Take what help you can get. Give yourself a break if necessary. The hard-line message that babies not exclusively breastfed from birth for a full year are at high risk of suffering harmful consequences or developing a weak infant–mother bond is quite simply wrong. Bonding takes more than just breastfeeding. All the other things we do to take care of our children affect it. And while breast milk is indeed the best nutritional option for infants, I support a more flexible approach to supplementing with either expressed milk or formula if this is what is needed. In fact, as I mentioned earlier in this chapter, supplementing can actually improve women's breastfeeding rates. A study reported by the journal *Pediatrics* showed that when formula was offered to babies struggling to gain weight, 79 percent of them were still being breastfed exclusively at the age of three months, while only 42 percent of infants who received no formula were still being exclusively breastfed by the same age. In sum, supplementing can improve women's long-term breastfeeding rates because it offers mothers and doctors alternative treatments to problems that can otherwise derail breastfeeding permanently, giving them a chance to fix problems and get everyone back on track.

With this in mind, when we are willing to teach our infants to take both breast and bottle, we introduce a wonderful way to give all the people in our baby's life a chance to spend some special time with her. Allowing other people to feed your child will never diminish your importance in her life. If you're tired, could you go to bed earlier and let your partner do a late evening feed? Could you allow Grandma to come over and watch and feed the baby while you take an afternoon nap or go to the spa and relax? If I mentioned this to parents, especially to fathers or partners, they would often look at me as though I had lifted the weight of the world off their shoulders. Some moms even cried in relief.

Not every mother was amenable. Occasionally I'd meet a woman who would look at me as though I'd spoken heresy. Then, despite her obvious fatigue, she would muster up a smile and assure me that things weren't really that bad and she'd get everything under control. I frequently noticed consequences to this response, though. Later their babies and toddlers showed signs of anxiety when cared for by others, even by close family members, including Dad. These were often the same mothers I heard express extreme fatigue and resentment for being saddled with such overwhelming responsibilities 24/7.

For this reason, I will always support any opportunity for dads to help with feedings, and the sooner the better. Studies have shown that men are much more supportive of their breast-feeding partners when they're allowed a role in their child's feeding care.

Mothers (and fathers/partners) need all the support they can get. As we've discussed in previous chapters, many other countries have networks in place that reflect their societies' understanding and appreciation for the importance of parenting and family life. They have also implemented programs to support breastfeeding efforts. In 2013, the UK started offering poor women shopping vouchers to breastfeed for at least the first six weeks of their baby's life; eligible Australian mothers (those who earn less than $150,000) receive up to eighteen weeks of government-paid minimum wage leave upon the birth of their children. Until we have the policies in place that make it easier for working mothers to breastfeed, we need to psychologically free them (and all mothers, whether they work or not) to do what works best for them, rather than imprison them with a rule that causes many to feel guilty if they don't or can't comply or that encourages them to persevere to the detriment of their health and sanity. Babies rarely get dysentery in this country; formula is not poison. Breastfeeding is undeniably beneficial. I would like more moms to be educated to be flexible about baby feeding so that they can allow themselves the chance to enjoy their time with their infants and start their journey together as a family in happier and healthier circumstances.

DR. JANE'S TIPS FOR BREASTFEEDING MOTHERS

Get Rid of Paraphernalia

Remember, your body and your baby's are designed to fit together perfectly when you sit him on your knee, whether when nursing or doing any other activity together. The stuff we don't need weighs on us. For example, if you received a popular nursing pillow as a baby shower gift, consider exchanging it for something else at the store. Some of these were made to fit around babies' bottoms to help steady babies as they learned to sit up. Turning it around your body and using it as a table to hold your baby is completely nonphysiological. When wrapped around a nursing mother's waist, these pillows encourage her to lay her baby down almost horizontally. Have you ever tried to eat lying down? It's not much fun. And as you've seen, it can exacerbate reflux and therefore breastfeeding difficulties.

Delegate

By five to seven days, it's okay to introduce a bottle nipple, especially if you know you are going back to work. In my experience, babies learn quickly and have never shown me any signs of confusing the bottle for the breast. By teaching infants both feeding methods you open up a whole new world and give yourself and your baby a wonderful opportunity to allow your baby's father, aunts, uncles, and grandparents to participate in nurturing the newest love of their life while allowing you—another love of baby's life—to get some much needed rest.

Consider Scheduling Your Feeds

For years the mantra has been that the only way to breastfeed properly is on demand. It works for some, but it's a practice that puts a huge demand on mothers, especially in this era. And has anyone ever stopped to consider how much work it entails for the baby? Think about it. Parents complain about being exhausted, but at least they are used to moving around, eating, and even breathing. While in the womb, babies do zero work. Then they get born, which is a lot of work. And then on top of that, they have to feed, pass stools, move, and cope with a barrage of new experiences like light, cold, and noise. We expect these poor little newborns who have never had to make an effort to do anything at all to suddenly work all day and all night to survive. At the same time, they're constantly being diapered, burped, and bathed; at least, they are when they're not being transferred from crib to car seat to carrier. All that commotion is tiring!

You know what else is tiring? Hunger. And a baby who is fed on demand will be hungrier more often than a baby who is given a scheduled feed. Here's why: It takes about two hours for mothers to produce a full feed. Human beings like the feeling of fullness and satiation. Babies don't get that by dribbling a little feed all the time, so understandably, they get frustrated. Imagine if I figured out what you should eat in a twenty-four-hour period, and then gave you only 1 tablespoon every hour. Do you know how upset you would be? You'd get your calories, but you'd never feel fully satiated or comforted. The thought behind breastfeeding on demand is that if the baby is allowed to feed whenever he wants to, he will feel satiated and not cry, which will decrease his stress and improve the mother–infant bond. After all, that's how they do it in Africa, and as attachment parenting advocates often point out, most African babies rarely cry. But African babies are worn against their mothers' bodies all day and all night. They can literally sleep against the breast every minute they're not feeding, and as soon as they wake up, there it is, ready and waiting. The vast majority of American mothers simply do not live a lifestyle that allows their baby that luxury. With exceptions for families living in urban hubs like New York City, at the very least most need cars to conduct the daily business of living and running a home. Many have to work outside the home.

Bottom line, a baby has no more than about 30 minutes of energy at any one time, about eight times per day. But if you're like most Western mothers, you're going to want or need to get up, go out in the car, and do things. It's really hard to stop in your tracks to feed a baby multiple times per day and still get anything done, even housework, meal prep, or nurturing other children. Scheduling your feeds every two to three hours not only will provide some structure to your life but will allow your baby to feel full and rested, happy and safe, which means he has little reason to cry.

How to Schedule Breastfeeding Sessions

You'll need to feed from both breasts, because one will not provide enough milk to keep a baby going happily for two to three hours. When you start with the first side, you'll hear your baby suck and swallow as it gets a mouthful of milk, and then after a few minutes, the rhythm will slow down. Your baby is getting only drops after that. Give her eight to ten minutes on the first breast, before she gets tired. Then take her off, do a quick burp, and latch her on the other side. In a total of twenty minutes, babies who feed actively on both breasts can get almost double the amount of milk in the same time that they could if they fed from only one breast. They will feel full once breastfeeding is established and are able to get the hind milk, and they will be able to sleep comfortably until the next feed. You then have two to three hours to do whatever it is you want or need to while your body builds up your milk supply. An unsatiated or snacking baby will sleep only an hour, maybe an hour and a half, at any one time. That just doesn't work well for the lifestyles of most modern women. Scheduled feedings, however, can provide all the benefits and bonding of breastfeeding on demand while still allowing you to retain some control over your life.

Your baby doesn't need a martyr; she needs a strong, confident, happy mother. Sometimes, try as we might, we parents can't do "perfect." And that's okay so long as we try to do our best. Instead of feeling terrible about what we cannot do, let's concentrate on providing our babies with the best experience possible, so we can bond and create a nurturing, happy environment for our families. That's how joyful, confident parents are born.

Make Mealtimes Fun

THE COUPLE SITTING before me in my small examination room were well-educated professionals in their mid-thirties. On his knee, the father dandled a baby boy dressed in a brown onesie with blue piping. His name was Chase, and as I scanned his chart, I read that he had been born full term and healthy and was developmentally normal in every way. One look at him, however, and I could see why he was here. At eight months old, he could have been mistaken for a four-month-old. His skin was nearly translucent, his eyelids a pale, purpley blue. I could see the veins in his tiny starfish hands. His chart told me that he had started life in the 50th percentile for newborn height and weight, but he now weighed just over thirteen pounds, which actually placed him under the growth chart, below the lowest percentile for his age group. Chase's parents, Erica and Nick, had traveled many miles to meet with me in my pediatric clinic. Repeated visits to their local physician had failed to reveal any reason why this otherwise healthy child should fail to thrive, a catch-all diagnosis for children whose stunted growth leave them far behind their peers. Chase's father smiled nervously, his eyes filled with hope that I would find the answer that would help his baby boy.

I did my best to put the parents at ease, letting Nick keep Chase on his lap while I gently examined him, listening to his heartbeat, running my hands over his sunken belly and his thin, bony little arms and legs. I found no abnormalities to suggest a serious pathology. As my hands moved over the tiny boy's body, I kept my tone light while I asked the questions that would give me a more complete understanding of his health, development and dietary history. How many diapers did Chase go through per day? How long were his naps? What were his stools like? What did he eat?

"That's the problem. He won't eat," said Erica.

I asked her what foods they had introduced.

"Lots of different things," she answered. "Tofu. Lima beans. Lentils. All organic, of course."

"We never give him that processed stuff," inserted Nick. The look he gave me made it clear we were surely of the same mind. "It's awful what some people will feed their kids."

As our conversation continued, I found out that at eight months, Chase had never sat in a high chair—his parents thought they could better prevent choking if he were on their laps. He had never been allowed to eat food with his fingers. Aside from formula, his diet consisted of purees made from the extremely limited number of organic vegetables available at the supermarket in Nick and Erica's town. No wonder the child wouldn't eat.

I told Erica and Nick that on their way home I wanted them to stop at the supermarket and buy an array of colorful fruits and vegetables, as well as some chicken and dairy products. If they could find organic versions, fine, but if they couldn't, they were to buy whatever looked fun and tasty. Then they were to go home, prepare it for themselves, chop a portion of it into small, bite size pieces, put Chase in a high chair and scatter the food in front of him. I insisted they let him play with his food, and leave him alone to figure out for himself how to get the food into his mouth. If he smeared it in his hair, more power to him. From now on, meal times were going to be fun social events, not battlegrounds. In addition, I suggested that the whole family start weekly feeding therapy sessions with a trusted therapist near my office.

Nick and Erica were visibly nervous but grateful to have a plan in place that they hoped would help their son. They were loving parents who wanted only to give their child the healthiest start in life. They knew something didn't seem right about the way Chase resisted what they fed him, but they had read dire warnings about what, when, and how to feed young babies, so they persisted with what seemed the most prudent approach. When I asked why they hadn't introduced Chase to different foods when he'd refused what was offered, Erica replied: "I didn't know what to do. I believed that I should be that perfect mom, and buy the best organic products. If they weren't in the store, I didn't give him any. I thought that milk was enough. He [is], after all, very young."

Chase's story is an unusual case, but many parents have probably entertained a smidgen of some of the doubts and fears that plagued his parents. There are few who won't confess to a twinge of guilt after pushing their shopping cart past the pasture-raised organic chicken eggs to pick up the cheaper factory-farmed eggs, or eschewed the pricy organic zucchini for its less expensive conventionally grown version. At the same time that we've become increasingly aware of the presence of pesticides and hormones in our mass-produced foods, we've also finally caught up to the rest of the world in understanding the importance of food, not just as a barometer of health, but as a cultural touchstone and social connector. And this is where we see an interesting divide between the rest of the world and us. In fact, nowhere can we find better evidence that what is "best" in one culture simply isn't always true for another than in the way we feed our children. Having lived among many different cultures and watched children react to food, I've concluded that children around the world are largely the same; it is the menu—and the parenting—that is different.

> Children around the world are largely the same; it is the menu—and the parenting—that is different.

HOW WE RAISE PICKY EATERS

Babies in America usually start off on solids like rice cereals mixed with breast milk or formula and pureed bananas before moving to a diet of relatively bland grains, vegetables, and chopped meats. Meanwhile, six-month-olds in Japan are often served minced natto (powerfully smelly fermented soybeans) and barley tea and usually after the age of two, sushi; Inuit children learn to chew on seaweed, nuk-tuk (seal blubber), and whale meat, sometimes raw; Nigerian babies enjoy egusi—melon seeds—pounded into smooth pasty balls or cooked into soups, and fermented cassava root; Koreans cut their teeth on rinsed kimchi; Polynesians feed their children poi-poi, a blend of coconut cream and breadfruit; and in Tibet, babies are weaned on tsampa, a blend of ground barley flour mixed with yak butter tea. Given the variety of foods that human babies will happily eat, there should be no reason why America should have a picky eater problem.

And yet, by all accounts, we do. In fact, one study showed that 50 percent of children aged four to twenty-four months were identified by their caregivers as picky. Some parents in other countries probably complain about their children's selectivity or food aversions, but I've never heard anything like what I encounter here. Is it possible American children have more delicate taste buds than other children around the world? While some research does suggest that some kids are biologically more sensitive to certain tastes and take longer to get used to strong flavors, it's unlikely so many more children in the States are biologically sensitive than kids in other parts of the world. Picky eaters surely exist elsewhere, but not in the same numbers.

Why do so many elementary-school children in this country refuse to eat vegetables or subsist on an entirely white-food diet? The most likely answer is that it's a matter of culture and learned behavior. Though the American palate has become far more sophisticated of late and our appreciation for different cuisines has broadened, we still tend to favor sweet tastes over savory, and as a whole haven't embraced many of the spicy, pungent, even sour flavors that are a staple in many dishes around the world. Many of us are put off by the idea of eating organ meats, though they are key ingredients in many countries, even in the West. Scotland has its haggis, France loves its pâté, and most countries, from Spain to Sweden to Germany, boast a version of blood sausage. However, there is a difference between disliking chilies or preferring broccoli over asparagus, and refusing anything with a sauce, or anything green, or anything that's not mac n' cheese.

In my experience, the battles so many families wage over

mealtimes are often caused by the same thing that seems to under-lie most parenting challenges today: stress and anxiety. It can start during infancy with difficulties such as breastfeeding, reflux, or lactose or milk protein intolerance. When the child gets older, par-ents are often faced with frustrating choices. For example, they can choose to wait patiently until the child decides to swallow that nutritious little bowl of breakfast quinoa or the nice dish of scram-bled eggs in the morning, or they can hand him a piece of toast or even a Pop-Tart that he can eat in the car so everyone can actually get to school and work on time. The same thing can happen in the evenings. Most parents are aware that young children need any-where from nine to twelve hours of sleep each day. They're likely not going to get it, though, if you make them sit at the dinner table until they agree to finish their plates. When mealtimes become a control issue between caregivers and children, the frustration takes its toll on everyone in the family. When it comes to food, many parents take the easy way out, and picky eating is the end result. Parents cave under the pressure and end up catering to the child's preference for starchy, fatty, or bland foods because it's eas-ier than fighting it, then shrug with embarrassment when their nine-year-old won't try anything new.

As a physician I can confirm that there is no biological cause for the vast majority of picky eating. If there were, children in other countries would also subsist on buttered pasta or rice and chicken. But they usually don't. Babies' tastes can be trained, and it's worth the effort to do it as early as possible, long before any expectations about food and mealtimes can set in. Teaching them to enjoy a broad variety of foods will not only make future mealtimes more pleasurable for you, it will ensure your children get the nutrition they need, and it will set them up to enjoy new

> Eating is
> supposed to
> be fun!

adventures and experiences with foods down the road. Eating is supposed to be fun!

Breast milk is sweet, so many scientists will agree that babies are born to prefer sweet tastes as a matter of survival. My anecdotal observations indicate, however, that by introducing savory or at least nonsweet foods in a particular order during infancy, you can establish a wider and more nutritious diet than the one consumed by many children in this country (and largely responsible for our high rates of childhood obesity). For instance, you might start a baby off with something bland like rice cereal mixed with breast milk or formula. Babies usually like it and it starts the whole eating experience off on a positive note. After a few weeks, you could follow up with a vegetable like pureed carrots or squash, and after you've let your child establish a good relationship with these foods, then you can introduce pureed natural fruits like mashed bananas and stewed apples. Avoid the syrupy prepared fruits, which are loaded with added sugars. When children are introduced to strong sweet flavors early, it can be very difficult to get them to accept other natural flavors.

I have seen examples of this happen unintentionally when young infants are admitted to the hospital with a diagnosis of gastroenteritis. Breastfeeding is the gold standard of treatment—breastfed babies don't vomit as much, even when they're sick. However, formula-fed infants in danger of dehydration often need to be given an electrolyte solution such as Pedialyte, which is usually sweet. I have seen babies who have needed this treatment reject their formula in favor of the sweeter Pedialyte. Some of these infants then have to be given a mixture of Pedialyte and formula before they will accept formula again.

FIRST FOODS

There are probably as many ways to introduce foods to children as there are different types of foods. That said, I have used this schedule successfully for many years and have followed many happy parents who have thoroughly enjoyed raising babies who not only love to eat but who prefer a varied and nutritious diet to a bland, boring one. As your baby grows, he will become ready to try different things. Each month or so, I like to add foods that have more texture, so that by the time babies are ten to twelve months old they are feeding themselves and eating almost all the same foods as the rest of the family. Infants can eat a full meal before they have their teeth, though they do need to have their foods cut up into tiny pieces for them.

I would love to see more children learn to eat like little Jared. I'll never forget him. He was his parents' firstborn, and when we started to discuss feeding his mother listened carefully and his dad took notes on his smartphone. Each time Jared was brought in for his well checks we talked about his progress. He was a model baby. He was happy, he slept well, and he ate literally whatever his parents offered him with a big smile on his face. His mother told me he had never rejected a single food she had offered him, but she never offered him candy. He loved fish like halibut, all vegetables including Brussels sprouts, fruits like kiwi, and dairy. He'd sit in his high chair anywhere they took him and he would finger feed himself, and when they took him to a restaurant, he ate off the real menu, not the kid menu.

Use this timeline as a guide to increase your chances of raising children who are unafraid to try new or different foods:

0 to 4 months: Exclusively breast milk, formula, or combination

4 to 6 months: For infants who are showing readiness (trying to grab your fork or following every bite you eat with her eyes), stick to one food type at a time, three to four weeks apart. Start with small amounts of rice cereal, followed by pureed yellow and then green vegetables, and then whatever looks good to you (mashed eggplant is a favorite for Iranian babies). Next, start offering pureed or mashed natural fruits like bananas and avocados. You can prepare your baby's meals yourself, but jarred baby food is fine (though more limited in options). This early feeding should be considered tasty and educational, not nutritive. The majority of your baby's needs are still being met by breast milk or formula.

6 months: Now things start to get interesting. Once your baby can sit up supported in a high chair, you should start by placing four to six soft, pea-size pieces of food on her tray or a small plate and let her play with it. It's best to start with things like cooked soft pieces of vegetables and chopped natural fruits. Don't be afraid to introduce foods with nice strong flavors like tomatoes and zucchini. In between baby's finger feeding, you can spoon-feed her with mashed foods, like potato, sweet potato, and cereals, until she has had enough. Go ahead and allow her to smush her food around and get it stuck between her fingers. This is how babies learn. You may be surprised how much of the food makes it into her mouth. Once her tray is clear and she still seems to want to eat, place some more choices on it.

Don't try to feed your baby entirely by yourself. Let her practice. She'll do great if she can model the rest of the group. Offer foods off your own plate so your children learn to enjoy what you enjoy. It is always best to feed her whatever you are serving for that meal; babies know if they are eating with the family and are often quite happy to have the same food as everyone else. Offer her a sippy cup to drink water like everyone else at the table. She may need help initially, but babies usually quite quickly get good at picking up the cup and drinking on their own. Although infants at this age still rely on milk for a significant part of their nutrition, they should not be drinking milk at the table while eating or they will fill up on milk and be unable to participate in the meal. Offer milk after the meal once you've given her a little while to digest the solid foods.

7 months: At this age, you can introduce white meats such as chopped cooked chicken, white fish, turkey, pork, and ham.

8 months: By now infants can handle ground meats, such as beef and lamb. In many British and European homes, eight-month-olds eat kidneys and liver, either cooked or in the form of pâté. Go ahead and try it! Organ meats are incredibly nutritious and delicious when properly prepared. Don't worry, your child won't need her teeth to eat—her gums are very strong and effective for chomping.

9 to 12 months: Now we're having fun. This is when I usually like to introduce dairy. The dairy department in the United States has exploded in recent years, so enjoy experimenting with all manner of cheeses, full-fat yogurts, puddings, and custards. And don't forget cooked eggs!

> **FAQ: What Is a Sensible Portion if I Want to Avoid Wasting Food without Forcing My Child to Clean His Plate?**
>
> Put out very small portions of each food and add as your child eats or serve him one spoonful of one of the dishes you have prepared for the family, and then add the others as your baby keeps eating. Favorites can be alternated with other foods that are a little less popular or less familiar.

DR. JANE'S TIPS FOR RAISING AN EASY EATER, GLOBAL STYLE

All Together Now

As soon as you start introducing solids, make sure that you or whoever is taking care of your child during the day brings him to the table to eat. Just by taking that step, you will be breaking with American tradition and following more in the footsteps of the international community. I've met many millennial moms who feel they do not have time to prepare a meal or are not skilled enough in home cooking to properly feed a family. I have heard children say that they think a home-cooked meal is eaten only in the homes of poor families who cannot afford to buy their meals from a store or restaurant. And I have learned that it is not uncommon for young families to have no tables or chairs in their homes at which to sit at for a group meal. We have to change our expectations and our norms. If you're accustomed to eating on the fly or takeout or on your feet, start taking steps to change your habits now, before your child knows any different, so that he will learn to enjoy a good mealtime experience at an early age.

In addition, feed your child what you eat, and feed him when you eat. Too often parents feed their children separately from the rest of the family. We'll feed them before we feed ourselves, often so we can get them to bed at an appropriate hour, and then take some quiet time over a real meal when a spouse or partner gets home from work. We're also notorious for preparing something completely different for our children from what the rest of the family is eating (it's not just restaurants that have a separate children's menu). The idea that children should eat apart from grownups and shouldn't be expected to eat what grownups eat would be baffling to families in most other countries. And it is so much work to prepare multiple meals! That's time that would be better spent in one-on-one time with your children or your partner every day.

In our attempts to combat our obesity epidemic, we've become obsessed with the nutritional value of food, and increasingly we teach our kids in school and at home that you are what you eat. Parents are encouraged to eat nutritious food in front of their children so they will want to eat it, too. That's commendable and well advised because babies do learn by modeling. Unfortunately, we often neglect to model the other important message about food, the one that comes first and foremost in most other cultures: Eating is supposed to be social and pleasurable, a time when people are meant to bond, share, talk, and relax. It is not a time to negotiate over whether Johnny can get away with eating only one of the three cauliflower florets on his plate. In fact, in most other countries, there is rarely any negotiating about food at all. Children eat what's put in front of them, period. If they eat poorly, then they do not get a special snack or big bowl of dessert or dry cereal to tide them over. They get to wait for the next meal! And when that expectation is modeled from the first day a child is served a real meal, children never think to argue with their parents about what or how much they're going to eat. They just eat, and they eat happily, which leaves the family much more time to enjoy each other's company.

> In most other countries, there is rarely any negotiating about food at all.

The importance of the communal meal is not just about modeling healthful eating habits, although it's an important part of that lesson. It's about bringing people together. In her book *Parenting without Borders*, Christine Gross-Loh includes a wonderful description of how the teachers at her three-year-old's Japanese preschool taught the children to savor their meals and enjoy the respite from their busy day:

> A typical school day for our three-year-olds stretched from nine to two, with nothing to eat during those hours but their obento lunch, since their meals were supposed to be substantial enough to sustain them. In *yochien*, children were taught carefully how to get out their lunches, spread out their lunch mats, sit with classmates at meals, and take the time to enjoy eating together and talking with each other and with their teachers, who were also modeling the art of sitting down to enjoy a meal.

They were taught to wait until everyone was ready to begin eating. After saying *itadakimasu*, (thank you for this food), everyone could start. Then the children were expected to wait at their seats until everyone was done with the meal.

We couldn't re-create this scenario in an American school if we wanted to. Gross-Loh writes that the children in the pre-school get a forty-minute lunch period per day; many American children get a twenty-five-minute lunch period if they're lucky. When even the American Academy of Pediatrics recommends a minimum of twenty minutes for eating lunch, it's clear that from a very young age we are being taught that food is fuel and that it needs to be ingested quickly. Not family or friendship, not a chance to practice good manners, not downtime, not pleasure. Yet the secret to raising healthy, adventurous, easy eaters is to incorporate all of those lessons into our mealtimes, and they have to be instilled long before children start attending school.

Focus and Celebrate

Treat mealtimes as a celebration. That doesn't mean you have to make much hoopla out of every meal. It merely means that meal-times should be regular and everyone in the house at that time should have expectations that they will join together at the table to eat. No standing at the kitchen counter eating over a napkin. No eating over the laptop while a child eats in front of the TV or swipes an iPad. This is a perfect moment for everyone to step back from the busyness of life. Let your brain and body rest. For at least thirty minutes or, even better, an hour, everyone's attention should be focused on the food and the people sharing it. If it's impossible for the whole family to be together at the same time in the evenings, make breakfast the family meal and encourage the kids to tell about their recent experiences. Even if everyone is just eating eggs and toast, it's a great way to connect and model good eating habits and socialization to the younger members of the family.

Let your baby watch you enjoy your food. Talk to your child and everyone else at the table while you eat. Make the whole eating thing look like fun! If there's one thing babies are really good at, it's noticing when other people are enjoying themselves. Inevitably, they're going to want to try doing that fun thing, too. Prime them to anticipate their meals, and the whole process of introducing new foods will be accepted without question. As I recommended in earlier chapters, think about how you want life to look when your children are older. Do you want to enjoy nice meals out together in public? Will you be happy if you're limited to "family friendly" restaurants? Do you want people to compliment you on your toddler's great manners? Would you have fun watching your child order new things off an unfamiliar menu? Now is the time to pave the way toward that future.

Let Them Eat What You Eat

I'm not a big fan of jarred baby food because I find the options limited. For example, I've never seen avocado puree in a baby food jar, but many babies love avocado. I also suspect that even the upscale organic labels aren't really superior to the ordinary supermarket brands. These companies are marketing convenience and nutrition, but it's really not hard to make your own baby food. It's also much, much cheaper! All you need is a food processor and a few ice cube trays. For purees, throw the food in a food processor and blend until smooth, adding a little water, low-salt broth, or milk until it reaches the right consistency. Place any leftovers in your ice cube trays and put them in the freezer until you're ready to use. If you use a microwave to thaw the food, just be sure to test the temperature with your wrist before spooning it into your baby's mouth, or wait five or ten minutes for it to cool. When your baby is older you can just mash the food or chop it into tiny pieces.

FAQ: I'm Vegetarian. Can I Raise My Baby to Be Vegetarian, Too?

Of course you can raise your child to be a vegetarian! Many Hindu and Buddhist families around the world have done so. You'll want to make sure that your baby's diet is not deficient in calcium, vitamin D, iron, zinc, and especially vitamin B_{12}. Start off with breast milk or soy formula. To ensure your baby gets adequate nutrition, you'll have to do some research on your current diet and likely add some other products to your meal rotation. As a backup I usually recommend vegetarian children take a multivitamin to be sure that everything is covered adequately.

There are excellent baby food recipe books you can buy or check out of the library, but for many busy parents, cooking baby food in addition to their own meals can feel like yet another burden. But that's the wrong attitude—you're not making anything in addition to your meal unless you prepare a really heavily spiced dish, in which case you do need to prepare a small separate portion with less intense flavor. But that doesn't mean you have to eat bland, boring food. Babies love flavor. You don't have to make anything special for your baby to keep her healthy or to satisfy her palate. You eat every day so presumably you have food in the home, and even if you've long relied on take-out or prepackaged meals to feed yourself, most people find it's financially impossible to keep that up once a family grows. It's more nutritious and cheaper to make your own meals. As your child grows, you will have to make some small additional portions anyway, so why not just start right now? Every time you make a meal, make a little bit extra. If your child is eating finger foods, just finely chop her portion and place it on a small plate. Better yet, let your baby see the food on your plate before transferring it to hers. Babies love to see that they're eating the same thing you are. Freeze any leftovers in individual portions.

Try, Try Again

You'll want to tame heavily spiced foods and make sure nothing is served too hot, but once your baby is close to a year old you can offer anything and everything. I know many little children who eat pickles and gherkins and all manner of different fruits like mangoes and kiwis. If you have been bringing your baby to the table and allowing him to eat your food, it is unlikely that he will wrinkle his nose at your ratatouille or risotto. However, if baby doesn't love something, be nice. Don't call much attention to it and if it is something you like to eat, keep making it, and keep offering small amounts to your child every time you do. Throwing in a comment on how much you enjoy it is always helpful. Make an effort to accompany it with something that you know your child does enjoy. If it takes a while for your child to appreciate the dish, don't stress, and definitely don't give up. When he does finally eat it, a nice compliment will be in order!

If your child refuses to eat, calmly clear the table when everyone else is finished and move on to the next part of the day. Make sure you do not reward him for refusing his meal by offering him a snack. Offer drinks of water, but make him wait until the next meal to eat, even if it is overnight. When your child is actually hungry, I promise you he will eat.

Set positive expectations and emphasize the conversation around the table more than the food. Never preface a meal with an apology like, "I know you might not like this so I gave you an extra helping of potatoes." If you are out visiting and someone offers your child something new to eat, you might let him know that you enjoy this food and that it would be great for him to try it. Whatever you do, don't beat your child to the punch by explaining that it's something he's unlikely to enjoy. I've heard conversations like this so many times: A host will offer something to a child—"Ava, would you like some cheese?"—and before the child can answer, the parent quickly interjects, "Oh, Ava, it's Brie. I don't think you're going to like it." Teach your children to assume that food will taste good unless they're proven wrong.

Insist on Manners

It's not nearly so important that a child knows which fork is for salad and which is for the main course as it is to teach him to recognize that almost every meal represents someone's time and effort. Every time we allow children to complain about the food they're served, we're allowing them to disrespect the person who took the time to make it. At the family table, it is acceptable to respectfully express one's preferences for one dish over another. ("Dad, I like that casserole with the rice better than this one." Not, "Ew, what is this stuff?") At anyone else's table, it is not acceptable. Teach children to eat what they're served with a smile. If you're going to someone's home for dinner, ask your child to please be polite and nice about the food even if it is not his or her favorite.

FAQ: I've Got a Picky Eater, and We're Invited to a Friend's House for Dinner. How Do I Ensure a Nice Evening for Everyone without Putting the Host to Any Extra Trouble?

If your host is considerate enough to ask what your child would like, especially if your child is picky, it is reasonable to offer some suggestions that would be really easy to add to a meal. I would not advise that you take snacks for your child. This might just facilitate the unsocial behavior and feel somewhat rude to the host. If you're not given the option to suggest a dish, let your child eat whatever he finds palatable, even if it's just a dinner roll or spoonful of rice, encourage him to be polite to the host, and feed him something light when you get home. Make it clear that these are special circumstances and that he shouldn't expect to eat a separate meal from the family on a regular basis.

The good news is, when kids have been primed since they were tiny to anticipate that food generally tastes good, they'll usually be excited to see what gets served for dinner no matter where they are, and they'll probably enjoy it. And if they don't, they'll live. That said, most people want to be good hosts and want to see their guests happy, and if they see a young child struggling to swallow food he doesn't like, they will likely offer him something else to eat. Just make sure your child knows that's not going to happen at home!

Don't Customize

One of the best things about America is our fierce belief in individuality and personal choice. Those concepts, however, need to take a step back from the dinner table while young children are learning to eat. You can offer the option of cheese or no cheese on a burger; instead of throwing them in a bowl, you can place the components of your salad on a large plate and let everyone take what they like (perhaps with a rule they must take some); you can omit your usual final squeeze of lemon from your child's portion of salmon. But other than easy adaptations like these that take no additional effort on your part, everyone at the table should be eating the same thing. Why? First, no parent should ever be reduced to short-order cook. Making separate meals to accommodate everyone's preferences simply takes more time and planning. There is no reason you should make your life harder (and unnecessarily add to your stress) by catering to everyone's food preferences, and it is a sure-fire way to set children up to eat very limited diets, which can compromise their health.

Second, customizing everyone's meal diminishes the power of the bonding experience inherent in sharing a meal and creates an expectation that one's individual needs always take precedence over those of the group. As Art Markman and Bob Duke at the University of Texas explained in an episode on food and food rituals for their podcast *Two Guys on Your Head*, sitting down for a meal is a holistic learning experience. You're not just learning how to properly hold a spoon and that you prefer ketchup to mustard, you're learning important social lessons:

> When everyone is having the same meal, you learn the art of compromise. You learn that we may be having one person's favorite meal tonight, and maybe it's not your favorite meal, but that's ok, it's still good healthy food. You learn to share that meal with everyone, so you don't get to take it all for yourself, and if there's something you all like you have to divide it up. There's an awful lot of social interaction that goes on when you're sharing, and when everyone eats his or her own thing you learn as a kid I can have whatever I want if I just scream loudly enough. It's all about me and getting my needs at this moment.

Don't bribe your children with dessert as a reward for eating their meal. First of all, this behavior sets up the meal as a time of frequent negotiation for something else. It removes the child's attention from the nice social occasion into a game of "Let's see what I can get out of this." From a medical standpoint, it is a recipe for childhood obesity. You're saying, "If you eat the whole plate of food I will give you more." The lesson rewards overeating.

In many other cultures, aside from a piece of fruit, dessert isn't part of the expectations of a regular meal. Most children raised to view a prepared dessert as an occasional treat and not a meal mainstay experience very few weight problems as adults.

If you still wish to have dessert, of course, perhaps you can serve yourself once your kids are in bed.

Get Everyone Involved

Since her children were very young, Jamie and her two children, Aaron, eleven, and Josie, nine, in Brooklyn, New York, have planned the week's meals together. First Jamie will go through her refrigerator, freezer, and pantry to see what she already has that can serve as the base for a few meals. With that information, she'll offer the kids a few suggestions and let them choose which they'd like to see on the menu that upcoming week. "They both have favorites and sometimes I'll say, pick something other than your favorite. I look through recipes—mostly online now—and sometimes I'll offer up choices and they choose what they want. Sometimes they put in their choices and then I will throw in a new recipe and after they eat it, they rate it as a keeper or not." Simplicity and efficiency are key for this working mom whose husband often travels for his job. But in this way, Jamie's kids are learning what it takes to plan and prepare healthful meals, and since they're given some say in the process, they're unlikely to complain about what's served.

Kids can also start helping in the kitchen at a young age. Toddlers love sifting flour or scooping measuring cups and spoons. Even young children with little eye–hand coordination can slice a banana with a dull knife or peel a cucumber. Let your child sit on the counter or in the kitchen with you while you cook so he can get a first-row view of all the action. Kids enjoy eating what they've made, and in this way, meal preparations become fun, social-bonding moments.

Mix Things Up

Every now and then, eat picnic-style on the floor, gather out on the deck in the backyard, or sit on the stoop or porch out front. It is always fun to add a new spin to a routine activity. The point is to be together sharing the meal and enjoying each other's company. Dinner can still be celebrated even when it's only sloppy Joes and salad.

Most of All

Make your motto, "Here, try this. I think it's yummy."

BUT WHAT ABOUT ALLERGIES?

One of the reasons many parents proceed with extreme caution when feeding their babies is a fear of allergies, and in particular anaphylactic shock. In truth, very few foods are likely to cause this extreme and dangerous reaction, which causes breathing problems and should be considered an emergency, requiring a dose of an antihistamine like Benadryl and a trip to the ER. It's easily one of the nightmare scenarios parents fear most. That said, food allergies usually make themselves known at first with a minor reaction such as a rash. If your child responds this way, then of course for now you would be wise to avoid the particular food that seems to be causing it. If a child develops a severe rash with hives, I would recommend taking him or her for a professional evaluation with their primary care doctor, who might suggest testing with an allergist.

There is reason to believe that it's our own hypercautious tendencies that have caused the rapid elevation in rates of food allergies. Our grandparents certainly didn't worry too much about them. Two decades ago, doctors started seeing more children with allergic reactions to foods like peanuts, eggs, and fish. In fact, the rate of children suffering from peanut allergies in the United States and the UK doubled in the ten years between 1997 and 2007. Pediatricians responded by suggesting we delay the introduction of those foods to give children's immune systems time to develop. Peanuts and tree nuts, especially, were strictly forbidden before a child's first birthday. Some parents were even told to wait two years before trying to introduce a bit of peanut butter.

Meanwhile, in parts of Africa where peanut stews and soups have always been popular, children ingest peanuts at extremely young ages. In Israel, one of the most beloved children's snacks is Bamba, which Miriam, whom we met earlier, described as a "peanut-flavored Cheeto" that easily dissolves in babies' mouths. Once they are ready for solids, at about seven months, Israeli infants are consuming about 7 grams of peanut protein per month. Scientists at King's College in London were so intrigued by the dramatic difference between the high peanut allergy rates of Jewish children living in the UK, many with genetic roots in Israel, who usually didn't try peanuts until the age of two years, and the low rates of peanut allergies in Jewish children being raised in Israel with regular access to peanut products, they decided to do a controlled study among children who might be at risk for a peanut allergy but had not yet developed one. The results were clear: Children exposed to peanut protein before the age of one year lowered their risk of developing a peanut allergy by as much as 81 percent.

Once again, by trying to prevent something terrible from

happening to our children, we most likely made the problem worse, and stressed out a lot of parents unnecessarily. Today researchers and doctors are starting to suspect a link between allergies and the state of the flora in the gut, but we're still a long way from finding any definitive answers.

Even though medically it would seem that gently sensitizing young children to foods that are well known for their ability to cause allergic reactions is probably helpful in decreasing allergies across a group, I strongly recommend that children with a highly allergic parent or close family member discuss this with their child's doctor for guidance on food introductions.

If your child doesn't have a family history of allergies it's unlikely you need to worry, but check your pediatrician's view on this while attending well-child appointments. A good precaution is to keep a bottle of liquid Benadryl in your home so you're prepared for any surprises.

IS ORGANIC REALLY WORTH IT?

The same anxiety that raises the specter of allergies drives parents to obsess over feeding their children with organic food. Until now, the problem for many who want to buy organic is that organic products at the supermarket have traditionally cost significantly more than conventional products. Now that even Wal-Mart sells organic produce, the cost barrier may be starting to come down. Still, it's not always easy to buy exclusively organic. But should we even be trying?

The thing about organic food, as I understand it, is that it is actually extremely difficult to produce. There are so many uncontrollable factors in food production it makes it almost impossible to grow food products completely free of every impurity we might want to avoid. Rather than worry about whether a food is organic, people would be better off if they just concentrated on eating real natural food, not processed variations of food. If everyone tried to avoid boxed or packaged ready-made foods and instead cooked real vegetables, real fresh unprocessed meats and fish, and added more fresh fruit to our daily menus, we would all be getting a more nutritious and healthier diet. I'd rather parents hand a conventionally grown banana to their children than an organic chocolate chip granola bar any day.

On the other hand, if you've ever traveled to Europe and found yourself around any children at about 4:00 P.M., you'll often see them with a small bar of chocolate or some other sweet or pastry in their hands. Though Europe has seen an increase in rates of obesity, their childhood obesity rates are still significantly lower than ours. Poverty and lower socioeconomic status often determines who will be overweight and who will not. In more highly educated families with more stable income, that chocolate bar is often the only processed sugar those children will eat throughout the day. Portion sizes matter a great deal, too. Small children should not be eating plates of food similar in size to that of their parents. Balance is everything.

We can't let worry and fear paralyze us the way it did Chase's parents, the couple we met at the beginning of this chapter, who became so terrified about what could happen if their son ate something he "shouldn't" they deprived him more than a commercially grown tomato ever would have. Not many families wind up in such dire straits, but too many families are confused by the processed food industry's marketing efforts and really do not understand how to eat well. An ideal diet is remarkably easy to achieve: eat a well-balanced blend of plants and proteins, carbs and fats, and "not too much" of any of it, as the food writer Michael Pollan famously wrote on the first page of his book *In Defense of Food*. But as in all things when it comes to parenting, no one should be expected to exclusively adhere to an ideal anything, and no one should castigate themselves when they either fall short or decide to sin. Just don't do it every day! I have never noticed a difference between children who eat organic and those who do not that couldn't easily be linked to environmental or financial inequalities.

Sugar is not the devil. Unless true allergies or intolerances have been diagnosed, there need be no debate over whether to allow a child to eat a piece of store-bought, circus-colored birthday cake every now and then. Research strongly suggests that children's long-term eating habits—including the ones that affect a child's likelihood of becoming obese—are shaped early in infancy, so what matters is that parents plan to avoid packaged products with large amounts of sugar, additives, dyes, and other artificial ingredients in their children's daily diets and, when reasonable, make the effort to feed their children real foods found in nature, not concocted in a factory. Just making that effort, even if not 100 percent successfully, can make a huge difference in children's overall eating habits and health.

As a nation we're making progress. For the first time in about forty years, the number of calories children consume each day has declined, with the obesity rate in children aged two to five years going down by about 40 percent. That means that nutritious eating is becoming more of a priority. And the more people change their diets for the better, the more people will be inspired to make the effort and will make it happen in their own home. Eating well and eating together are definitely more work than pulling out a packaged family-style dinner and popping it in the oven or microwave and letting everyone eat while watching their favorite YouTube videos. But the long-term social, physical, and emotional benefits of cooking your own meals and sitting down at the table are priceless for you and your children.

Around the time I was writing this chapter, my grandchildren came over for a visit. As usual, my husband, the primary cook in our home, was preparing the meal. *The Voice* had just come on the television. We are a music-loving family—my grandmother Ann, in whose house I grew up in Kenya, had wanted to be an opera singer—and I decided to do something special for the kids by suggesting that we all convene in the great room to watch the show while eating dinner.

To my surprise, my fifteen-year-old grandson immediately said he would prefer not to. Instead he set the dining room table as we customarily do, hit the record button on the DVR, and called the remainder of our family to the table. In just a few minutes someone was telling a story, and we were all laughing, eating, and having a grand time. It reaffirmed my belief that the practice of bringing people together around a table never grows old and may be one of the most powerful experiences a family can have together.

8

Slow Down to Discipline

IN THE SPRING of 2014, the *Huffington Post* published an article written by the mother of a three-year-old girl. In it, she explained that the terrible twos have got nothing on the tyrannical threes. The reason three-year-olds are more difficult than any other creature on the planet, she said, is that they just don't care (actually, she used far more explicit, colorful language). As an example, she explained how her daughter would pitch a fit if the pink pants she wanted to wear were dirty and she had to wear her blue pants instead. The article, titled "Three-Year-Olds Are Assholes," made social media waves. Thousands of parents took the opportunity to commiserate about what little monsters their two- and three-year-olds could be. Most people read the article and laughed. I really didn't find it amusing.

The article made me angry and concerned. Did parents really feel this way about their children? It bothered me that no one seemed to question whether the child might have good reason for acting out in such a scenario. The author's intent was to reassure parents that the unkind, inappropriate thoughts that sometimes race through their minds are universal and understandable. I believe she was trying to help. But to my mind, all she did was perpetuate the idea that little children are inherently difficult, challenging, and deserving of our rage. After all, they *know* they're behaving poorly, and they know they're making you mad. They just don't care. But none of that is true. I saw no humor in an article that showed me how little parents understood how it felt to be a child or how they could improve their own behavior. Children of this age normally do care about pleasing their caregivers. If more parents understood this, they might be able to intervene and prevent the kind of behavior that would make even the most patient parents tear out their hair.

THE TODDLER'S MISSION: TEST CAUSE AND EFFECT

As much as your life changed the day you brought your precious baby home from the hospital, nothing can prepare you for the surprises you'll face once your child starts toddling about on her own. On that day, the whole world becomes her laboratory, a place to experiment with cause and effect. "I wonder if I can fit inside the kitchen cabinet if I pull out all these pots and pans?" "This bright crayon lets me make pretty pictures in my coloring book. Mommy has pictures on the wall; what kind of pictures can I make on the wall?" "I keep asking Mommy to play with me but she keeps talking on the phone. I am lonely. What will get her to spend time with me? Perhaps she will hear me and spend time with me if I bang my stroller against the car." "Hey, when I cry and hold my breath, Mommy looks scared, and then hugs me and gives me anything I want." This is normal behavior, especially for children who don't feel they are getting enough attention or are bored or don't feel like their needs are being heard. But many times parents respond with anger and choose to believe that their children are trying to be difficult. This makes our children feel helpless. Not having any other recourse, they then repeat the behavior, many times with even more vehemence.

We get frustrated and the whole situation spirals out of control. Suddenly we're at a loss. Most of us have been led to believe that as parents we're supposed to be endless fonts of wisdom, patience, and encouragement, a combination of *Friday Night Lights*'s Tami Taylor, Mr. Rogers, and the Weasleys of Harry Potter fame. But as children assert their independence and begin to express their needs and opinions and even test their boundaries, parents often find themselves feeling helpless, they resort to punishing the child and end up exhausted when neither time-outs nor countdowns nor yelling nor any other disciplinary tactic seems to work.

HAVE WE GONE SOFT?

I've heard parents sometimes wonder, Did previous generations have it right all along? Would the occasional spanking be so bad? Parents in many other countries might wonder at our doubt, especially those in more traditional, group-oriented societies. Some Hispanic cultures take corporal punishment for granted, enough so that a YouTube video spoofing the habit of mothers using *la chancla*—a flip-flop—as a disciplinary tool went viral, spawning op-ed pieces questioning the tactic and social media threads in which people bragged about their mothers' ninja-like *chancla* skills. Caning is still a common practice in Singapore and Malaysia, and even if a family doesn't heed the philosophy of "I hit you because I love you. The more I hit you, the more I love you," many Asian parents do subscribe to a strict tradition of harsh discipline, heralded as the secret to the Asian immigrant success story in Amy Chua's best-selling and hotly debated *Battle Hymn of the Tiger Mother.*

The fear of a spanking can definitely make some kids behave. More to the point, it's fast. Parents who aren't afraid to spank probably don't spend too much time negotiating with or cajoling their kids. Here in the States, however, among many parents, especially the middle and upper classes (research has found that social class has more effect on parental values that dictate how we raise our children than does race, religion, region, and national background combined, especially for fathers) these "tough love" tactics have been widely dismissed as old-fashioned and harmful, even abusive. Is that why we have trouble disciplining our kids?

Not likely. More than thirty countries, including Denmark, have placed outright bans on corporal punishment. Another one of those countries is Kenya. Growing up there, I spent a lot of time surrounded by young African families. One thing that struck me early on was how seldom the mothers scolded their small children. Between the precautions necessary due to legitimate concerns for the security of a little white girl growing up during an anticolonial uprising, and my traditional British upbringing with its high expectation of conduct, I was unable to enjoy the same kind of unsupervised freedom of my native African friends. Yet though they were loosely supervised, most of them were polite to their elders, well behaved, and stayed out of trouble—just like me. In retrospect, I was seeing how two distinct cultures and parental expectations could produce similar results.

How does the Kenyan method, so different to the one I was raised in and also so different from the parenting gold standard in the United States, reliably produce such cooperative, even-tempered toddlers? From my observations, the Kenyan method of child-rearing might be summed up as follows:

- Limit your rules.
- Be consistent.
- Ask for what you want, not what you don't.
- Offer limited choices.
- Ask why.

Let's examine these one by one and see why they work and how they might be useful.

LIMIT YOUR RULES

If you want your children to hear you and heed you, keep your rules to a minimum. Focus on protecting their safety, the safety of others, and instilling respect and good manners. Don't worry much about anything else except what really matters to you.

Urging parents to loosen up a bit is not to say we should relax our standards or dispense with rules altogether. No one likes to be around little hellions who insist on having their way and give no one any peace. That's exhausting, and this book is about finding ways to raise happy, healthy kids without wearing ourselves out. Perhaps if we stopped implementing so many rules and instead thought more about what *kinds* of rules we want our kids to follow, and why, we'd be more effective. Instead of telling kids to do things, we might ask them to do things and explain why it's a good idea. When there are only a few rules to keep track of, and everyone is clear on why they exist, you might find you have very little need to discipline your children at all.

Here's what I mean. In Kenya the mothers I observed didn't have to chastise their children repeatedly for breaking rules or disobeying because there were very few rules to break in the first place. The rules the children were expected to follow were generally in place to keep them safe, keep others safe around them, and to establish a hierarchy of respect. For some, it will seem counterintuitive that a relatively hands-off approach could instill in a child the sense of respect necessary for him or her to willingly obey a parent or other authority figure. It's not, though, when you are consistent with your expectations. It also means that when parents do give direction, the children usually listen.

BE CONSISTENT

Think about this: What do you do when someone repeats himself for the tenth time? You tune him out, right? Children do, too. Constant reprimands and repetition eventually become background noise—children don't even hear it anymore. But adults, especially tired adults, will usually blow a gasket pretty quickly when their child doesn't respond to them. That's how a simple request for your child to pick up his socks in the living room escalates into World War III. Often we wind up doing the neglected chore ourselves, which is frustrating, or we get the child to mind by raising our voices and dishing out a punishment that is completely out of proportion to the banal task we asked the child to do in the first place. Now we've modeled inconsistency and introduced drama into the home over something of truly minimal consequence. We shouldn't be surprised, then, when our children model the same.

One thing we can do is reduce the opportunities for friction. For example, an easy place to start is to stop controlling what our children wear. So what if we don't think their clothes match? Is it really unacceptable for a child to wear the same pants for two days in a row if they aren't stained or smelly, or are you just concerned about what the teachers at school will think? When my children did not want to heed my warnings that it was cold enough to wear a coat, I would suggest they go outside to check out the weather. Their usual response was to come back in and retrieve their coats. By using psychology instead of insisting I was right, I gave them a semblance of control and avoided an upsetting fight before heading out for the day.

Does it really matter if your children's room is a mess? We have to accept that young kids are going to remember things one day and forget them the next. You can tell them your expectations, but it's unreasonable to demand they be fully responsible for managing their own chores and obligations until they're really ready, and for some kids that might be later than you anticipated.

> Modeling is far more effective than almost any other parenting technique.

If your kids are working on an art project at the table, it's acceptable to ask them to tidy up when they're done. It's good to ask them to place their clothes in the laundry basket and not on the bedroom floor. But if it doesn't happen every single time, don't lose your cool, and don't punish. After all, it's unlikely you are always 100 percent compliant yourself. Just take a moment to remind the kids of what they're supposed to do, tidy up, and move on to more important things. Modeling is far more effective than almost any other parenting technique. End of story. I have found that parents who talk respectfully to their children, treat them politely, and respond consistently when there is an issue tend to have children who are calm, caring, and reasonable.

Work with your children and allow them to express their individuality and experiment within reason. So many things that seem the norm to us are far from the norm in other cultures. What's the harm if your children want soup for breakfast? It's a common breakfast item around the world, among them the Chinese jook, Bolivian changua, and Tunisian lablebi. Remember that the rules and values we hold dear are not the same everywhere else. (I didn't eat my first hamburger until I was thirty-five years old and living in the States!) Before saying no always ask yourself, Is this worth fighting about? Are we arguing over something that is important and will make my child a well-rounded person in the future? Letting go of the things that are unimportant in the long run will go a long way to reducing the daily turmoil and stress in your home.

Consistency, not severity, is the key to instilling good discipline. You can run a relaxed home and still make it clear that the rules might differ at school or elsewhere and you expect your child to respect them. Focus on curbing really unsafe or violent behaviors, teach empathy and respect, and ignore the little things that don't make a scrap of difference. When you set very few rules, it gives children the freedom to learn without a doubt what's really important to you and your family until they're old enough to understand *why* the rules need to be followed. That's when you can start holding them more accountable and

> The less you nag, the more your children hear you.

expecting more of them. I've found that the less you nag, the more your children hear you.

ASK FOR WHAT YOU WANT, NOT WHAT YOU DON'T

Children under the age of two years don't really understand a negative sentence. For example, when you tell a small child not to do something, you might as well be telling them to do it. Say you were walking down the street with your eighteen-month-old and you noticed a puddle of water on the pavement. A child's natural instinct would be to stomp in it. Under many circumstances, I would urge you to let them—I'd love to see more children be free to get dirty, for reasons I'll explain in the following chapter on play. But let's say you're on your way to a religious service and you want your child to stay neat and tidy. When you notice your child heading toward the puddle, your initial reaction might be to yell, "Stop! Nathan, don't go near that puddle, you'll get dirty!" But it would be more effective if you said, "Nathan, I want to see if you can walk with me around that puddle." Now the child knows exactly what you expect of him and more than likely he will oblige, especially if you can redirect him to something else that would be fun, like kicking the leaves or jumping like a bunny rabbit.

OFFER LIMITED CHOICES

I've noticed that many parents assign their children a chore or task that they don't want to do themselves. This is definitely laying the groundwork for a battle. A better idea would be to ask the child what chores she'd like to do, especially if you're not actually looking for help, but rather assigning tasks to teach her how to be a helpful family member. It will help your child succeed more if you allow her to select the task for which she will be responsible. If you tell her she must load the dishwasher, but she really wants to feed the dog, why not just let her feed the dog? She'll succeed a lot more frequently and peace will reign. Since most children would like to pick the clothes they wear, let them and make a practice of asking them to pick out an outfit with you preferably in the evening—and then actually let them do it! Don't criticize their choices, though you certainly can make suggestions. Unless his outfit is completely off the wall, if your child feels strongly about it let his decision stand. Alternatively, you could set out a few outfits and let him pick the one he likes best. If you have a child who resists picking up her toys, challenge her to a race to see who can pick up the most toys in five minutes. It is amazing how much fun this sudden game can become.

The more control you can give children over their own decisions and actions within a safe setting, the more amenable they will be to participating in the daily tasks of family life and your requests for help. But we will find ourselves very frustrated if we expect children to remain aware of the time and stop what they are doing at the correct hour to do whatever tasks they have been made responsible for, or that you've asked them to do, on their own. Even teenagers often need a prompt to be aware of the time.

One thing I like to suggest to parents is that if you're going to ask children to help, try to find outdoor jobs. Better yet, have them help you or your partner outside after school or on the weekends. Outdoor work is going to tend to be a bit physical, and the jobs you can find for kids will be more enjoyable to them because they can get dirty and they may get a chance to play with water or dirt. Once they're older they can learn a skill such as running the mower, edging, or the like. Children can help out indoors as well but I don't subscribe to the idea that they should have routine obligations or chores to make our lives easier. As the adults, we have the responsibility to organize our lives to function with or without our children's' help. Our children's main priority should be to learn, and our priority for them should be to provide opportunities for them to learn and gain skills. This does not mean we can't ask for their help when we need it. In fact, I wholly support this idea. But we are out of line to get mad when our children don't live up to our adult expectations. They're going to forget and fail sometimes. They're going to need reminders, probably more than you think they will. Keep in mind that they don't have the same concentration or the same memory ability as we do.

In my home, once the kids were of school age, the whole family, all six of us, would work together for a couple of hours Saturday mornings. I would delegate the spaces that needed cleaning or the jobs (such as vacuuming) and assign them by what was appropriate for each age. We all knew that after we were done we would go out as a family for a whole day of fun and play, such as going water skiing, having a picnic, or hitting the ski slopes. It worked really well; the house was clean, everyone did his or her share, and there were no complaints.

Our job as parents is to teach our children how to do things, allow them to try, and then make sure that we offer any help they need to succeed and be successful. They already have lots of responsibility related to learning how to manage themselves and their school or activities. Other than that, when we ask them to do something, our objective should be to teach them to work with us, not for us. And if you can do all of this teaching with a sense of humor, you might be amazed at how much faster your children learn. They may even come to enjoy working together to keep the home clean.

ASK WHY

We are human, and no matter how good our efforts are to stay calm, occasionally we're going to lose our cool. But I've had families come to me in despair, feeling like they've not only lost their cool but lost control of their children, too. The problem has been going on so long, they've started generalizing, saying the child is unmanageable because she's choosing to be difficult, stubborn, or willful; to have temper tantrums; or to refuse to sleep. Often by this time they've started using threats and punishments to get the behavior they want. Sometimes those threats and punishments even work for a short time, but eventually the behaviors start up again. Instead of trying a different tack, they double down on the punishments, assuming that if the behavior hasn't changed, it must be because they're not being strict enough. After all, that's the general message we get, isn't it? We've almost all been on the receiving end of a judgmental sideways glance when our children act up in public or heard a tone of reproach from a well-meaning mother or mother-in-law who informs us how things were done back in her day. If our children are misbehaving or not minding us, they imply, it must be because we haven't established our authority.

There is no such thing as an inherently challenging child unless there is a medical, genetic, neurological, or psychosocial problem going on. But there are many children whose needs are not being met by their environment. No one, including children, behaves in a vacuum. When children act out, they're almost always trying to tell us they're frustrated, and we can't help them or improve the behavior unless we know why. Unfortunately, some parents don't bother to ask. They jump to conclusions, deciding that undesirable behavior is always attributable to caprice or that the child is spoiled or selfish. Many parents do try to reason from their own perspective with their children but get nowhere, which leads them to the same conclusions. This is unfortunate because most of the time, there really is a reason children behave the way they do. And you don't need to be a child psychologist to figure it out. Just ask!

> Most of the time, there really is a reason children behave the way they do.

It's About Time

What you do need is time. You've got to take the time to talk to your child and in a calm tone ask what is wrong before emotions—yours and theirs—get out of control. And as we've discussed, time is one of the things most parents just don't think they have. In fact, time constraints are probably one of the biggest reasons for confrontations between children and parents. The parents are trying to get out the door to go to work, or they're trying to finish making dinner, or get children to bed, or get one last email written, or get somewhere on time, or beat rush-hour traffic. It's not like it was when I was growing up in England, when school and work started at 9:00 A.M. and most people lived close to both. Everyone could wake up at seven and still have plenty of time to wash up, eat a comfortable sit-down breakfast, and get dressed before catching a bus or getting in the family car. My friends and I rarely, if ever, headed out in the morning with the sounds of our parents yelling at us to hurry up still echoing in our ears. Unfortunately, life has sped up tenfold. The opening bell rings at many elementary schools at 7:45, and some kids are dropped off as early as seven. That way parents can get to work early and then leave work early enough to pick the kids up from school instead of paying for afternoon day care.

A whole book could be written about how our country is falling short of supporting children and working families, to its detriment. But until enough families vote for change, these schedules—and the overstimulation and pressure that accompany them—are the reality of our days. My suggestion, then, is to try honestly to prioritize what really needs to be done and simply ignore anything that does not positively affect you or your family.

For example, if your morning routine has you frustrated every day, what you are doing is not working and you need to evaluate it. You could get up thirty minutes earlier so that you can get yourself ready and finish any other preparations for the day, like lunches, before the kids are even awake. This will allow you to focus entirely on them and keep the morning routine running smoothly and calmly. You may feel like your kids should be capable of handling themselves without your help, but if you find yourself screaming every morning because they are running slow, it may be time to put principle behind practicality and give them a hand. It will be worth it so that everyone, you included, can start the day on a positive, optimistic note. As soon as we begin to feel like we're running against the clock, we get impatient and we start pushing children to do things before they've had a minute to process what they're being asked to do (or stop doing). And when parents are in a rush, we usually stop listening. We don't—we can't—take the time to find out what's at the root of children's slowness, obstinacy, or anger (often they're just plain exhausted, just like you).

Now imagine how you might start to react if every time you expressed a negative emotion you were essentially told to suck it up because no one had time to hear about it.

When I was working in a pediatric clinic, I took care of an adorable baby named Jacob. His mother, Anne, was a dream, too. At every appointment, we'd talk about Jacob's growth and progress, and I'd tell her what to expect in the next month or so. Jacob was an easy, sweet baby with a delightful disposition. Then Anne gave birth to her second child, a daughter. She was doing everything as I had taught her to do with her first child, but her little girl, Ella, was feisty and difficult, throwing tantrums at every turn. By the time she came in for Ella's eighteen-month well visit, Anne was tired and frustrated and, as she told me, horrified at how resentful and angry she was starting to feel toward her daughter.

The situation brought home just how easily our emotions can cloud our sight. This mother had always been calm, sensible, and intuitive. But a prolonged period of poor sleep and daytime stress was keeping her from seeing what was perfectly obvious to me listening to her story. I pointed out that of course everything that worked with Jacob wasn't going to work exactly the same with Ella. From the very first day of life, Ella had been required to share. Jacob didn't. Ella was not getting nearly the same quality of time with her mother or dad that Jacob did. I advised Anne to make a point of giving her daughter one-on-one time and told her that the next time she felt herself getting angry with Ella's behavior, she should be sure to compensate by giving Ella a little extra time or help. Sure enough, once Anne started responding to Ella with compassion and attention instead of frustration and resentment, the tantrums went away.

I believe time might also have been at the root of the conflict between the author of the *Huffington Post* piece we discussed in the beginning of this chapter and her daughter who wanted to wear pink pants. In a follow-up interview, the author explained her angry response to her daughter's capriciousness: "Look, we have to get going, and if you're going to behave in a way that is counterproductive to that, you're going to have to deal with whatever consequences come with that." Many parents of toddlers would sympathize as most of us have experienced this particular showdown. You're in a hurry and suddenly your child refuses to put on the brand-new shoes he picked out himself or decides that he hates long sleeves and has to change into his favorite Teenage Mutant Ninja T-shirt. Our initial reaction is often to roll our eyes and tell the kid to get over it. But what if, instead of responding negatively, we asked why the shoes have lost favor and responded sympathetically. Even when the reasoning seems silly to us, it's rarely silly to a child. Giving your child a chance to figure out his feelings and then acknowledging them will likely help you decompress the situation.

In a culture that prizes self-sufficiency as much as we do, we really need to put things in perspective so that parents and children feel empowered rather than end up struggling over issues of independence. Finding the right balance between encouraging children to solve their own problems and accept help when they need it can feel like a tightrope act. One day a child will fiercely insist "I do it!" when you try to help her tie her shoes, and the next she'll wail because she suddenly lost the ability to put the shoes on the right feet. So often, though, we do things for our children when they can and want to do it themselves, but then we insist they do things when they don't feel capable. We've got to listen better. Just because a child is capable of doing something herself doesn't mean you shouldn't help her when she asks you to. A three-year-old who knows her left from her right is still new to that knowledge. Maybe she's embarrassed that she has forgotten which shoe is which. Maybe she's just feeling insecure that day. Try to not get frustrated, and do your best to give yourself enough leeway so that when all of a sudden your child is acting helpless and slowing you down, you have time to understand and acknowledge your child's emotions, fix the problem, and get out the door with everyone feeling good about themselves. It will usually take you far less time to help the child than to face her down. In addition, it's not worth it when a confrontation will leave both of you starting your day feeling irritable.

When a school-age child asks you to do things she's capable of doing, it's appropriate to ask, "What is the problem? Do you need me to stop what I am doing or do you think you can give it a try first?" If the child persists, help out quickly and move on.

There is never a reason to emotionally duke it out with a three-year-old. At this age, what's important is to help our children to succeed. That doesn't mean you have to spoil them or let them take advantage of you. Help them, but don't reward undesirable behavior, whether by yelling (which is attention, even if it's negative attention), begging, or even worse, giving in.

> There is never a reason to emotionally duke it out with a three-year-old.

TAMING TANTRUMS

Still, sometimes the fireworks explode and you've got a tantruming child on your hands. What to do? Don't argue and don't waste time telling your children off. The best thing to do is to remove them to a safe area such as their bedroom. The problem could simply be that they are tired and need some down time. Once they have no audience, they will probably stop performing. When they have calmed down, you can let them come back and join you. They will quickly learn that the behavior won't get them the results they want.

FAQ: Time-Outs Defuse Tantrums in the Moment, but the Threat of a Time-Out Isn't Enough to Deter My Child from Exploding with Rage When She Doesn't Get Her Way. What Am I Doing Wrong?

If you decide a time-out is necessary, remove your child to another area where she cannot disrupt you or the remainder of the family. Make sure she understands that the privilege of returning to be near you or anyone else depends on her getting her act together. Don't yell and don't threaten. After she has calmed down, try to talk about what happened, making sure to engage in a dialogue, not a one-way conversation from you to the child. Explore what the problem is and take the opportunity to point out how you feel when your child behaves this way. Suggest other ways of behaving that are more acceptable to you when she feels frustrated or angry in the future. For example, you could give her permission to scream into her pillow when she's angry or go outside into the yard, weather permitting, to stomp out her frustration.

Time-outs, like any other punishment, will not be effective if used too frequently because they lose their meaning. If time-outs stop working, try taking away a privilege or an item that means something to her (but not something that offers comfort, like a favorite stuffed animal).

WHINING

Whining occurs when a child figures out that if he just keeps up a low level of complaint, his parent or caregiver will cave. See, kids are really good about being consistent. It's parents who have a hard time with it. So here's what you do.

For the small things that really don't matter: If you know that eventually you will give in to a request if your child keeps begging or nagging, just agree to it the first time and be done with it. You'll spare yourself and the whole family a lot of annoying behavior and stress.

For the big things that are not negotiable: Stay strong. For the things you absolutely do not want your child to do or have, whether it's eating snacks right before dinner or playing with your tablet or climbing on your patio chairs, then stick to those. In every other case, try not to react to every request with a knee-jerk no. Calmly weigh the pros and cons and then give a single, clear answer with a reason, and make sure that you are consistent. And once you've given that answer, make sure to end the conversation. If you can help your child move on to something more fun, do so, and if you can't, it's okay if your child is unhappy with your decision. Kids rebound quickly. Give them time and they'll find something else that will engage them.

AGGRESSION

Aggression can have several causes. Sometimes it's modeling aggressive behavior in the home, but sometimes it's a child's response to feeling victimized in group settings outside the home, such as day care or school. For older children aggression can be a reaction to the frustration of managing schoolwork. Whenever you see aggressive behavior, before jumping in with a disciplinary action it is always important to talk to the child and see if you can find out what is bothering him or her. Even a small child can often tell you. Many children are scared to talk about feelings that make them aggressive or they don't quite understand why they are so upset, but speaking to children gently will probably help you get to the bottom of the problem faster than if you threaten or punish. That will often just make the child feel backed into a corner, which can make him lash out even more and exacerbate the problem. If you are unable to find out the source of the problem quickly, get help from your pediatrician, who will likely recommend a consultation with a child psychologist or child psychiatrist, depending on the situation.

PREPARE TO BE TESTED

No strategy is perfect every time. Even kids who know their boundaries will test them until you figure out how to stop them. Sometimes you can politely ask for what you want until you're hoarse and it won't make a difference. Then you need to stop the behavior in a different way. It happens to pediatricians, too. When I was in medical school my eldest son made me late several days in a row by playing instead of getting dressed like his siblings, and as a result my children missed their buses and I had to drive them all to their respective schools, which made me late for my classes. My son was six at the time, and we had been doing this morning routine for a while, so he knew very well that this behavior would allow him to miss the bus and get a ride from Mom. I decided to tell him that in the future if he was not ready I would take him as he was. The next day, when I picked up my keys to leave, despite my reminders I saw that again he was not dressed. I insisted that he get into the car and I took him to his bus stop. To his horror, and that of the bus driver, I carried him up the stairs into the bus still wearing his pajamas. The other children in the bus thought it was quite funny. I followed the bus to school, and when it arrived I parked behind it and handed my son a change of clothes. I got his attention and from then on I got the behavior I needed from him in the mornings without having to yell and scream. He never tested me again. At least, not on this issue.

The first time a child doesn't heed your request, stay calm and ask again. Children usually want to be helpful but are easily distracted. It is entirely possible your child intended to do as you asked but forgot. By the second or third time, it would be natural to start feeling irritated, but keep it in check. Instead of getting angry, quietly interrupt whatever activity it is that your child is choosing to do instead of listening to you. Turn the television off, gently take away the iPad, or put the Legos away. Explain that you are disappointed with her and expected more. Very few children aren't affected when they feel they have disappointed or hurt their parents' feelings.

If the real problem with a certain behavior is that it's making you late for work or delaying bedtime, remove the distraction or be sure to allow more time. Many families have a "no screens" policy during the week. Have your children pick out their wardrobe the night before. I've heard of some families putting their children to bed in fresh clothes for the next day so the only thing left to do in the morning is eat breakfast, brush their teeth, and put on their shoes. I am not sure I love this idea as I think children probably feel more energized for the day when they have a chance to clean up and transition from night to day, but it is a modern practice and if it works for you, why not? Be creative! Do what it takes to make your life easier, even if it's a bit unusual, so long as it doesn't sacrifice anyone's well-being.

Some parents respond to the challenges of toddlerhood by retreating from the world, so worried that their children won't behave in grown-up public settings they either leave them at home when going out to non-child-centered settings or stick a tablet in their hands so they won't make any noise. But neither strategy teaches kids to behave appropriately. More parents need to venture out with their children, not hide them. We need to give our children more free reign to succeed, and not get angry when they fail. At this age, the consequences are minimal. Yes, it may require a little more effort in the beginning when you want to relax with a glass of wine and talk to your friends and instead you have to make sure your child isn't being noisy or getting into something he shouldn't. But go in with a strategy, share the work with your partner if you can, and keep at it. Children learn your expectations very quickly, and they love to be a part of your life. The more chances you give them to practice, and the more positive reinforcement they get from other adults and from you for being a lovely, interesting, well-mannered child, the easier it will be to take them anywhere.

Here's a tip for a pleasant night out: If you plan to take your children out to an adult setting, ensure that they have had a chance to exercise first. It's amazing how mellow they can be after some high-energy playtime. Also, if you have more than one child relatively close in age, try to separate them by seating one with a parent, a much older child, or a baby so that they can't antagonize each other.

We need to change the way we think about discipline. It's not about implementing restrictions and punishing bad behavior but about teaching and modeling kindness, respect, manners, and compassion. It's about helping children learn to navigate the world in a way that's acceptable to the common norm while still hanging on to their individuality. It's certainly not about command and control. In fact, it's exhausting and ultimately fruitless to try to control another human being, even a young one.

A valuable trick to a calm family life is to prioritize. Decide what is most important to you and your loved ones, and concentrate your energy on that. Your home does not need to be spotless; it's okay if your child decides to wear an unusual outfit to his doctor appointment. I think we could ease a great deal of stress in a lot of people's homes if we stopped spending so much time on things that quite simply do not matter. In sum, once you establish what is usually a short list of what has to get done, and jettison all the things that you only *think* need to get done, you'll find that you'll have to spend less time disciplining and more time having fun with your children than you ever thought you could.

And please don't worry about what other people think. Everyone is going to tell you how great their children are, how responsible, and how accomplished. Having worked in the medical field with children and parents for several decades I know for a fact that many of these people have the same struggles as you, they just choose not to tell you about them. Our children are much more likely to reach their full potential when raised in a loving, harmonious home where the parents enjoy each other and where the kids feel good about themselves because their parents are in tune with their abilities and strengths and challenge them accordingly, rather than in a home where everyone is expected to live up to some unrealistic, even fictional idea of the perfect family, and is reminded of their failure to do so on a daily basis.

9

Play!

DANIEL KISH LOST both of his eyes to retinal cancer when he was just a toddler. Kish is known as "the Batman" because he relies on echolocation—the act of bouncing clicks off hard surfaces to "see" one's environment, like a bat—to get around. It allows him to do everything seeing people do, such as hike the hills of his native California, travel, and perhaps most extraordinary, ride a bike. When his mother, Paulette, realized her son would never see, she realized, as she explained in an interview on *This American Life*, that she had a choice: "Wrap him in cotton so that he didn't get hurt" or "put away" her fear and let him experience the world like any other child. Daniel taught himself echolocation, or as he now calls it, FlashSonar, at an extremely young age. Yet, even when her son got in trouble with the police for climbing a neighbor's fence, even after he knocked out his front teeth by running into a pole at school, and even after he smashed into a metal streetlight after riding downhill full speed on his bike, Paulette stuck to her decision to give him his freedom. Of course everyone kept asking, "How can you let him do that?" But when they did, "she'd look at his smiling face and think, 'How can I not?'"

If Paulette can find the courage to let her blind child ride a bicycle—a child who then grew up to hold two master's degrees and become a role model, teacher, media star, TED Talk lecturer, and founder and president of a nonprofit, World Access for the Blind—then surely the parents of almost every other child in the country should be able to find the courage to let their children do something as simple as cross the street in their own neighborhood or play unsupervised in their front yard, or spend time on their own with friends. Yet that doesn't happen very often. Our fearful culture causes parents to overprotect their children and limit them in every way, from exploring their physical environment to making their own decisions. We don't take the time to let kids try and fail, then try and fail again. Social critics and even some college administrators have lamented that overprotective parents are raising a generation of entitled young adults incapable of making decisions without checking in with Mom and Dad. And it's true that the freedom to experiment and take risks is necessary to promote creativity, innovation, courage, confidence, and grit—the very characteristics for which Americans are famous. But my concern is not only the loss of our national character. My concern is that there are indications that the increasing limits we impose on our young children's freedom are altering their minds as well as their bodies.

As we discussed in chapter 3, our tendency to limit babies' movements has resulted in a 600 percent increase in plagiocephaly, or flat head syndrome, and may even be partially contributing to the childhood obesity epidemic. But there's more. I've seen an increase in young patients suffering from asymmetry, weakness, and problems with balance. Without adequate movement during the first year of life, motor endplates—the neurological connection between the nerves and the muscles—will not develop appropriately; without adequate stimulation, children can't develop the fast twitch muscles necessary for building speed and quick reflexes. It makes me wonder whether we will see a dearth of star athletes one day.

Most disconcerting, however, is that we're seeing a rise in childhood cognitive and behavioral disorders, such as anxiety, depression, and particularly ADHD. What's causing it? There is certainly a genetic component, but why are these conditions exhibiting themselves so much more now than only two or three generations ago? Could it be something in our food? Something in the air? Many researchers and doctors, myself included, believe the uptick may be due in some way to the cultural shifts that are stifling children's freedom, movement, and development.

I suspect that the severity of many of these disorders, and especially many of the common discipline problems parents regularly face when raising children, could be minimized if we increased the amount of unstructured play in this country. The fact is there just isn't enough of it. Babies join a Gymboree Play & Music program; young school-age children unleash themselves in indoor bouncy house facilities; and older children participate in organized sports and take extracurricular classes in gymnastics, martial-arts, and soccer. So they're moving. But they're not *playing*—not the way humans were meant to play: outdoors, unfettered, and after a certain age, without close supervision. Even way back when children were expected to work and contribute to the family income, before the 1950s, children were regularly masters of their free time and left to their own devices to create their own entertainment—most of which took place away from home and hidden from adult eyes.

In many cases the reasons for the decline in free outdoor play are easy to identify. In disadvantaged urban neighborhoods, side-walks are often in disrepair and amenities like parks and play-grounds are few, making it rare to see kids outside doing kid things (and their families certainly can't afford Gymboree Play & Music classes). Where violence is truly rampant, parents under-standably limit their children's time outdoors to keep them safe from danger. But for reasons we explored in chapter 1, parents living in suburban middle-class neighborhoods have also locked their children behind closed doors, convinced by a sensationalist media that danger is everywhere. More working mothers also means fewer kids at home in the afternoons, which means fewer packs of children roaming yards and parks enjoying safety in numbers. Today children are monitored 24/7, and their days are scheduled sunup to sundown. And during the downtime they do have, they're generally reaching for an electronic device to fill the silence. That's not to say there isn't a place for tech in children's lives or that digital entertainment is a bad thing. But too much can easily become an addiction, especially when it constantly fills in those moments children used to typically spend in contempla-tion, or being bored, or even getting into a little trouble here and there. And without those empty moments and those periods of silence, many important components of childhood development that enable problem solving, creativity, and social skills are at high risk of being lost.

When I was growing up in Kenya, I noticed the African fam-ilies imposed very little structure on their little ones. While the men and women worked, the children ran around them playing games that usually seemed made up on the spot. Eventually everyone would settle down for a bit to share something to eat, but there were no fixed timetables, and few rules. When the children returned from school they were free to run around and play for quite a while. I was more supervised than my friends as a young girl, but even then no one interfered with my play. My grandmother's home was a rich and lively environment. There were monkeys bouncing around in their cages together, giant tortoises I could ride, parrots who enjoyed talking to me, and many other exotic tropical creatures. I spent my days with these creatures, and with my friends, and I knew that when I started having my own children, I would want to immerse them in the same comfortable, easygoing environment that allowed children to be children, even if an adult was in the background.

When I was raising my first two babies in the South African desert I was often alone while my husband traveled long distances into the field for his work as a geologist. At the time I was a stay-at-home mom, living in a trailer with a tiny propane-powered refrigerator, but with no running water or power, let alone a phone, dishwasher, or washing machine. I was busy all the time. Everything was done by hand, so we employed Rachina, a young lady who grew up in the bush, to help me during the day (in chapter 2 I introduced her as the woman who shocked me by showing up at my door ready to work a few hours after giving birth to her first child). I loved watching her interact with my children. There were no roads, but we would go for walks, and I'd watch her stop every few feet to break a leaf off a plant and let the children smell it, or dig in the dirt to show them something wriggling about. She would run ahead with my older boy, dancing and singing at the top of her voice to the songs coming from the little radio she carried with her. She showed the children how to make their own fun. During the day, we took turns watching the children, for they were very young and the area had its fair share of snakes and scorpions. We made sure they were safe, but they always had plenty of time and space to roam aimlessly and poke holes in the dirt, chase bugs, and lay on the ground to count clouds.

Their world changed dramatically when we left the desert. After a short stint in the UK, we moved to Colorado. My oldest son was four, his little brother two and a half, and baby Julianne was ten months. We bought a house, chosen for its large front- and backyard, where we imagined the children could continue to play freely. We had not stopped to think, however, that raising the boys out in the desert with no traffic or even neighbors for miles meant they had not developed one shred of street sense. Nor, as it turned out, any respect for doors or locks. Within a day they were racing out of the house into the street, never looking for cars. I called a fencing company whose owner at first told me he couldn't make time to help us for at least a month. I begged him to come and see the situation for himself. It took less than thirty minutes to change his mind once he saw the safety problem. He put all his other jobs on hold and built us a fence within the week.

The children quickly learned urban survival skills, and even as our family changed and grew—my husband and I divorced, I remarried and had my fourth child, David—like all the other parents at the time we made it a point to continue to give them as much freedom as we could. By the time they were school age, we had an understanding with the children that when they heard my husband whistle they were to whistle back and immediately return home. The kids would head out with their friends on their bikes, and as darkness fell, Jim would go out on the porch and whistle. Within seconds, we would hear four whistles back, and know that in a few minutes all four kids would straggle in ready to wash up for dinner. We were not the Waltons living in the middle of rural farmland—it was an average, safe middle-class suburban neighborhood. But we believed it was important that our kids learn to use their good judgment without us hovering over them, that they figure out how to manage their friendships without our input, and that they learn their own physical limits. At the time we were not alone. All the neighborhood children were free to play without adult supervision within reason. (At the time, I found American parents already remarkably stressed, but only later did they add to their anxiety with constant worry about their children's safety.)

These are important lessons that many children simply don't get to learn anymore, despite the fact that children are actually safer in this country today than they have ever been. They're no longer allowed to explore the boundaries of their neighborhoods; their playgrounds are bland and unchallenging for all but the smallest tots; their sports are organized and moderated by adults. Parents rely on camps and extracurricular classes to provide the character-building experiences that were once natural rites of passage. We reassure ourselves that our kids aren't missing out on anything because play is play, and it's not the play that's changed, just the setting. But that's just not the case. By bringing play indoors and imposing our constant close supervision, the play itself has changed significantly. The reevaluation of what's best for kids shouldn't be limited to how much or how little playtime our children should get, but the *type* of play they're allowed to experience. It's not just about getting exercise; it's about allowing children to navigate their own worlds without interference from adults.

Some Western countries are recognizing the need to reintroduce unstructured play into childhood. In Wales, "adventure playgrounds"—which could pass for junk yards and where kids are free to build forts and are even permitted to light fires—are gaining popularity as a movement builds to provide children with a place to make their own rules without any direction from adults. In these experiments, an adult is actually observing these children from a distance, but the children are unaware this is happening. The results have been very good. New Zealand is experimenting with relinquishing all traditional playground rules in favor of more free-form play, having discovered that when kids think they're engaged in dangerous play, they're less likely to get in trouble or to play recklessly and get hurt.

Of course children have always entertained themselves with dolls and small action figures, cards and puzzles. They have spent hours curled up with books. But in addition, even the youngest children spent a great deal of time outdoors where they could engage in gross muscle movement. The human body didn't develop its gross motor skills indoors with toys. Children are built to move and feel and bounce and spend most of their time running, jumping, walking, and lifting. Naturally, few adults will tolerate that kind of big physical behavior indoors and therefore often redirect their kids to line up their cars or play with Legos. Cars and Legos are excellent games, but they develop only fine motor skills. While important, they should be part of short rest periods in between lots of big movement. We're taking bodies that were meant to move and forcing them to sit still and quietly for the majority of their days, even before our kids start school.

Most of us remember a time when school didn't mean the end of play. Day care and preschool used to be almost all crafts, songs, games, and free play. So was kindergarten, for that matter. Now in addition to and sometimes instead of teaching three- to five-year-olds how to use their words and tie their shoes, we're teaching them to read. But at what cost? As one kindergarten teacher lamented in an article for *Scholastic Teacher*, "While young students' reading and math scores are soaring, there is little assessment of the effect of the intensified academic focus on kids' motivation to learn, creativity, motor skills, social skills, or self-esteem. The risk is children who are already burned out on school by the time they reach third grade. School should be a fun place and play is how children learn. There should be more of it in the upper grades, not less in the lower."

Fat chance. Even as America's position in global academic rankings continues to fall, education reformers and politicians, finding it politically inexpedient to tackle the real culprits—poverty, low entry standards for the teaching profession, and this country's lack of respect for teachers and academic life in general—continue to shorten recess and PE for school-aged children, eliminate nap times for kindergarteners, and curtail lunch periods in the name of academic rigor and discipline.

What's interesting is that on any given school day in many of the countries that surpass us academically, children actually enjoy more playtime than ours do. Take Finland, one of the top academic performers for the past several decades. Children don't even start going to school there until age seven, and students and teachers take a fifteen-minute break between forty-five-minute classes. The day is structured much the same way for elementary-age students in Asia. In fact, in a concerted effort to preserve China's competitive edge, which will require heightened levels of creativity and innovation, the Chinese Ministry of Education is encouraging more play into the school day, for example by partnering with Lego Education "to enable 'learning by playing'" and has indicated a need for parents and schools to take steps to "lighten the burden on children . . . giving them more time to play."

We are a nation obsessed with improving our children's cognitive functions so they can compete in an ever-intensifying scramble for limited resources, academic placement, and career opportunities. But it's truly counterproductive to elevate study and practice at the expense of free play. The development of the young immature brain is connected to development of the body; movement and muscular development and those connections to the central nervous system have a huge role affecting everything from balance to logic. Play and gross motor movement are as vital to the cognitive development of an eighteen-month-old as are read-aloud bedtime stories and listening to music. In fact, the cognitive will always be stronger if you attend to the motor development. Always. You have to strike an equal balance.

> It's truly counterproductive to elevate study and practice at the expense of free play.

Delaying formal education until the age of seven so kids get more free playtime during their early years isn't feasible in this country. However, there are easy ways parents can incorporate more free play, supervised when necessary, unsupervised when possible, into their children's days.

TURN OFF THE SCREENS

My first piece of advice probably won't be a big surprise: mini-mize the amount of time your kids spend in front of screens. As we've already discussed, ideally children under the age of two should have minimal exposure to television or computer screens. It is simply not good for the development of the central nervous system. But inevitably, your older child is going to want to watch TV, and you're going to want to let her. There may be no greater moment in new parents' lives than the day their chil-dren are old enough to pour themselves a bowl of cereal and turn on the television while the adults sleep in on the weekends. But we've become a society that purposely introduces screens to keep our children sedentary and quiet at all hours of the day, often to allow us to get as much done as possible, like a home-cooked meal, a workout, or a last-minute spreadsheet. They're not just spending an hour here and there in front of a TV, lap-top, tablet, or phone; on average children up to age eight years are spending about two hours a day on screens. This wouldn't be a problem if the children were spending much of the rest of their time outdoors or moving around, but they're not. Kids have got to have more opportunities to practice their gross motor skills, not just the fine ones that can see improvement from time spent on the computer. Of course, some screen time is fine. I see little kids coming in to the clinic with smartphones or tablets all the time. A doctor's office is a perfectly appropriate place to use an electronic device, especially if it helps distract the child and ease her anxiety. But she needs to play more often with other humans—face to face, without a screen acting as the conduit.

She needs to throw balls, hop, sprint, and scream at the top of her lungs.

THINK HOME FREE

When at home, young children should be playing in the physical world, not the virtual one; so often tablets, smartphones, and TVs are used to keep children out of trouble while the adults are too occupied to supervise closely. But if you've taken the proper precautions to safeguard the environment, you only need to monitor your child with periodic check-ins. Of course you'll have to be prepared for small messes. It's entirely possible your toddler will find it super fun to unroll the toilet paper and trail it as far as it will go down the hall. Take a picture—come on, you have to admit it's funny—and reroll it as best you can. It's still good. If you don't want to find your kitchen turned upside down, install baby-proof latches on the cabinets (especially below the sink) but leave one drawer or cupboard filled with Tupperware and plastic containers available for your children to explore.

When I was in medical school and needed to study, instead of requiring the kids to play quietly indoors so they'd stay out of trouble while I worked, I found it much easier to let them play freely out in the back. I'd perch myself with my computer or book either under a tree or on the deck with a good view of the yard. That way I could look up periodically and watch their play without interfering, and when a kid wanted to show off something I could smile with approval and make him or her feel great. I found I could do this most days, even when the weather wasn't perfect, and the kids didn't mind as long as they were dressed accordingly.

What are the real risks to your child's safety you need to take seriously? I can count on one hand the truly serious recurring childhood injuries that I've seen in more than twenty-five years of practicing medicine.

Falls

Most parents know to baby-proof their home as soon as their children become mobile, but a number of the patients I treat for concussions or severe head contusions haven't even learned to crawl yet. Many of these accidents occur because safety devices give parents a false sense of security. They'll bring their child in from the car still strapped into the car seat, and then place that car seat on a counter or a bed. But those car seats are not stable when they're not locked into place. When the baby grows bigger and moves, the car seat can fall upside down onto the floor with the child in it. Sometimes the baby isn't strapped in, and with one wiggle he flips out of the car seat, often suffering significant head injuries or complex arm or leg fractures as a result. I treated one five-month-old for a terrible bump on his head he got after falling onto a hard tile floor. His parents had placed him in a Bumbo, a squat, squishy chair that when used properly is wonderful for keeping babies sitting upright. The parents, however, had placed the Bumbo onto a dining room chair, and he fell right out.

Dr. Jane's Safety Tip

Always use a car seat when transporting an infant in a car, but if you use the car seat to carry him inside, do not place the car seat anywhere but the floor. Besides, as we discussed in chapter 3, children should be removed from their car seats whenever they're not traveling.

Burns

It's second nature for parents to caution young children to steer clear of the stove when they're cooking and to refrain from placing children within proximity of boiling water. (Be mindful of where you rest your colander of drained hot pasta, too.) But while parents generally remember the boiling pot, they often forget about the cup of steaming hot coffee or tea. It's very easy for a young child to reach a mug placed near the edge of a kitchen table, especially if they're using the table to balance as they toddle by.

If you use a curling iron, be careful where you put it down. Bathroom vanities are relatively low, and kids can easily wrap their hands around the metal barrel. They can also yank on the cord and bring the hot iron down on their head or face.

Finally, few people can resist the dancing glow of a fireplace, especially little ones who see it at eye level. Make sure any gate you put around the perimeter of the fireplace is clipped or bolted down securely and immobile, because otherwise small children can pull the guards onto themselves. If purchasing a glass enclosed gas fireplace, look for one equipped with a mesh to help keep children's hands away—the glass door can get so hot it will melt skin and can cause third-degree burns.

Dr. Jane's Safety Tip

Assume all heat-emitting tools and appliances are on until you have confirmed otherwise. Make it a habit to treat all pots and mugs as though they contained hot liquids.

Poisonings (Including Skin Irritations)

Children are curious. They want to poke and peer and explore, leading with their hands, and often following with their mouths. Brightly colored bottles filled with (toxic) splashy liquid and containers full of (caustic) fluffy powder are natural draws. Some medicines are brightly colored or smell sweet, inviting further investigation. Kitty litter, which can carry toxoplasmosis, is often mistaken for a small sandbox.

Dr. Jane's Safety Tip

Move all household cleaners from underneath the sink to a hard-to-reach location. That includes laundry detergent pods—children have been known to choke on them. Make sure medicine cabinets can be locked, even the ones above the bathroom sink, for children love to climb up to explore what's behind the cabinet doors. If you own a cat, particularly one allowed outside, change its litter daily and keep the litter box contained to an area inaccessible to children.

Drownings

A child can drown in just a few inches of water. I've seen cases where a parent was giving a child a bath, ran downstairs for just a minute, and when he or she got back the child had slipped beneath the surface. There is nothing so important that it can't wait until bath time is over.

Swimming pool accidents are extremely common, too. Some municipal pools require a ratio of one adult to one child under the age of six. While there may be fewer distractions in a private pool than in a public pool, it's not unwise to hold yourself to the same safety standards. But many times, unsupervised children drown in pools because no one knew they were there. Kids simply decide to go play in the backyard without alerting their parents, and they accidentally fall in. Sometimes they will decide on their own to go for a swim or sneak into their neighbor's pools. For this reason, a childproof locked pool gate should surround all private swimming pools. In addition, it's not overkill to place a safety cover over the pool when it's not in use or to install an alarm that goes off whenever anyone enters the pool.

Dr. Jane's Safety Tips

Never leave a child under the age of four alone in a bathroom while the tub is filling. No exceptions.

Never leave a child under the age of four unattended in a bathtub, not even in a child safety seat or baby bath. No exceptions.

Empty the tub as soon as bath time is over. No exceptions.

Never leave a child unsupervised near a swimming pool, not even if he can swim (children can slip and fall unconscious into the water), not even if older children are around, and not even for a minute. No exceptions.

Dog Bites

The CDC reports that about 4.5 million Americans suffer from dog bites per year; half of those cases are children. However, while any dog can unexpectedly display aggression, the majority of dog bites are a result of encounters with strange dogs, not with the family pet. There is no reason to teach children to be afraid of dogs, but you should supervise when a small child is interacting with any animal.

Dr. Jane's Safety Tip

Read up about introducing your established dog to a new baby. Pets can feel quite jealous initially. Teach your children how to interact safely with a pet and supervise very young children when they're around the animal. Even non-aggressive dogs can bite and cats will scratch when caught off guard.

Each of these five common childhood injuries can be prevented with a few simple precautions.

WHAT YOU REALLY NEED

The baby industry wants you to believe that you need to invest hundreds of dollars to baby proof every surface, door, and item of furniture in your home. But here's a list of the only products you really need once your child starts to crawl, pull up, and walk:

- safety gates—one to block access to the stairs if you live in a multilevel home and one to block access to the fireplace
- cabinet locks for any low cabinets where you might store sharp objects, medicines, or chemicals
- electrical outlet covers
- cable organizers and clips, to tuck away and hide loose wires
- a swimming pool fence if you have a pool
- window guards for upper story windows, especially in older homes

For good measure, get on your hands and knees and look at your home from a small child's perspective to see if there is anything clearly dangerous that you might have missed. If you have tall cabinetry or a large TV, bolt it to the wall to prevent children from pulling it down on top of themselves if they decide to try to climb it. Along with any adjustments you need to make for your particular living arrangement, and a car seat, these are really the only purchases you need to make to provide a safe, secure environment for your child. That's not to say your children will never get hurt. They will. Children between twelve and eighteen months frequently have small bruises and sustain minor lacerations. That's normal! Do not allow your imagination to run away with you—you and your children will be calmer, happier, and more confident for it. Kids do crazy things so you need to be alert and watchful. Even if they don't end up with a serious problem, it can be painful, stressful and expensive to deal with.

GET OUTSIDE

Make a concerted effort to help your child go outdoors every day. There is a growing body of research that indicates outside play is not just about giving kids a chance to blow off steam but is mentally restorative and promotes better cognition. (Remember that Finnish children, who score so admirably in school, get seventy-five minutes of free play, usually outside except during the most frigid weather, during the school day.) If you live in a home with a large, secure, child-proof backyard, this shouldn't be a problem, of course. Once your child is four or five years old, you can let him go play by himself. You can check on him by looking out the window off and on, or sit outside and allow him to feel he is exploring the world on his own terms, then join him so you can have fun together. Being outdoors is a stress release for both parents and children, and if there's one message I hope you take away from this book, it's that it's imperative that we work to diminish the amount of stress, anxiety, and overstimulation in our lives. If you're at home with your children, instead of planning your days around errands and classes, make the time you set aside to spend outdoors the highlight of the day and schedule everything else around it. Visit your area parks; take walks with the dog; take walks without the dog; do whatever you can to find places to roam, wander, and explore.

There's no doubt that this recommendation is far easier for stay-at-home parents to follow than for those who work outside the home. But this is where good accredited day care and even after-school care can be a marvelous thing, even part-time. It's a perfect environment for a combination of indoor quiet play and outdoor rambunctiousness. And precisely because the adult-to-child ratio will necessarily be higher (though ideally not more than 1 to 10 for children aged four to five years) than if the children were at home with their parents, the kids get a chance at an early age to safely explore their world a little on their own and develop relationships without their parents' input. Ahn from Vietnam sent her daughter to day care for a while, and said she'd never seen her so happy. "She could play and run as much and as long as she wanted. But then I couldn't afford it." She paid a family member to come and watch the girl after that, but although she knew her daughter was in good, loving hands, she was sure continuing with the day care would have been a better experience for her.

Regardless of who is watching your children, make sure that part of the caregiver's job includes taking your children out every single day, rain or shine, cold or hot. And if you are your children's caretaker, follow the same rule. It doesn't have to be for long, but fresh air is a marvelous tonic for everyone, young and old.

Think of this time with your child as your workout. In fact, if you're crunched for time and physical fitness is a priority, consider replacing your regular workout with time spent in your own backyard playing ball or hopping on a bike with the kids. I guarantee your four-year-old can help you work up a sweat. By the time my oldest was six I could barely keep up with my kids; I was sweating and exhausted after playing in the yard with them. Start this habit early, when your children are babies and just little bundles rolling around on a blanket in the grass, so that they never know any other way. You have to condition your children from an early age to crave the outdoors, so that they approach it as a natural part of their day, not something forced on them. With any luck, you'll start to feel the same way about this special time. It's a mind-set that's extraordinarily nourishing for children and parents and so much fun. You'll be combining the mental decompression of yoga with the aerobic exercise of the treadmill. It's very easy to work up a sweat and get your heart rate going when chasing little kids around. And it's much better than pumping iron or riding a bike in the gym.

Sometimes you're just not going to be in the mood to play, but I urge you to push yourself the same way you would if you had to talk yourself into going to the gym. You'll be amazed at the destressing capabilities, not to mention the workout, of a good game of tag. Parents will find that their family life will be easier and more pleasant if they find ways to get the children out of the house for unstructured play. If they're older, they'll be better students, and overall nicer kids to have around. That should be all the incentive you need.

ENCOURAGE CALCULATED RISK

As your children get older, encourage them to take reasonable calculated risks and challenge themselves. Kids will learn to be safer if you give them the chance to test themselves. Push your girls, in particular, to play rough-and-tumble. I see many more girls than boys coming in with fractures because they don't have as much experience being physical. Boys, who tend to get more exercise and get more experience with falling, roll when they fall, but girls tend to put out an arm to cushion their fall, breaking it in the process. Give all of your children plenty of encouragement to learn their physical limits and practice self-preservation.

That's a hard thing to ask of parents today, I know. We live in a world rife with malpractice suits. The playground equipment most of us knew as children—merry-go-rounds, tall slides, see-saws, even diving boards at the neighborhood pool—have disappeared. Yet in trying to prevent our worst nightmares, we threaten to limit not only our kids' motor skills but also their cognitive and emotional growth. At the same time, we risk our children's lives more every time we put them in an automobile than when we send them to the playground or a neighborhood park.

Kids will seek out risk no matter how much you try to protect them from it. If you see your children taking the opportunity to challenge themselves physically, take a breath and assess, asking, Is the risk they are taking life and death? Stop yourself from robbing them of important life lessons. Learning to handle fear and risk is important. If a minor accident occurs, don't interpret it as a failure on your part, or your child's. It's a lesson. I cannot tell you your children will never get hurt if you take this approach to child-rearing—they probably will. Children get hurt whether you try to protect them or not. That's how each of us learns—falling and knowing that you can get up again. Our imaginations lead us to believe that catastrophe could wait around every corner, but if we lived our lives that way we'd never do anything interesting.

Let's not impose a negative outlook on our children. If we learn to accept the small bumps and bruises with a little more equanimity, it might be easier for us to live without fear and, more important, we need to teach our children to live without it, too. They'll be stronger and smarter for it. Give them the freedom to become strong, independent, and fearless, all qualities that will help them succeed later in life. And you—start making more time to play, alone and with your children. The more we decrease parental stress and increase children's playtime, the closer we will be to turning the tide on many of the most baffling and heartbreaking problems plaguing families today.

Final Thoughts

WHEN MY SON Cameron was about five years old he shimmied out an open car window while I was driving so he could ride the roof rack. Not long after, he skied down my snow-covered roof. So it shouldn't have surprised me that as he grew up he refused to take any traditional path. When he was about sixteen years old we were discussing his future, and I suggested he'd make a wonderful doctor. He looked at me and said, "Become a doctor? No, it's not for me! There are many easier ways to make money and have a fun life." I'd never felt that I wasn't having fun doing work I love, but, obviously, everyone has a different perspective. I smiled and said, "Well, Cam, go grab life by the horns." And he did. This boy, born in the desert and raised with the spirit of Africa, ultimately became an entrepreneur—and a classic American success story.

I would never suggest we should let our children ski down our rooftops. But I'm glad my son did and that he did not get hurt, and I'm glad that I raised all of my children to be unafraid to take some risks, to play hard, and to experiment. Each of them has taken a completely different approach to life than I did, and they've each succeeded marvelously. The one thing they all have in common is that they have refused to live by anyone else's rules but their own. I believe that's the end result of the relatively unusual freedom they enjoyed as children. They're creative, productive, and adventurous, and I see many of the same traits in their own children. I'm never happier than when I have them all together under my roof. But then, that's been the case since the day they came into my life. Parenthood hasn't always been without challenge, of course, but it never brought me to the level of stress, anxiety, or fear that I see so many parents grappling with today. If you're one of them, it is my sincere hope that by sharing my global perspective and professional knowledge, I can help ease some of that burden from your shoulders.

You don't need to be afraid. In fact, you can be fearless, and teach your children to be, too. Understanding that most of the fears driving parenting trends today are irrational and unfounded will go a tremendous way toward allowing you to be the parent you want to be. From stomach bugs to less-than-stellar report cards, parenting will always have its challenges, but with life as complicated and busy as it is today, we need to actively take steps to lessen the friction and tension in our homes. It should be our oasis from the madness of the outside world. Let's make our moments with our children relaxed and happy, so that we don't reach the end of the day wishing for a do-over. This time is short—we should make it as enjoyable as we can. We are so lucky that we live in an era where we have the luxury to enjoy our children. Let's not waste it.

You don't need to be afraid.

The changes recommended in this book don't require that families reject everything that makes Americans so . . . American. Ambition, self-sufficiency, and a strong can-do spirit are distinctly American characteristics, and this country is better for it.

But we do have to acknowledge the effects that our distinctly American tendency to pursue everything at full throttle is having on our children. Leaning in may be the way to a fulfilling career, but in the parenting sphere, leaning out is the way to a fulfilling and rewarding experience.

It's natural to want to give our children as much as or more than we had when we were young, but I promise that if you can't your children won't suffer. They will suffer, however, if you're not your best self because you're so busy and stressed by everything you have to do to provide those advantages you think they deserve or that are supposedly the new requirements for success. If this starts happening, take a look at how you could change the allocation of your resources so that you're spending your money and your time where it will actually count and in ways that will allow you to parent in a positive, fun-loving way. This isn't a call to downsize or switch to a less demanding job or move into a less expensive home, though for some, that may be a solution. It's a call to recognize what is really necessary for a child's healthy development aside from the basics of food and safe shelter. The list is short: family, friends, and play. These are the fundamentals. And so easy!

In the end, this is my prescription for improving the state of American parenthood and improving the health of our children:

Reject the fearmongering.
Adopt best practices.
Slow down.

Could it really be that simple? In my experience, it is. As someone who has treated children of every age, from babies in the NICU to high-school teenagers, I can promise that the vast majority of the time, your nightmares will not come true. Empower yourself to reject the brand of high-stakes, fear-based parenting that has become our gold standard and adopt the simpler, less-all-consuming child-rearing methods that are still in practice all over the world. It would be a shame to spend the short years you get to enjoy living with your children worrying about what could go wrong instead of appreciating everything that's already right.

Parents have important obligations and responsibilities, and they have every right to pursue work that fulfills them and interests that have nothing to do with their children. But when life with a baby starts feeling difficult or overwhelming, try to stop worrying about getting everything done and just worry about getting done what needs to get done; your stress levels will decrease and the overall tenor of family interactions will improve. Turn off the screens a lot more. Make time to get on the floor and let your babies roll around freely. Later, make time for one round of Candy Land before bed. As soon as possible, allow your children to be a part of the effort to keep home life calm and relaxed. If dinner needs to be made, show your toddler how to use the salad spinner. If dishes need to be washed, do it side by side with your five-year-old . . . or leave the dishes in the sink until later or tomorrow. And above all, when you are with your children, be with your children—not "mostly" with your children except for the part of you that is texting, tweeting, and checking your Instagram account.

I hope I have given you reasons and strategies for reducing the stress and guilt that our culture imposes on parents so you can feel more confident, have more fun, and remember that being a parent is supposed to be a joy, not a job. This book likely did not teach you how to be a perfect parent, but I hope it did teach you to be happy being the best parent you can be.

Acknowledgments

Thank you to my four children, who in the last few years have joined me in a business that allows me to continue living my passion so that I can spend the remainder of my working life helping children—I owe you!

I am grateful to Stephanie Land, who worked so hard to help me write this book. Thank you, Stephanie. My deep appreciation goes to my agent, Brandi Bowles, at Foundry Literary & Media, and to my editor, Marian Lizzi, at TarcherPerigee, for their invaluable editorial insight and constant support.

I have the incredible good fortune to count Lydia Miller as part of my village. Your friendship and support during the years I attended medical school mean the world to me.

I am indebted to all the parents who have allowed me to care for their children over the years, especially to those who shared their stories with me for this book.

Many thanks to all the educational institutions, hospitals, and clinics that have given me the opportunity and knowledge to serve my patients, including:

ACC Littleton, Colorado

University of Colorado, Denver, Colorado

Duke University Medical Center, Durham, North Carolina

St Joseph's Hospital, Denver, Colorado

St. Luke's Magic Valley Medical Center, Twin Falls, Idaho

Physicians Center, Twin Falls, Idaho

Pediatric Care Nightly, Highlands Ranch, Colorado

Notes

Chapter 1

such as the Austin woman: Kari Anne Roy, "It's All Fun and Games Until Your Neighbor Decides That She Is the Boss of Fun and Games," *Haiku of the Day*, September 9, 2014, haikuoftheday.com/haiku_of_the _day/2014/09/it-was-a-monday-late-morning-hotter-than-hot-we -were-not-even-24-hours-home-from-vacation-and-i-was-going -through-the-pil.html.

the Maryland couple charged: "Silver Springs Parents Charged with 'Child Neglect' for Allowing Kids to Walk Home Alone," ABC News, March 8, 2015, wjla.com/articles/2015/03/silver-spring-parents-charged-with -child-neglect-for-allowing-kids-to-walk-home-alone-112094.html.

1 in 68 children diagnosed with autism spectrum disorder: "Autism Prevalence on the Rise: 1 in 68 Children Diagnosed with Autism Spectrum Disorder," American Academy of Pediatrics, March 27, 2014, aap.org/en-us/about-the-aap/aap-press-room/Pages/Autism-Prevalence -on-the-Rise-1-in-68-Children-Diagnosed-With-Autism-Spectrum -Disorder.aspx.

1 in 8 children diagnosed with an anxiety disorder: "Facts and Statistics," Anxiety and Depression Association of America, last updated September 2014, www.adaa.org/about-adaa/press-room/facts-statistics.

increased rates of asthma: Alice Park, "Parental Stress Increases Kids' Risk of Asthma," *Time*, July 22, 2009, content.time.com/time/health/article /0,8599,1912184,00.html.

a 50 percent increase in ADHD diagnoses: Maggie Severns, "ADHD Diagnoses Increased More Than 50% in a Decade," *Mother Jones*, April 2, 2013, www.motherjones.com/blue-marble/2013/04/study -diagnoses-adhd-are-more-50-percent-over-ten-years.

increased levels of juvenile depression: University of Washington, "Kids' Anxiety, Depression Halved When Parenting Styled to Personality," EurekAlert!, August 1, 2011, www.eurekalert.org/pub_releases/2011 -08/uow-kad072811.php.

a 35 percent increase of type 2 diabetes and hypertension: Alba Morales Pozzo, MD, "Pediatric Type 2 Diabetes Mellitus," Medscape, updated May 12, 2014, http://reference.medscape.com/article/925700-overview.

The Korowai tribe of New Guinea: Paul Raffaele, "Sleeping with Cannibals," *Smithsonian Magazine*, September 2006, www .smithsonianmag.com/travel/sleeping-with-cannibals-128958913/?all.

at one point back in the 1970s: Bee Wilson, "Honey, I Poisoned the Kids," *The Guardian*, August 25, 2005, www.theguardian.com/science/2005 /aug/25/health.society.

On average, there are only 80 to 100 cases of infant botulism reported: Jeremy Sobel, "Botulism," *Clinical Infectious Diseases* 41, no. 8 (2005): 1167–73, http://cid.oxfordjournals.org/content/41/8/1167.full#ref-19.

Botulism spores can be found in dirt, water, and dust, including the dust from your vacuum cleaner: American Society for Microbiology, "Vacuum Dust: A Previously Unknown Disease Vector," ScienceDaily, September 20, 2013, www.sciencedaily.com/releases/2013/09/130930 152745.htm.

Even if a child does contract infant botulism: California Department of Health Services, "Frequently Asked Questions (FAQs) about Infant Botulism," n.d., infantbotulism.org/general/faq.php.

Miriam, who grew up in the States but now lives in Israel: Miriam A., personal interview, October 13, 2015.

In one study conducted by researchers: Sara F. Waters, Tessa V. West, and Wendy Berry Mendes, "Stress Contagion: Physiological Covariation between Mothers and Infants," *Psychological Science*, December 21, 2013, pss.sagepub.com/content/early/2014/01/29/0956797613518352 .abstract.

As writer Erika Christakis said: Cited in *What Is the Goal of Parenting*, Aspen Ideas Festival, July 2, 2012, video, aspenideas.org/session /what-goal-parenting#.

Kate, an Australian who frequently visits her American mother's large extended family: Kate G., personal interview, October 12, 2015.

For Borgit, an American who lived in Guatemala and Venezuela: Borgit
O., personal interview, October 14, 2015.

**over a four-year period, the US Consumer Product Safety Commission
received reports:** "CPSC Warns: Pools Are Not the Only Drowning
Danger at Home for Kids—Data Show Other Hazards Cause More Than
100 Residential Child Drowning Deaths Annually," US Consumer
Product Safety Commission, May 23, 2002, cpsc.gov/en/Newsroom
/News-Releases/2002/CPSC-Warns-Pools-Are-Not-the-Only-Drowning
-Danger-at-Home-for-KidsData-Show-Other-Hazards-Cause More
-than-100-Residential-Child-Drowning-Deaths-Annually.

a $250 baby monitoring sock: John Biggs, "Owlet, The Smart Baby Bootie,
Raises 1.85 Million," TechCrunch, April 22, 2014, techcrunch.com
/2014/04/22/owlet-the-smart-baby-bootie-raises-1-85-million.

one of the main predictors of unintentional injuries and fatalities:
"Unintentional Injury Risk for Children" SafeKids of Gainesville/Hall
County, 2013, safekidsgainesvillehall.org/unintentional-injury-risk
-for-children.html.

Chapter 2

it's been identified as one of the key causes: Victoria M. Indivero, "Classes
Reduced Pregnancy Complications for Stressed Mothers," Penn State
News, June 26, 2014, news.psu.edu/story/319359/2014/06/26/research
/classes-reduce-pregnancy-complications-stressed-mothers.

tests are now available to screen for more than 800 genetic disorders: Jane
E. Brody, "Breakthroughs in Prenatal Screening," *New York Times,*
October 7, 2013, well.blogs.nytimes.com/2013/10/07/breakthroughs
-in-prenatal-screening.

Studies show that mothers with higher-than-normal cortisol levels:
Indivero, "Classes Reduced Pregnancy Complications."

ultrasounds are a routine part of every prenatal visit: Erica, date n/a,
interview with Ameena Gorton, "Having a Baby Abroad—Global
Differences Series: Japan," *Mummy in Provence Blog,* n.d., www
.mummyinprovence.com/having-baby-japan-expat.

some doctors have been known to call a woman's employer:
Naly, Comment posted on November 17, 2014, to "Please Have
Your Baby during Working Hours: 10 Tips on Giving Birth in
Japan," Elizabeth Tasker, *Gaijin Pot,* September 30, 2013, injapan
.gaijinpot.com/featured-photo/2013/09/30/10-facts-about-giving
-birth-in-japan.

"a 2011 study published by nurses at the University of Illinois at Chicago": Melinda Wenner Moyer, "The Truth about Epidurals," *Slate*, January 11, 2012, www.slate.com/articles/health_and_science/medical _examiner/2012/01/the_truth_about_epidurals.html.

some nurses are being trained to dissuade mothers: Julie Deardorff, "Baby Nursery vs. 'Rooming In' Is a Debate for Some New Moms," *Chicago Tribune*, November 17, 2013, articles.chicagotribune.com/2013-11-17 /news/ct-rooming-in-promo-20131115_1_nursery-moms-rooming-in.

In Bali, new mothers are expected to stay out of the kitchen: Hilary Brenhouse, "Why Are America's Postpartum Practices So Rough on New Mothers?" The Daily Beast, August 15, 2013, thedailybeast.com /witw/articles/2013/08/15/america-s-postpartum-practices.html.

they and their baby can expect daily massages: Cheryl Murfin, "Lying In," *Seattle's Child,* March 2, 2012, www.seattleschild.com/Lying-In.

Miriam raved about her experience in Israel: Miriam A., personal interview.

12 percent of US workers having access to paid family leave: "DOL Factsheet: Paid Family and Medical Leave," US Department of Labor, updated June 2015, dol.gov/wb/PaidLeave/PaidLeave.htm.

a quarter of the 71 percent of mothers who work outside the home: Sharon Lerner, "The Real War on Families: Why the US Needs Paid Leave Now," In These Times, August 18, 2015, inthesetimes.com/article /18151/the-real-war-on-families.

Even new mothers in Colonial America: Richard W. Wertz and Dorothy C. Wertz, *Lying In: A History of Childbirth in America* (New Haven, CT, and London: Yale University Press, 1989), pp. 3–4.

an article in the *Washington Post* in 2014: Amy Joyce, "Would You Hire Someone to Be with Your Baby at Night?," *Washington Post*, July 15, 2014, washingtonpost.com/news/parenting/wp/2014/07/15/would -you-hire-someone-to-be-with-your-baby-at-night.

Chapter 3

developmental milestones are often shaped by what a culture decides is most important: Joseph Henrich, Steven J. Heine, and Ara Norenzayan, "The Weirdest People in the World," *Behavioral and Brain Sciences* 33, nos. 2–3 (2010): 61–83.

infants raised in traditional Kenyan villages: Charles M. Super, "Environmental Effects on Motor Development: The Case of 'African

Infant Precocity,'" *Developmental Medicine and Child Neurology* 18, no. 5 (1976): 561–67.

in Papua, New Guinea, babies born to the Au: Kate Gammon, "Crawling: A New Evolutionary Trick," *Popular Science*, November 1, 2013, www .popsci.com/blog-network/kinderlab/crawling-new-evolutionary-trick.

In a nomadic society or one at risk from predators or parasites on the ground: Dan Johnson, "Discovery: Will Baby Crawl?," *National Science Foundation*, July 21, 2004, www.nsf.gov/discoveries/disc_summ.jsp?cntn _id=103153.

almost 50 percent of infants ages seven to twelve weeks are affected: A. Mawji, A. R. Vollman, D. A. McNeil, and R. Sauvé, "The Incidence of Positional Plagiocephaly: A Cohort Study," *Pediatrics* 132, no. 2 (2013): 298–304.

Infants with flat head syndrome are at risk: Robert I. Miller, MD, and Sterling K. Clarren, MD, "Long-Term Developmental Outcomes in Patients With Deformational Plagiocephaly," *Pediatrics*, vol. 105, issue 2 (2000), pediatrics.aappublications.org/content/105/2/e26

***The New England Journal of Medicine* recently released statistics:** Cited in Gina Kolata, "Obesity Is Found to Gain Its Hold in Earliest Years," *New York Times*, January 29, 2014, www.nytimes.com/2014/01/30/science /obesity-takes-hold-early-in-life-study-finds.html?_r=0.

with the cerebellum: Linda Chang, Thomas M. Ernst, Steven D. Buchthal, et al., "Novel Study Maps Infant Brain Growth in First Three Months of Life Using MRI Technology," UC San Diego Health, August 11, 2014, health.ucsd.edu/news/releases/Pages/2014-08-11-study-maps -infant-brain-development.aspx.

Jamaican mothers use bath time to stretch: B. Hopkins and T. Westra, "Maternal Handling and Motor Development: An Intracultural Study," *Genetic, Social, and General Psychology Monographs* 114, no. 3 (1988): 377–408, ncbi.nlm.nih.gov/pubmed/3192073.

Mothers in the Mithila region of India and Nepal: Nadja Reissland and Richard Burghart, "The Role of Massage in South Asia: Child Health and Development," *Social Science & Medicine* 25, no. 3 (1987): 231–239, community.dur.ac.uk/n.n.reissland/publication%20files/The%20role% 20of%20massage%20in%20south%20asia.pdf.

the uptick of children in their care experiencing motor delays could be traced: "Lack of 'Tummy Time' Leads to Increased Motor Delays in Infants, PTs Say," American Physical Therapy Association, last updated June 3, 2013, apta.org/Media/Releases/Consumer/2008/8/6.

Some research suggests bold contrasts are restful: Dr. S. Ludington-Hoe, *How to Have a Smarter Baby* (New York: Bantam Books, 1985), p. 75. Cited in HuggaMind, "Infant Brain Stimulation," www.huggamind .com/highcontrast.php.

Babies as young as three to five days old are already mimicking: Birgit Mampe, Angela D. Friederici, Anne Christophe, and Kathleen Wermke, "Neworns' Cry Melody Is Shaped by Their Native Language," *Current Biology* 19, no. 23 (2009): 1994–97.

newborns only hours old showed a greater interest: "Newborns Know Their Native Tongue, Study Finds," LiveScience, January 2, 2013, livescience.com/25908-newborns-learn-native-language.html.

As early as three months old: "News: Babies Tune in to Human Voices Even When Asleep," King's College London, January 7, 2011, kcl.ac.uk /newsevents/news/newsrecords/2011/06June/Babies-tune--human -voices-even-when-asleep.aspx.

Around the world, lullabies are remarkably similar: Nina Perry, "The Universal Language of Lullabies," BBC News Magazine, January 21, 2013, bbc.com/news/magazine-21035103.

Mary Martini, a professor at the University of Hawaii: Mei-Ling Hopgood, *How Eskimos Keep Their Babies Warm* (Chapel Hill, NC: Algonquin, 2012), p. 197.

As one Nairobian woman said in response: Emily Wax, "An Idea Still Looking for Traction in Kenya," *Washington Post*, May 18, 2004, washingtonpost.com/wp-dyn/articles/A34654-2004May17.html.

the vast majority of kids over the age of four: Victoria Rideout, *Learning at Home: Families Educational Media Use in America*, A Report of the Families and Media Project (New York: Joan Ganz Cooney Center at Sesame Workshop, 2014), p. 6, www.joanganzcooneycenter.org/wp -content/uploads/2014/01/jgcc_learningathome.pdf.

Studies have shown that young children who spend time: Juana Summers, "Kids and Screen Time: What Does the Research Say?" NPR, August 28, 2014, www.npr.org/sections/ed/2014/08/28/343735856/kids-and -screen-time-what-does-the-research-say.

Chapter 4

I remember a conversation I once had with Anh: Personal interview, February 2015.

millennial mothers with children under the age of 18: Suzanne Woolley, "This Is the Most Stressed-Out Person in America," Bloomberg Business,

February 4, 2015, www.bloomberg.com/news/articles/2015-02-04
/this-is-the-most-stressed-out-person-in-america.

"It is not enough to want to be a good parent": Sobonfu E. Somé,
*Welcoming Spirit Home: Ancient African Teachings to Celebrate
Children and Community* (Novato, CA: New World Library, 1999),
p. 141.

In Denmark, whose citizens repeatedly land: Vanessa Loder, "Why
American Mothers Have Less Leisure Time and Find Ourselves
Overwhelmed and Exhausted," Huffpost Parents, July 29, 2014, www
.huffingtonpost.com/vanessa-loder/why-american-mothers-have_b
_5630825.html.

In Belgium, most kids start preschool: Julian Herman, Sasha Post, and
Scott O'Halloran, "The United States Is Far Behind Other Countries on
Pre-K," Center for American Progress, May 2, 2013, www
.americanprogress.org/issues/education/report/2013/05/02/62054
/the-united-states-is-far-behind-other-countries-on-pre-k.

not even 50 percent of three-year-olds are enrolled in preschool: Ibid.

**Danish moms—most of whom work—routinely get about ninety minutes
of child-free time:** Brigid Schulte, *Overwhelmed* (New York: Picador,
2014), p. 216

**A study published in the April 2014 issue of the *Journal of American
Marriage and Family*:** Brigid Schulte, "Making Time for Kids? Study
Says Quality Trumps Quality," *Washington Post*, March 28, 2015, www
.washingtonpost.com/local/making-time-for-kids-study-says-quality
-trumps-quantity/2015/03/28/10813192-d378-11e4-8fce-3941fc548f1c
_story.html?tid=pm_local_pop.

It's during adolescence: Ibid.

Research shows that a child under the age of six: Ibid.

"Working makes me a better parent": Kate G., personal interview,
February 2015.

In a *New York Times* article: Sam Roberts, "Divorce after 50 Grows More
Common," *New York Times*, September 20, 2013, www.nytimes.com
/2013/09/22/fashion/weddings/divorce-after-50-grows-more-common
.html?_r=1.

"It's not something you can put on the back burner": Ibid.

"If a child grows up with the idea": Sobonfu E. Somé, *Welcoming Spirit
Home*, p. 141.

Same-sex couples seem to be better: Lourdes Garcia-Navarro, "Same-Sex
Couples May Have More Egalitarian Relationships," interview with
Robert-Jay Green, NPR, last updated December 29, 2014 www.npr.org

/2014/12/29/373835114/same-sex-couples-may-have-more-egalitarian
-relationships.

fathers in general reportedly get about three hours: Wendy Wang, "The
'Leisure Gap' between Mothers and Fathers," Pew Research Center,
October 17, 2013, pewresearch.org/fact-tank/2013/10/17/the-leisure
-gap-between-mothers-and-fathers.

Then the couple can work together to find: Alexandra Bradner, "Some
Theories on Why Men Don't Do as Many Household Tasks," *The
Atlantic*, March 11, 2013 http://www.theatlantic.com/sexes/archive/2013
/03/some-theories-on-why-men-dont-do-as-many-household-tasks
/273834/.

Chapter 5

A recent study from the University of Michigan: "Only One-Third of
Parents Follow Doctors' Orders for Kids All of the Time," University of
Michigan Health System, March 18, 2013, www.uofmhealth.org/news
/archive/201303/only-one-third-parents-follow-doctors%E2%80%99
-orders-kids-all-time.

**admonishments from nineteenth- and even twentieth-century
pediatricians:** Therese Oneill, "'Don't Think of Ugly People': How
Parenting Advice Has Changed," *The Atlantic*, April 19, 2013,
theatlantic.com/health/archive/2013/04/dont-think-of-ugly-people
-how-parenting-advice-has-changed/275108.

In her best seller *Bringing Up Bébé*: Pamela Druckerman, *Bringing Up Bébé*
(New York: Penguin Press, 2012), pp. 39–40.

By the age of six months, Dutch babies: Kay Hymowitz, "Why Are
American Parents So Unhappy: A Theory," *Family Studies*, June 9,
2014, family-studies.org/why-are-american-parents-so-unhappy
-a-theory.

She suggests that from the beginning new parents teach: Ibid.

**she points to a comparative study between Dutch and American
mothers:** Ibid.

Ferber insists that CIO as interpreted: Editors of Parenting.com, "The
Truth about the Ferber Method," *Parenting Magazine*, n.d., parenting
.com/article/the-truth-about-ferberizing.

**One author, Dr. Alicia Lieberman of the University of California, San
Francisco, insisted:** Cited in Jeffrey Kluger, "The Science behind Dr.
Sears: Does It Stand Up?" *Time Magazine*, May 10, 2012, ideas.time
.com/2012/05/10/the-science-behind-dr-sears-does-it-stand-up.

babies who share a bed with their mothers: Antonia Hoyle, "The New
Parenting Fad Experts Fear Could Kill Your Baby," *Daily Mail*, last
updated August 22, 2013, www.dailymail.co.uk/femail/article-2399238
/Co-sleeping-new-parenting-fad-experts-fear-KILL-baby.html.

One report that drew together the results of five studies: James R. Hood,
"Bed-Sharing with Baby: Fun but Not Safe," ConsumerAffairs, August
26, 2013, www.consumeraffairs.com/news/bed-sharing-with
-baby-fun-but-not-safe-082613.html.

Out of over 8,000 cases of unexplained infant deaths: Jeffrey D. Colvin,
Vicki Collie-Akers, Christy Schunn, and Rachel Y. Moon, "Sleep
Environment Risks for Younger and Older Infants," *Pediatrics*, 134, no. 2
(2014): e406–12, pediatrics.aappublications.org/content/134/2/e406.

Chapter 6

many cultures around the world supplement breastfeeding: Amy Tuteur,
"Viewpoint: The Breastfeeding Police Are Wrong about Formula," *Time*,
May 13, 2013, ideas.time.com/2013/05/13/viewpoint-the-breastfeeding
-police-are-wrong-about-formula.

for millennia it was tradition for many cultures across the globe: Michel
Odent, *Birth and Breastfeeding* (West Hoathly, UK: Clairview Books,
2007), pp. 81–84.

Native populations of Guatemala, Korea, and Sierra Leone: Jan Riordan
and Karen Wambach, *Breastfeeding and Human Lactation* (Burlington,
VT: Jones and Bartlett Learning, 2010), p. 806.

women who blog about their experiences giving birth in Japan: "Mother's
Milk—and Others' Milk—in Japan," *Breastfeeding without BS* blog,
December 20, 2012, breastfeedingwithoutbs.blogspot.com/2012/12
/mothers-milk-and-others-milk-in-japan.html.

Some of the beneficial proteins found in breast milk: Marie Biancuzzo,
Breastfeeding the Newborn: Clinical Strategies for Nurses (Herndon, VA:
Gold Standard Publishing, 2002).

increasing the duration and exclusivity of breastfeeding: R. M. Martin, R.
Patel, M. S. Kramer, et al., "Effects of Promoting Longer-Term and
Exclusive Breastfeeding on Adiposity and Insulin-Like Growth Factor-I
at Age 11.5 Years: A Randomized Trial," *Journal of the American Medical
Association* 13, no. 309 (2013): 1005–13, ncbi.nlm
.nih.gov/pubmed/23483175.

breastfed children appear to be at higher risk for asthma: Emily Caldwell,
"Breast-Feeding Benefits Appear to Be Overstated, According to

Study of Siblings," Research and Innovation Communications, Ohio State University, February 25, 2014, researchnews.osu.edu/archive /sibbreast.htm.

According to Cynthia Colen, associate professor of sociology at Ohio State University: Cited in Caldwell, "Breast-Feeding Benefits Appear to Be Overstated."

A 2005 study of siblings: Cited in Julie E. Artis, "Breastfeed at Your Own Risk," *Contexts*, November 12, 2009, contexts.org/articles/breast feed-at-your-own-risk.

infant mortality rates of many countries plagued with poor sanitary conditions: "Breastfeeding Report Card," Centers for Disease Control and Prevention, 2014, www.cdc.gov/breastfeeding/pdf/2014breast feedingreportcard.pdf.

their long-term breastfeeding rates are actually quite high: Cited in Tuteur, "Viewpoint: The Breastfeeding Police Are Wrong about Formula."

when formula was offered to babies struggling to gain weight: Cited in Tuteur, "Viewpoint: The Breastfeeding Police Are Wrong about Formula."

In 2013, the UK started offering poor women shopping vouchers: Nick Triggle, "Breastfeeding Mothers Offered £200 in Shop Vouchers," BBC News, November 12, 2013, bbc.com/news/health-24900650.

eligible Australian mothers (those who earn less than $150,000): Department of Human Services, "Parental Leave Pay," Australian Government, last updated March 2016, humanservices.gov.au /customer/services/centrelink/parental-leave-pay.

Chapter 7

six-month-olds in Japan: Vanessa Beddoe, "Baby Food around the World," ReachMe, June 13, 2012, www.reachme.co.nz/Articles-Blogs/Food -and-Recipes/Baby-Food-Around-the-World.aspx.

50 percent of children aged four to twenty-four months: Betty Ruth Carruth, Paula J. Ziegler, Anne Gordon, and Susan Barr, "Prevalence of Picky Eaters among Infants and Toddlers and Their Caregivers' Decisions about Offering a New Food," *Journal of the Academy of Nutrition and Dietetics* 104, suppl. 1 (2004): 57–64.

some research does suggest that some kids are biologically more sensitive: Francine Russo, "Picky Eaters Are Not All Alike," *Scientific American*, July 1, 2015, www.scientificamerican.com/article/picky -eaters-are-not-all-alike.

A typical school day: Christine Gross-Loh, *Parenting without Borders* (New York: Penguin Group, 2013), pp. 65–66.

American Association of Pediatrics only recommends: L. Turner, M. Eliason, A. Sandoval, and F. J. Chaloupka, *Most US Public Elementary Schools Provide Students Only Minimal Time to Eat Lunch*, BTG Research Brief (Chicago: Bridging the Gap Program, Health Policy Center, Institute for Health Research and Policy, University of Illinois at Chicago, 2014), bridgingthegapresearch.org/_asset/0h178v/BTG _lunchtime_brief_Oct2014_FINAL.pdf.

When everyone is having the same meal: Dr. Art Markman and Bob Duke, "Diets, Dieting, and Food Rituals," *Two Guys on Your Head* podcast, KUT News 90.5, NPR, July 30, 2015, npr.org/podcasts/381443482 /two-guys-on-your-head.

With that information, she'll offer the kids a few suggestions: Email, October 2015.

the rate of children suffering from peanut allergies: Dr. James Aw, "How Medical Science Got It Exactly Wrong on Childhood Food Allergies," *National Post*, April 9, 2013, news.nationalpost.com/health/how -medical-science-got-it-exactly-wrong-on-childhood-food-allergies.

at about seven months, Israeli infants are consuming: George Du Toit, Graham Roberts, Peter H. Sayre, et al., "Randomized Trial of Peanut Consumption in Infants at Risk for Peanut Allergy," *New England Journal of Medicine* 372 (2015): 803–13, nejm.org/doi/full/10.1056 /NEJMoa1414850#t=article.

Children exposed to peanut protein before the age of one year: "Popular Snack Bamba May Explain Why So Few Israeli Kids are Allergic to Peanuts," *Haaretz*, February 24, 2015, haaretz.com/life/science -medicine/1.644028.

Poverty and lower socioeconomic status often determines: "Obesity Update," Organisation for Economic Co-Operation and Development, June 2014, oecd.org/health/Obesity-Update-2014.pdf.

"not too much": Michael Pollan, *In Defense of Food* (New York: Penguin Press, 2008), p. 1.

children's long-term eating habits: Laurence M. Grummer-Strawn, Ruowei Li, Cria G. Perrine, Kelley S. Scanlon, and Sara B. Fein, "Infant Feeding and Long-Term Outcomes: Results from the Year 6 Follow-Up of Children in the Infant Feeding Practices Study II," *Pediatrics* 134, suppl. 1 (2014):S1– S3, pediatrics.aappublications.org/content/134/Supplement_1/S1.full.

For the first time in about forty years, the number of calories: Margot Sanger Katz, "Americans Are Finally Eating Less," *New York Times*

Magazine, July 24, 3015, nytimes.com/2015/07/25/upshot/americans
-are-finally-eating-less.html?abt=0002&abg=1.

the obesity rate in children aged two to five years: Sabrina Tavernise,
"Obesity Rate for Young Children Plummets 43% in a Decade," *New
York Times,* February 25, 2014, nytimes.com/2014/02/26/health
/obesity-rate-for-young-children-plummets-43-in-a-decade.html.

Chapter 8

the *Huffington Post* published an article: Sarah Fader, "3-Year Olds Are
A**holes," Huffpost Parents, last updated April 29, 2014, www
.huffingtonpost.com/sarah-fader/threeyearolds-are-asshole_b
_4784416.html.

a YouTube video spoofing the habit of mothers using *la chancla*: "*La
Chancla,*" YouTube video, June 1, 2012, www.youtube.com/watch
?v=CMij9AKLvog.

social media threads: "For Those of You Who Don't Know What a 'Chancla'
Is," Reddit, July 27, 2013, www.reddit.com/r/videos/comments/1j61ug
/for_those_of_you_who_dont_know_what_a_chancla_is.

"I hit you because I love you": Yilu Zhao, "Cultural Divide over Parental
Discipline," *New York Times,* May 29, 2002, nytimes.com/2002/05/29
/nyregion/cultural-divide-over-parental-discipline.html.

social class has more effect on parental values: J. R. H. Tudge, D. M. Hogan,
I. A. Snezhkova, N. N. Kulakova, and K. E. Etz, "Parents' Child-Rearing
Values and Beliefs in the United States and Russia: The Impact of Culture
and Social Class," *Infant and Child Development* 9 (2000): 106.

In a follow-up interview, the author explained: "Mom Gets Real about the
Serious Challenges of 3-Year Olds," HuffPostLive video, n.d., on.aol
.com/video/mom-gets-real-about-the-serious-challenges-of-3-year
-olds-518140189.

Chapter 9

Daniel Kish lost both of his eyes to retinal cancer: Ira Glass, "Batman,"
This American Life, January 9, 2015, www.thisamericanlife.org/radio
-archives/episode/544/transcript.

FlashSonar: Daniel Kish, "FlashSonar: Understanding and Applying Sonar
Imaging to Mobility," *Future Reflections,* winter 2011, nfb.org/images
/nfb/publications/fr/fr30/1/fr300107.htm.

even when her son got in trouble with the police: Glass, "Batman."

New Zealand is experimenting with relinquishing all traditional playground rules: Hana Rosin, "The Overprotected Kid," *Atlantic Monthly*, April 2014, www.theatlantic.com/features/archive/2014/03/hey-parents-leave-those-kids-alone/358631.

"While young students' reading and math scores are soaring": Jen Scott Curwood, "What Happened to Kindergarten," *Scholastic Teacher*, n.d., www.scholastic.com/teachers/article/what-happened-kindergarten.

Children don't even start going to school there until age seven": Tim Walker, "How Finland Keeps Kids Focused through Free Play," *Atlantic Monthly*, June 30, 2014, www.theatlantic.com/education/archive/2014/06/how-finland-keeps-kids-focused/373544.

in a concerted effort to preserve China's competitive edge: Zhao Xinying, "Education Ministry, Lego Education Group Ink Agreement," *China Daily*, last updated September 29, 2014, www.chinadaily.com.cn/china/2014-09/29/content_18681775.htm.

"lighten the burden on children . . . giving them more time to play": Didi Kirsten Tatlow, "Gingerly, Chinese Parents Embrace the Value of Fun," *New York Times*, January 25, 2011, www.nytimes.com/2011/01/26/world/asia/26iht-letter26.html?_r=0.

on average children up to age eight years: "Zero to Eight: Children's Media Use in America 2013," Common Sense Media, October 28, 2013, www.commonsensemedia.org/zero-to-eight-2013-infographic.

Finnish children, who score so admirably in school: Samuel E. Abrams, "The Children Must Play," *New Republic*, January 27, 2011, newrepublic.com/article/82329/education-reform-finland-us.

Index

accidents, *see* injuries
ADHD, 4, 216
advice and warnings from others,
    23–24, 26–27, 86
Africa, xii–xiii, xiv, xv, 24, 25, 39,
    45–46, 76, 77, 89, 103, 185,
    218–19, 237
    see also Kenya
aggression, 209–10
allergies, *see* food allergies and
    intolerances
American Academy of Pediatrics
    (AAP), 67, 79, 131, 132,
    133, 175
anaphylactic shock, 184
ankyloglossia, 40–41
anxiety, *see* stress and anxiety
anxiety disorders, 4
Aspen Institute, 16–17
asthma, 4, 143, 144
Atlantic Monthly, 105
attachment parenting, 60,
    61, 160
autism spectrum disorders, 4
Au tribe, 56

BabyBjörn, 60
baby monitors, 19
baby-proofing the home, 226, 231
baby showers, 84–85
baby wearing, baby carriers, 21,
    60–61, 66, 75–77, 160
Back to Sleep campaign, 59, 61, 62,
    65–67
Bali, 42
bassinets, 123–24, 136
bathroom cabinets, 227, 228
bathtubs, 229–30
Battle Hymn of the Tiger Mother
    (Chua), 193
bed sharing and co-sleeping,
    117–24, 136
bedtimes, 122–23, 128
behavioral disorders, 216
Belgium, 90
birth, *see* childbirth
blankets, 118, 131
bonding, 39, 52, 53
    breastfeeding and, 155, 160, 161
    crying and, 116
    medical interventions and, 75

bottle-feeding:
  with breast milk, 141, 142, 145–46, 147, 155
  combining breastfeeding with, 158
  with formula, 139–45, 151, 155–57, 168
botulism, 9–10
brachycephaly, 59
  see also flat head syndrome
Bradner, Alexandra, 105
brain:
  electronic media and, 79–80
  fever and, 11, 12
  growth of, 64–65
  see also cognitive development
breastfeeding, 139–61
  and allowing others to feed the baby, 52–53, 156, 157, 158
  anxiety and, 152–53
  author's tips for, 158–61
  baby falling asleep during, 41–42
  bonding and, 155, 160, 161
  bottle-feeding and, *see* bottle-feeding
  burping and, 154
  colic and, 148–51
  combining bottle feeding with, 158
  crying and, 11, 12, 53, 139–40, 160
  cultural differences in, 142–43
  on demand, 159–60
  emphasis and pressure on importance of, 139–42, 145–47, 155
  fathers and, 53–54
  foods to avoid while, 152
  gastroenteritis and, 168
  guilt and, 155
  health and cognitive advantages of, 143–45
  hospital and, 38, 39, 39–41
  hunger and, 126–27, 159
  lactation consultants and, 39–41, 132

lactose intolerance and, 151
lying-in and, 47
medical intervention and, 75
milk protein intolerance and, 151
pacifiers and, 132, 133
pain medications and, 33, 34, 36–37
paraphernalia for, 158
partner and, 53–54, 156, 157, 158
positions for, 149–50, 158
problems with, 139–42, 145–56, 167
reflux after, 117, 127, 145, 148–52, 158, 167
scheduling, 12, 159–61
sleep and, 112, 117–19, 122–23, 126–27, 136
sudden infant death syndrome and, 20
tongue-tied baby and, 40–41
touch and, 74
breast milk, 142–47, 155, 168
  bottle feeding with, 141, 142, 145–46, 147, 155
  colostrum in, 143
Bringing Up Bébé (Druckerman), 113
Bumbo, 226
burns, 227–28
burping, 154
busyness, 59, 80, 81, 99, 113, 128, 146, 239
  time constraints, 202–6

cabinets, 227, 228, 231
calcium, 11, 13
cancer, 11, 12
cardiac conditions, 36
career opportunities, 17, 223
car seats, 59–60, 61, 66, 76, 77, 83, 226–27

cats, 230
    litter boxes for, 228
Centers for Disease Control and
        Prevention (CDC), 9, 10, 230
childbirth, 23–25
    epidurals and, 33–34
    home, 32
    hospital and, 31–35
    hospital care following, 35–41
    idealized vision of, 32–33
    natural, 32, 33, 34
    physical recovery from, 49–50
    plan for, 33
childcare and caretakers, 21, 90–93,
        96–97, 108
    after-school care, 233
    co-ops for, 108
    day care, 90–91, 92, 108,
        222, 233
    prioritizing and, 98–102
Child Protective Services, 3
child restraint seats, 59–60, 61, 66,
        76, 77, 83, 226–27
China, 42, 48, 223
Christakis, Erika, 16–17
Chua, Amy, 193
class, social, 6–7, 57, 193
classes, structured, 82
clothing, 196, 199, 205
cognitive development, 57, 58, 64,
        67, 82, 85, 223, 232, 235
    breastfeeding and, 145
    motor development and, 223
    see also senses
cognitive disorders, 216
Colen, Cynthia, 144
colic, 148–51
colostrum, 143
community, 106–8
computers and electronic media,
        78–81, 217, 224–25, 240
Coontz, Stephanie, 94–95
corporal punishment, 192–93
cortisol, 29, 33–34

cribs, 62, 66, 69, 71, 131, 136
    co-sleepers, 117–18, 123–24, 136
crying, 116, 154
    breastfeeding and, 11, 12, 53,
        139–40, 160
    tummy time and, 67
crying, sleep and, 109–11, 112, 125
    Crying It Out (CIO), 114–17, 119,
        135–37
C-section, 23, 24, 35, 38
cultural differences, 5, 21, 113, 197
    author's experiences around the
        world, xi–xvi, xviii, 2, 5–6,
        24, 238
    breastfeeding and, 142–43
    developmental milestones and,
        56, 58
    discipline and, 192–94
    food and, 165–66, 167, 197
    in lying-in practices, 42–48
    "natural" techniques and, 21–22
    safety standards and, 8, 9
    sleep and, 113, 117, 128
curling irons, 227

day-care programs, 90–91, 108,
        222, 233
    choosing, 92
dehydration, 168
Denmark, 90
depression, 4, 153, 216
development, 55–58
    cognitive, *see* cognitive
        development
    flat head syndrome and, *see* flat
        head syndrome
    milestones in, 55–56, 58
    motor, *see* motor development
    see also senses
diabetes, 4, 28, 143
digital media, 78–81, 217, 224–25, 240
discipline, 5, 190–213, 216
    aggression and, 209–10

and asking for what you want, not
what you don't, 198
and balance between helping and
encouraging independence,
205–6
and child's reasons for actions,
190, 201 6
and child's testing of boundaries,
210–11
and child's testing of cause and
effect, 191–92
clothing and, 196, 199, 205
consistency in, 195–98
constant reprimands and nagging
in, 195, 197–98
corporal punishment in, 192–93
cultural differences and, 192–94
and modeling behavior,
196–97, 212
morning routines and, 202–6
and offering limited choices,
198–201
prioritizing and, 212–13
and reducing opportunities for
friction, 196
rules in, 194–95, 197
and taking children out to an adult
setting, 212
tantrums and, 5, 204–5, 207–8
threats and punishments in, 201
time constraints and, 202–6
time-outs and, 207–8
whining and, 208–9
dog bites, 230
dolichocephaly, 59
drowning, 229–30
in toilets, 18–19
Druckerman, Pamela, 113
Duke, Bob, 182

education, continuing, 86–87, 91
electronic media, 78–81, 217,
224–25, 240

empathy, 81
epidurals, 33–34
esophageal sphincter, 127,
148–49, 151
exercise, 233–35
expecting best outcome, 28–29
eyes and vision, 61, 64, 65,
69–71, 80

falls, 226–27
family leave, paid, 44–45, 157
fathers, *see* partner
fear, 17, 62, 235, 238
fear-based parenting, 2, 3–5, 13–18,
19, 23, 215, 238–40
feelings, as contagious, 93–94
Ferber, Richard, 114, 115, 117
fever, 11, 12
Finland, 222–23, 232
fireplace, 227
flat head syndrome, x, 4, 19, 59–65,
77, 215
remedies for, 68–69
Tortle and, 19, 61–62
food allergies and intolerances, 11,
184–86, 188
anaphylactic shock and, 184
milk, 151, 167
peanut, 185
food and meals, 5, 162–89
author's tips for, 172–84
baby food, 176–78
bottle-feeding, *see* bottle-feeding
breastfeeding, *see* breastfeeding
cultural differences and, 165–66,
167, 197
desserts, 182–83
enjoyment of, 176, 179
first foods, 13
flavors in, 168, 178
focus and celebration in,
175–76, 184
fun ideas for, 184

food and meals (*cont.*)
  group meals, 172–76, 181–82, 189
  as guest at someone else's home,
    180–81
  home-cooked meals, 172–73, 189
  honey, 9–10, 21, 142
  manners and, 179–80, 182
  milk, *see* milk
  negotiating about, 174, 182
  nutrition and, 173, 188
  obesity and, 62, 143, 144, 168, 173,
    182, 187, 188
  organic foods, 163–65, 186–88
  picky eaters and food aversions,
    163–68, 174, 178–81
  planning and preparing meals
    together, 183, 240
  portions in, 172, 187
  processed foods, 163, 187–88
  rice cereal, 11, 13, 168
  school lunch periods, 174–75, 222
  separate meals and customizing,
    173, 177, 180, 181–83
  stress and anxiety and, 167
  sugar and, 188
  sweet tastes and, 168
  timeline for introducing foods,
    169–72
  vegetarian, 177
formula, 139–45, 151, 155–57, 168
fractures, 226, 234–35

gastroenteritis, 168
gradual extinction method,
  115–16, 117
Gross-Loh, Christine, 174–75
Guatemala, 43
guilt, 3, 21, 87, 88, 90–91, 96,
  99, 240
  breastfeeding and, 155
  easing, 95–97
  foods and, 164

head:
  flat, *see* flat head syndrome
  injuries to, 19, 226
health monitors, 19
hearing, 61, 64, 71–73
help and support, 29, 88–89,
    102–3, 157
  allowing others to feed the baby,
    52–53, 156, 157, 158
  asking for and accepting, 51,
    107–8
  child-rearing as shared
    responsibility, 89, 90–93
  from community, 106–8
  with household tasks, 103–6
  from partner, 29–30, 103–6,
    156, 157
  see also childcare and
    caretakers
honey, 9–10, 21, 142
hospital, 31–35, 42
  after birth, 35–41
  breastfeeding and, 38, 39,
    39–41
  lactation consultant in, 39–41
  length of stay in, 35–36
  natural birthing suite in, 32
  pain medications and,
    36–37
  rooming in at, 38–39
  well-baby nursery in, 37–39
household cleaners, 228
household tasks:
  children's participation in,
    196–97, 198–201
  outdoor work, 199–200
  partner's participation in, 103–6
Huffington Post, 190, 205
hunger:
  breastfeeding and, 126–27, 159
  sleep and, 126–27
Hymowitz, Kay, 113
hypertension, 4

illnesses, 19
immobilizing infants, 58, 59–61, 65,
    215–16
    see also flat head syndrome
immune system, 144
In Defense of Food (Pollan), 188
India, 65, 117
infant development, *see* development
infant mortality rates, 25, 31*n*, 146
infections, 36, 49
injuries, 20, 226–30
    burns, 227–28
    dog bites, 230
    drowning, 18–19, 229–30
    falls, 226–27
    fractures, 226, 234–35
    head, 19, 226
    minor, 235–36
    poisonings and skin
        irritations, 228
Internet and social media, 11, 14, 56
    medical issues and, 15–16
    pregnancy and, 27–28
    screening tests and, 29
IQ, 145
Iran, 42, 170
Iraq, 117
Israel, 14–15, 42–43, 185

Jamaica, 65
Japan, 31, 90, 117, 143, 165
jaundice, 141, 145
*Journal of American Marriage and
    Family,* 91

Kaufman, Joan, 116
Kaufman family, 8
Kenya, xii–xiii, 24, 56, 65, 193–94,
    195, 217–18
    Mau Mau uprising in, 25
kindergarten, 222

Kish, Daniel, 214–15
kitty litter, 228
Korowai tribe, 8

lactation consultants, 39–41, 132
lactose intolerance, 151, 167
language, 72, 73
Latin America, 128
lawsuits, 15, 235
learning, 81, 82–83, 85, 200
    play and, 222
Lego Education, 223
Lieberman, Alicia, 116
lying-in period, 42–54, 87–88, 89

Markman, Art, 182
Marquesans, 75–76
Martini, Mary, 75–76
Mau Mau uprising, 25
Maya Wrap, 60
Mayer, Marissa, 47
meals, *see* food and meals
milk, 11, 13
    allergy or intolerance to, 151, 167
    breast, *see* breast milk
Mimo, 19
Moken people, 8
money, spending on babies, 83
monitoring devices, 19
morning routines, 202–6
motor development, 57, 64, 66, 67,
    82, 216
    cognitive development and, 223
    play and, 77–78, 221, 223,
        224–25, 235
motor endplates, 216
movement, 58, 62, 65–66, 83,
    221–22, 223
    see also motor development
movement, restriction of, 58, 59–61,
    65, 215–16

movement, restriction (*cont.*)
 swaddling, 130–32
 see also flat head syndrome
music, 71, 73, 80
 singing, 72
 sleep and, 134–35

naps, 123, 126, 127–30
"natural" techniques, 21–22
Nepal, 65
newborn, 23–54
 bonding and, 39, 52, 53, 75
 going out with, 49
 hospital and, 35–41
 hospital nursery and, 37–39
 lying-in period and, 42–54,
  87–88, 89
 visitors and, 48–49
New England Journal of Medicine, 62
New York Times, 94
New Zealand, 221
NICU (neonatal intensive care unit),
 xv, 26, 31, 46, 47, 59

obesity, 62, 143, 144, 168, 173, 182,
 187, 188, 215
OB/GYNs, 28–29, 31
optimism, 26
 expecting best outcome during
  pregnancy, 28–29
 in parenting, x, xix, 1, 2, 22
 social opportunity and, 17
organic foods, 163–65, 186–88
outdoors:
 household jobs, 199–200
 play, 216–21, 225, 232–34
 sun exposure and, x, 11, 12
Owlet, 19

pacifiers, 132–34
pain medications, 36–37

breastfeeding and, 33, 34, 36–37
 epidurals, 33–34
parental leave, 44–45, 157
parenting, 1–22, 238–40
 attachment, 60, 61, 160
 author's global perspective on,
  xi–xvi, xviii, 2, 5–6, 24, 238
 class and, 6–7, 57, 193
 cultural differences in, *see* cultural
  differences
 fear-based, 2, 3–5, 13–18, 19, 23,
  215, 238–40
 healthy principles for, 5–6
 modeling behavior in,
  196–97, 212
 "natural" techniques and, 21–22
 optimistic, confident approach to,
  x, xix, 1, 2, 22, 161, 240
 rules in, 3, 7–13, 139
Parenting without Borders
 (Gross-Loh), 174–75
parents:
 busyness of, 59, 81, 99
 having a life beyond the children,
  93, 95–96, 108, 138
 needs and interests of, 22, 91,
  95–96, 108
 quantity and quality of time spent
  with children, 91–92, 99–100
Parents Magazine, 11
partner:
 feeding and, 53–54, 156, 157, 158
 help and support from, 29–30,
  103–6, 156, 157
 relationship with, 94–95, 97, 105,
  119, 138
 separation anxiety and, 96
 tummy time and, 68
Patz, Etan, 14
peanut allergies, 185
Pedialyte, 168
Pediatrics, 118, 156
peer pressure, 30
perspective, 18–21

PICU (pediatric intensive
    care unit), 59
plagiocephaly, 59
    see also flat head syndrome
play, 198, 200, 212, 214–36, 237
    learning and, 222
    motor skills and, 77–78, 221, 223,
        224–25, 235
    outdoor, 216–21, 225, 232–34
    overprotectiveness and, 215
    safety and, 215, 217, 219–21
    school and, 222–23
    television and computer screens
        and, 224–25
    unsupervised, 3, 215, 216–21,
        223, 225
playgrounds, 15, 220, 221, 235
poisonings and skin irritations, 228
Pollan, Michael, 188
pools, 229, 230, 231
pregnancy, 23, 26–30
    advice and warnings from others
        during, 23–24, 26–27
    expecting best outcome in,
        28–29
    hospital and, 31–35
    peer pressure and, 30
    screening tests during, 28–29
    social media and, 27–28
    stress and, 25, 29
    support from partner during,
        29–30
preschool, 90, 91
prioritizing, 98–102, 212–13
processed foods, 163, 187–88
punishment, 201
    corporal, 192–93
    time-outs, 207–8
    see also discipline

reflux, 117, 127, 145, 148–52,
    158, 167
rice cereal, 11, 13, 168

risks, reasonable, 215, 234–36, 237
risks and dangers, 3
    injuries, *see* injuries
    media and, 14, 217
    perspective on, 18–21
    play and, 215, 217, 219–21
rolling over, 62
rules, 238
    discipline, 194–95, 197
    parenting, 3, 7–13, 139
    safety, 9, 194, 195

safety, 3, 4
    baby-proofing the home,
        226, 231
    calculated risk and, 215, 234–36
    cultural differences in standards
        of, 8, 9
    play and, 215, 217, 219–21
    rules on, 9, 194, 195
    see also injuries; risks and
        dangers
safety devices, 19, 20, 226, 231
Scholastic Teacher, 222
school, 222–23
    lunch periods in, 174–75, 222
    play and, 222–23
    preschool, 90, 91
screening tests, 28–29
screens:
    electronic media, 78–81, 217,
        224–25, 240
    television, *see* television
senses, 57–58, 66, 69–75, 77–83, 85
    electronic media and, 78–81
    hearing, 61, 64, 71–73
    smell, 73–74, 80
    touch, 74–75, 77, 80
    toys and, 70, 77–78
    tummy time and, 66–67
    vision, 61, 64, 65, 69–71
separation anxiety, 5, 96–98
shower gifts, 84–85

SIDS (sudden infant death
    syndrome), 19, 20, 59–60, 66,
    118, 131, 132
sight, sense of, 61, 64, 65, 69–71, 80
sleep, sleeping, 5, 109–38
    allowing others to take care of the
        baby during the night, 52–53
    on back, 19, 59–62, 65–67
    bassinets and, 123–24, 136
    bedtimes, 122–23, 128
    blankets and, 118, 131
    breastfeeding and, 112, 117–19,
        122–23, 126–27, 136
    common problems with, 126–29
    consistency and routine in, 124–25
    co-sleeping, 21, 38
    cribs and, *see* cribs
    crying and, 109–11, 112, 125
    cultural differences and, 113,
        117, 128
    first few days and, 111, 120
    hunger and, 126–27
    music and, 134–35
    naps, 123, 126, 127–30
    noise and, 135
    pacifiers and, 132–34
    and reclaiming yourself, 137–38
    reflux and, 117, 127
    regression in good sleepers, 137
    and sharing a room, 120–22, 123
    SIDS and, 19, 20, 59–60, 66, 118,
        131, 132
    stimulation and, 113–14
    swaddling and, 130–32
    teaching child to sleep without
        you, 135–37
    too much or too little, 127–29
sleep training, 111–12, 114–20
    author's method, 120–25
    co-sleeping and bed sharing,
        117–24, 136
    Crying It Out (CIO), 114–17, 119,
        135–37
    gradual extinction, 115–16, 117

smell, sense of, 73–74, 80
social class, 6–7, 57, 193
social media, *see* Internet and social
    media
social norms, 121, 197
social safety net, 17
social skills, 81, 91, 217
    table manners, 179–80, 182
Somé, Sobonfu E., 89, 103
Spain, 128
spanking, 192–93
stay-at-home mothers, 87, 90
stimulation:
    overstimulation, 80, 81, 203, 232
    of senses, *see* senses
    sleep and, 113–14
stove, 227
stress and anxiety, 3, 17, 21, 88, 90,
    93, 94, 102, 138, 204, 216, 232,
    238–40
    breastfeeding and, 152–53
    children's absorption from parents,
        5, 16, 72, 99, 152
    easing, 95–97
    fear-based parenting and, 3–5, 23
    mealtimes and, 167
    pregnancy and childbirth and,
        25, 29
    and screening tests during
        pregnancy, 28–29
strollers, 76, 77, 83
sudden infant death syndrome
    (SIDS), 19, 20, 59–60, 66, 118,
    131, 132
sugar, 188
sun exposure, x, 11, 12
support, *see* help and support
swaddling, 130–32
swimming pools, 229, 230, 231

table bumpers, 19
tantrums, 5, 204–5, 207–8
television, 79, 92, 224, 225

horror stories and medical dramas
  on, 11, 28
sleep and, 135
temper tantrums, 5, 204–5, 207–8
This American Life, 214
thumb sucking, 134
tidying up, 196–97
time constraints, 202–6
time-outs, 207–8
toilets, 18–19
tongue-tied baby, 40–41
torticollis, 61
Tortle, 19, 61–62
touch, 221
toxic substances, 228
toxoplasmosis, 228
toys, 83, 221
  picking up, 199
  sensory development and, 70,
    77–78
tummy time, 62, 65, 66–68, 69, 132
  senses and, 66–67
Two Guys on Your Head, 182

US Consumer Product Safety
  Commission, 18

vegetarian diet, 177
Vietnam, 87–88, 155
vision, 61, 64, 65, 69–71, 80
vitamin D, x
vomiting, 149, 168

Wales, 221
Walsh, Adam, 14
warnings and advice from others,
  23–24, 26–27, 86
Washington Post, 52
weight gain and obesity, 62, 76,
  143, 144, 168, 173, 182, 187,
  188, 215
Welcoming Spirit Home (Somé), 89
whining, 208–9
work, 21, 88, 90, 91, 93–94
  parental leave from, 44–45, 157

About the Authors

Born in Mombasa, Kenya, Dr. Jane Scott attended the University of Western Australia Medical School in Perth at the age of sixteen. She subsequently lived in the Australian outback, England, Ireland, and the South African desert. Years later after moving to the United States, she attended the University of Colorado Medical School and completed her residency in pediatrics and fellowship in neonatology at Duke University while simultaneously raising four young children. After serving as a staff neonatologist at St. Joseph's Hospital in Denver for six years, she led the effort to transition St. Luke's Magic Valley Hospital NICU in Twin Falls, Idaho—the only NICU within a 120-mile radius—from a Level 1 unit to a Level 3A unit capable of treating many of the area's smallest, sickest newborns.

Dr. Jane returned to Colorado in 2010 and practiced urgent care pediatrics in Centennial until December 2014. She is the inventor of the Tortle, an FDA-cleared infant repositioning device designed to prevent and eliminate flat head syndrome, and is the founder of Tortle Products, LLC, which sells and distributes the Tortle as well as other products to help hospitalized infants with optimal head positioning. The Tortle has been adopted by pediatrics departments and NICUs in more than thirty hospitals around the world, and Dr. Jane's medical device products are being researched by university and hospital NICUs and outpatient clinics, including Duke University and Newman University in Pennsylvania. This is her first book.

Stephanie Land is a half-French, half-American writer, book editor, and mother of two who has collaborated on several *New York Times* bestsellers and ghostwritten for many entrepreneurs, entertainers, and television personalities. She lives with her family and two dogs in Austin, Texas.